Edexcel International GCSE

Spanish

EDEXCEL CERTIFICATE IN SPANISH

Jacqueline López-Cascante

Editor: Judith O'Hare

Series Editor: Mike Thacker

Hodder Education, an Hachette UK company, 338 Euston Road, London NW1 3BH

Orders

Bookpoint Ltd, 130 Milton Park, Abingdon, Oxfordshire, OX14 4SB
tel: 01235 827827
fax: 01235 400401
e-mail: education@bookpoint.co.uk

Lines are open 9.00 a.m.–5.00 p.m., Monday to Saturday, with a 24-hour message answering service. You can also order through the Hodder Education website: www.hoddereducation.co.uk

ISBN 978-1-4441-8108-1

First printed 2013
Impression number   5   4   3   2   1
Year   2017   2016   2015   2014   2013

In order to ensure that this resource offers high-quality support for the associated Edexcel qualification, it has been through a review process by the awarding body to confirm that it fully covers the teaching and learning content of the specification or part of a specification at which it is aimed, and demonstrates an appropriate balance between the development of subject skills, knowledge and understanding, in addition to preparation for assessment.

While the publishers have made every attempt to ensure that advice on the qualification and its assessment is accurate, the official specification and associated assessment guidance materials are the only authoritative source of information and should always be referred to for definitive guidance.

No material from an endorsed resource will be used verbatim in any assessment set by Edexcel.

Endorsement of a resource does not mean that the resource is required to achieve this Edexcel qualification, nor does it mean that it is the only suitable material available to support the qualification, and any resource lists produced by the awarding body shall include this and other appropriate resources.

All efforts have been made to trace copyright on items used.

Illustrations by Emily Hunter and Jim Watson

Cover photo: Fotolia

Inside photographs are reproduced by permission of: Azucena Herrero (p. 109); César Ballestros (pp. 93 d, e, 103, 113, 127 a, i and o); Chris Robinson (p. 93 g); Emily Hunter (pp. 12 (top), 93 f, 110, 127 h); Felix Absoram (p. 135 top); Fernando de Dios (p. 135 bottom); Francesca Streatfield (p. 81); Hannah Thacker (p. 96, 127 b); Image Library (pp. 50, 120); Ingram (p. 34); Mike Thacker (pp. 41, 64, 72, 76, 93 a, b, c, h, i, 97, 100, 127 c, d, e, f, g, j, k, l, m, n, 128, 131, 133); Sebastián Bianchi (p. 100 bottom right); TopFoto (pp. 12, 21, 25, 39, 46, 48, 49, 52, 98, 112, 136, 137); Greek photonews/Alamy (p. 47), Corbis Super RF/Alamy (p. 59), Chris Fredriksson/Alamy (p. 105), dbimages/Alamy (p. 117), BE&W agencja fotograficzna Sp. z.o.o./Alamy (p. 117); Fotolia (pp. 29, 59).

Typeset by Aptara, Inc.

Printed in Italy

Hachette UK's policy is to use papers that are natural, renewable and recyclable products and made from wood grown in sustainable forests. The logging and manufacturing processes are expected to conform to the environmental regulations of the country of origin.

Contents

How to make the most of this book

This book provides all you need to prepare for your **Edexcel International GCSE in Spanish** or **Level 1/ Level 2 Certificate in Spanish** qualification. It also teaches you about the way of life of the people in the Spanish-speaking world and about the language they speak.

Each of the five modules contains a sequence of texts and activities that enable you to discover the language and use it effectively. Each section includes the following features:

At the beginning of each section, a list of the unit's topic content and the main **grammar** items covered

Lots of **listening** activities to practise skills

☑ Talk about myself, my family and friends
☑ Revise the present tense of key verbs
☑ Prepare a presentation on this topic
☑ Use adjectives

Tasks to ensure effective **writing** in Spanish

Up-to-date **reading** passages based on life in Spanish-speaking countries

Varied activities to practise **speaking**

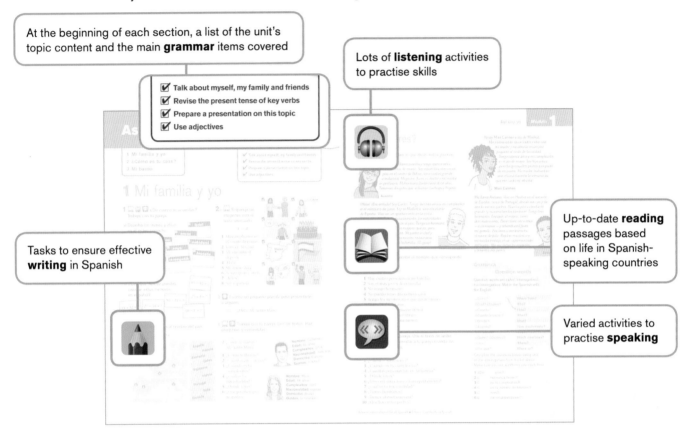

Watch out for these special features throughout the book too:

GRAMÁTICA These sections explain the key grammar points you need to know to communicate successfully in Spanish.

LENGUA CLAVE Under this heading, important language points (e.g. how to use certain phrases) are highlighted.

¡OJO! These sections offer tips on how to use and improve your Spanish.

CULTURA Items of interest relating to the culture and language of the Spanish-speaking world are included here.

At the end of each module you will find:

Exam Corner Specific preparation for the kind of tasks that you have to complete in the exams.

Vocabulario Lists of key vocabulary relating to the main topic areas covered in the module.

Towards the end of the book are:

Gramática A summary of all the grammar that you need to know with handy verb tables for quick reference.

Vocabulario A combined list of all the key vocabulary used in this book, in alphabetical order.

Enjoy the course!
Jacqueline López-Cascante   Judith O'Hare

The examination

The **International GCSE in Spanish** and **Level 1/Level 2 Certificate in Spanish (UK schools)** qualifications are made up of three compulsory papers that test the four language skills. Each paper is taken at the end of the course.

Exam practice and guidance on how to prepare for each paper are given in the Exam Corner sections at the end of every unit. The content and questions are the same for both qualifications.

Here are some general questions that you should ask yourself about the four skills:
- In which of the four skills do you feel most confident?
- Is there a skill that you need to improve more than the others?
- Which strategies, so far, have helped you to improve your skills?
- What do you think you can do to improve in all the skills?

Share your thoughts with others in your class.

Paper	Skill	Marks	Timing	Proportion of qualification
1	Listening	50 marks	40 minutes plus 5 minutes' reading time	25%
2	Reading and writing	60 marks (30 marks for reading and 30 marks for writing)	1 hour 30 minutes	50%
3	Speaking	40 marks (20 marks for Section A and 20 marks for Section B)	10 minutes	25%

Topics

You need to cover the topics listed below.

- **Topic area A**   Home and abroad
- **Topic area B**   Education and employment
- **Topic area C**   House, home and daily routines
- **Topic area D**   The modern world and the environment
- **Topic area E**   Social activities, fitness and health

You also have to learn about Spanish grammar, including nouns, adjectives, adverbs, pronouns, prepositions, conjunctions, numbers, verbs and their tenses (present, perfect, preterite, imperfect, immediate future, and pluperfect) and moods (indicative, imperative, conditional and subjunctive). All these grammar points and the topics are covered in this book.

- Think about how you revise best in Spanish.
- Share your ideas with your fellow students.
- Have you used any websites to help you revise? If yes, which ones have been most useful?

Paper 1: listening

The instructions are written in both Spanish and English. The material that you listen to contains several short recordings that get longer as you work through the paper. You are assessed through tasks such as completing a grid, a form or a plan, multiple choice, box ticking, note taking, gap filling, true or false, matching and summary. You hear each recording twice.

Paper 2: reading and writing

The instructions are written in both Spanish and English. The paper starts with three reading questions, followed by the first extended writing task. Two more reading questions are set, followed by the second extended writing task.

Reading

You are required to read a *range* of texts of differing length related to the topics in the specification. The texts require the use of different reading techniques, such as skimming, scanning and in-depth reading. The questions are varied in type: multiple choice, true or false, box ticking, matching, and completion of a plan, form or grid.

Writing

In the first extended writing task you have to write about 50 words in Spanish on a topic related to the preceding reading passage.

In the second extended writing task you select one task from a choice of three. You have to write about 150 words in response to this task. This task includes a variety of writing styles and formats. You will earn marks for communication and content, knowledge and application of language and accuracy.

Paper 3: speaking

The speaking test is divided into two sections. The whole test lasts a maximum of 10 minutes.

Section A: single picture

You choose a topic. In a maximum of 4 minutes you give a 1 minute presentation on a picture you have chosen. This is followed by a 3 minute discussion with your interviewer about the same picture.

Section B: conversation

You take part in two conversations that each last approximately 3 minutes. The conversations are about two topic areas that the interviewer chooses.

Así soy yo

1 **Mi familia y yo**

2 **¿Cómo es tu casa?**

3 **Mi barrio**

1 Mi familia y yo

1 📖 ✏️ 💬 ¿De cuánto te acuerdas?
Trabaja con tu pareja.

a Descifra los meses y dilos
en el orden correcto.

4 **brial**

3 **erone**

1 **ijnuo**

2 **verbeniom**

8 **mebiderci**

5 **razom**

6 **ostago**

7 **amyo**

12 **brucote**

9 **boferre**

10 **luijo**

11 **remespetib**

b ¿Con qué rapidez puedes
calcular estos números
en español?

$65 + 40 = ?$

$25 \times 4 = ?$

$90 - 11 = ?$

$15 + 12 = ?$

$21 + 34 = ?$

$50 - 7 = ?$

c Empareja la letra con el nombre del pais.

Ejemplo: **a** — *Inglaterra*

España

Francia

Alemania

Gales

Inglaterra

Irlanda

Portugal

Italia

Escocia

2a 📖 Empareja las
imágenes con el
texto adecuado.

Ejemplo: **1 — d**

1 Mi cumpleaños es
el veinte de enero.
2 Vivo en Madrid.
3 Me encanta el
deporte.
4 ¡Hola!
5 Me llamo Ana.
6 Tengo quince años.
7 ¡Adiós!
8 Soy española.

b 💬 Escribe un pequeño párrafo para presentarte
a alguien.

Ejemplo: *¡Hola! Me llamo Mark…*

c 📖 💬 Trabaja con tu pareja. Lee los textos. Haz
preguntas y contéstalas.

Ejemplo:
1 *¿Cómo te llamas?*
Me llamo María.

1 ¿Cómo te llamas?
2 ¿Cuántos años tienes?
3 ¿Cuándo es tu
cumpleaños?
4 ¿Cuál es tu
nacionalidad?
5 ¿Dónde vives?
6 ¿Qué pasatiempos
te gustan?

Nombre: Guillermo
Edad: 16 años
Cumpleaños: 31/4
Nacionalidad: mejicana
Domicilio: Cancún
Gustos: el fútbol

Nombre: Maria
Edad: 16 años
Cumpleaños: 12/7
Nacionalidad: inglesa
Domicilio: Bristol
Gustos: la natación

¿Quién eres?

3  📖 Escucha y lee lo que dicen estos jóvenes.

¡Hola! Me llamo Juanita y tengo quince años. Nací el once de marzo. Soy española y vivo en un piso en el centro de Bilbao, una ciudad grande e industrial. Mi padre, Juan, es médico y mi madre es profesora. Mi hermano Javier tiene doce años. Tenemos dos gatos que se llaman Lechuga y Pepino.

Juanita

¡Hola! ¡Encantado! Soy Carlos. Tengo dieciséis años y mi cumpleaños es el veintiuno de junio. Soy de Mallorca, una isla al este de España. Vivo en un apartamento en la costa. Es muy bonito. Desafortunadamente, las autoridades no nos permiten animales en el piso. Tengo un hermano y una hermana. Los dos son mayores que yo, pero nos llevamos todos muy bien. Mi padre es chef y mi madre trabaja con él en nuestro restaurante. En verano ayudamos toda la familia. ¡Es guay!

Carlos

Yo soy Mari Carmen y soy de Madrid. Mis padres están divorciados y vivo con mi madre y mi abuela en un piso pequeño al oeste de la cuidad. Tengo catorce años y mi cumpleaños es el dos de mayo. Soy hija única, pero tengo muchos primos por parte de mi padre. Mi madre trabaja en una oficina durante la semana así que me cuida mi abuela.

Mari Carmen

Me llamo Antonio. Vivo en Huelva en el suroeste de España, cerca de Portugal, donde nací yo y de donde son mis padres. Nuestro piso es bastante grande ¡y nuestra familia también! Tengo tres hermanos. Enrique, el mayor, tiene diecinueve años; Elena tiene once años — es la menor — y además está Juan, mi gemelo. Nacimos a medianoche el nueve de julio. Papá es mecánico y mi madre trabaja en un supermercado del barrio. Me encantan los animales y tenemos dos perros.

Antonio

a 🏛 ¿Qué dicen? Escribe el nombre que corresponde con cada frase.

Ejemplo: **1** — *Juanita*

1 Hay cuatro personas en mi familia.
2 Soy el más joven de la familia.
3 No tengo hermanos.
4 No puedo tener mascota en casa.
5 Tengo la misma edad que mi hermano.
6 Vivo al lado del mar.
7 Solo tengo un hermano menor.
8 Mi padre no vive conmigo.
9 Tengo una hermana menor.
10 No soy español.

b 🏛 Trabaja con tu pareja. Usa el texto de arriba para ayudarte a entrevistar a tu pareja usando las preguntas siguientes.

1 ¿Cómo te llamas?
2 ¿Cuántos años tienes?
3 ¿Cuándo es tu cumpleaños?
4 ¿Cuántas personas hay en tu familia?
5 ¿Dónde vives?
6 ¿Vives en una casa o en un apartamento?
7 ¿Cuál es tu nacionalidad?
8 ¿Tienes hermanos?
9 ¿Tienes mascota en casa?
10 ¿Qué hacen tus padres?

GRAMÁTICA

Question words

Question words are called 'interrogatives', *los interrogativos*. Match the Spanish with the English.

¿Cómo?	Where from?
¿Cuál? ¿Cuáles?	Who?
¿Cuándo?	How?
¿Cuánto/a/os/as?	When?
¿Dónde?	What?
¿Adónde?	How much/many?
¿De dónde?	Why?
¿Quién? ¿Quiénes?	Which one/ones?
¿Qué?	Where?
¿Por qué?	Where to?

Complete the questions below using one of the interrogatives from the list above. Make sure you use a different one each time.

1 ¿De _____ eres?
2 ¿ _____ hermanos tienes?
3 ¿ _____ es tu cumpleaños?
4 ¿ _____ es tu número de teléfono?
5 ¿ _____ eres?
6 ¿ _____ nacionalidad tienes?

4 🎧 Listen and then copy and complete the table in English.

	A	B	C	D
Nombre				
Edad				
Cumpleaños				
Nacionalidad				
Domicilio				
Familia				
Mascotas				

abuelo abuela

madre padre   tía tío

hijo   hija

5a 📖 Trabaja con tu pareja.

¿Qué significan estas palabras?
Usa el diccionario para ayudarte.

1. bisabuelo
2. primo segundo
3. cuñado
4. madrastra
5. novia
6. nuera
7. suegro
8. hermanastra

b ✏️ Escoge una palabra del recuadro para completar cada frase.

tía   primo   hermano   abuela
marido   madrastra   hija   mujer

*Ejemplo: La madre de mi padre es mi **abuela**.*

1. La madre de mi padre es mi _____ .
2. La hermana de mi madre es mi _____ .
3. El hijo de mi tío es mi _____ .
4. La segunda mujer de mi padre es mi _____ .
5. Mi madre es la _____ de mi padre.
6. Mi padre es el _____ de mi madre.
7. El hijo de mi madre es mi _____ .
8. Mi hermana es la _____ de mi madre.

LENGUA CLAVE

¿Qué tal tu pronunciación?

A	a	J	jota	R	ere
B	be	K	ka	S	ese
C	ce	L	ele	T	te
CH	che	LL	elle	U	u
D	de	M	eme	V	uve
E	e	N	ene	W	uve doble
F	efe	Ñ	eñe	X	equis
G	ge	O	o	Y	i griega
H	hache	P	pe	Z	zeta
I	i	Q	cu		

Ahora practica tu pronunciación, repitiendo estas palabras.

A	*gracias*	LL	*ella*
E	*inglés*	Ñ	*español*
I	*si*	R	*hora, Costa Rica*
O	*doctor*	RR	*arroz*
U	*uno*	V	*vídeo*
B	*bebida*	Y	*cinco y media*
C	*ciudad*	Z	*diez*
CC	*accidente*	Que	*¿Qué pasa?*
D	*ciudad*	Qui	*quince*
G	*general*	Gua	*guay*
H	*hotel*	Gue	*guerra*
J	*jamón*	Gui	*guitarra*

Los animales

1. Tengo un conejo.
2. Me gustan los caballos.
3. Prefiero los perros.
4. Me dan igual los peces dorados.
5. Odio las arañas.
6. Me encantan las chinchillas.
7. Mi gato es inteligente.
8. No tengo un hámster.

¿Qué animal es? Empareja las imágenes con las frases correctas.

a b c d

e f g h

Una encuesta. ¿Tienes un animal en casa?

Tengo…

6 ¿Cuál es tu opinión? Adapta cada frase para ti.

Ejemplo: **1** *Me parezco a mi madre o*
No me parezco a mi madre.

1 Me parezco a mi madre.
2 Me llevo bien con mi padre.
3 No me llevo bien con mi hermano.
4 Mi abuela me trata como a un adulto.
5 Mi hermana mayor me trata como a un niño.
6 Mis padres son bastante estrictos.
7 Me molesta mi hermano menor.
8 Discuto mucho con mi hermana.
9 Mi hermano y yo somos muy parecidos.
10 No me parezco físicamente a los demás de mi familia.

¡OJO!

Remember to use connectives to make what you say and write more interesting.

y	and	*porque*	because
que	that, which, who	*si*	if
también	also	*cuando*	when
además	besides	*ni…ni*	neither…nor
pero	but	*sin embargo*	however
o	or	*siempre*	always

Escoge una palabra de la lista arriba para formar una frase más larga.

Ejemplo: **1** *Tengo un hermano. No tengo hermanas.*
> Tengo un hermano, pero no tengo hermanas.

1 Tengo un hermano. No tengo hermanas.
2 Mi padre tiene el pelo moreno. Mi padre tiene los ojos azules.
3 Tenemos muy buenos amigos. Se llaman Maite y Ramón.
4 No me gusta jugar al fútbol. No me gusta jugar al rugby.
5 Soy alto y delgado. Mi hermana es alta y delgada.
6 Mi hermana menor me molesta. Me coge todas mis cosas personales. En general es una chica buena.
7 Me encantan los animales. No nos permiten tener un animal en el piso.
8 Soy muy deportista. Los lunes juego al tenis. Los jueves monto en bicicleta.
9 Hablo portugués. Mi madre es portuguesa. Hablamos portugués en casa.
10 Mi abuelo es muy alto. Tiene el pelo gris. Es alegre. Resulta gracioso.

7 Listen to what Ana says about her family. Answer the questions in English.

1 How old is Ana?
2 Where is she from?
3 What does she say about the English language?
4 How many people are there in her family?
5 What does she say about her mother?
6 What does she say about her father?
7 What does she tell you about her brother and her sisters?

GRAMÁTICA

The present tense of four key verbs

When talking about yourself and your family the following key verbs are used. Learn them well.

1 *llamarse* (to be called)		**2** *tener* (to have)
me	*llamo*	*tengo*
te	*llamas*	*tienes*
se	*llama*	*tiene*
nos	*llamamos*	*tenemos*
os	*llamáis*	*tenéis*
se	*llaman*	*tienen*

3 *vivir* (to live)	**4** *ser* (to be)
vivo	*soy*
vives	*eres*
vive	*es*
vivimos	*somos*
vivís	*sois*
viven	*son*

¡Atención! In Spanish, when giving your age you say 'I **have** X years.'
Tengo *catorce años.*

Completa las frases siguientes usando el verbo y la persona correctos.

Ejemplo: **1** *Mis hermanos* **se llaman** *Juan y Martín.*

1 Mis hermanos _____ Juan y Martín.
2 Mis padres y yo _____ en Madrid.
3 ¿De dónde _____ tú?
4 Mi padre _____ cuarenta años.
5 Mi mejor amiga _____ Ana.
6 Pablo y Juan _____ mis hermanos.
7 ¿Dónde _____ tu madre?
8 ¡Hola! _____ Juanita, ¿y tú?
9 Mis padres _____ muchos amigos.
10 En mi familia _____ cuatro personas.

8a 🎧 ¿En qué trabajan sus padres? Escribe las palabras adecuadas en la tabla.

1	2	3	4
cocinero	enfermera	profesora	ingeniero

5	6	7	8
mecánica	ama de casa	peluquero	auxiliar de vuelos

9	10	11	12
dentista	dependienta	hombre de negocios	bombero

13	14	15	16
taxista	recepcionista	periodista	cartero

17	18	19	20
electricista	granjeros	fotógrafa	secretaria

Madre	Padre
Ejemplo: secretaria (20)	*hombre de negocios (11)*

b 💬 ✏️ Pregunta a tus compañeros de clase en qué trabajan sus padres. Escribe un pequeño párrafo para explicar tus resultados usando las siguientes frases para ayudarte.

Haz la pregunta siguiente a X personas:
¿En qué trabajan tus padres?

Aquí están los resultados de mi encuesta:
- X trabajan en el sector empresarial (work in business).
- X trabajan desde casa (work from home).
- X están en el paro/no trabajan (are unemployed/don't work).
- En el futuro me gustaría trabajar _____ porque _____ .

9 📖 ✏️ Escribe una respuesta al correo electrónico siguiente.

Fichero Edición Inserción Formato Instrumentos Mensaje

¡Hola!

Me llamo Manuel. Tengo quince años y nací el ocho de agosto. Soy español y vivo en Granada en el sur de España. ¿Y tú? En mi familia hay cuatro personas. Tengo un hermano que se llama Tobi. Vivimos en un piso grande. Tengo un perro y un gato y ¡nada más!

¡Hasta luego!

Manuel

10 💬 Ahora prepara una breve presentación de ti mismo y de tu familia. Menciona lo siguiente:
- nombre
- edad
- cumpleaños
- nacionalidad
- domicilio
- familia
- mascotas

¿Cómo eres?

11a 📖 Lee el texto. Empareja cada persona con la descripción adecuada.

Ejemplo: 1 — e

1 Soy alta y delgada con ojos azules y el pelo largo, rubio y rizado.
2 No soy ni alto ni bajo. Tengo ojos azules y el pelo corto y pelirrojo.
3 Llevo gafas. Tengo el pelo corto y castaño.
4 Soy muy baja con el pelo largo, liso y negro.
5 Tengo ojos azules y pecas. Tengo el pelo medianamente largo y castaño.
6 Tengo el pelo gris y llevo barba. Tengo los ojos marrones.
7 Soy muy alta con el pelo ondulado y largo. Tengo los ojos marrones.
8 Soy calvo y tengo bigote.

b 💬 Trabaja con tu pareja. Descríbete a ti mismo y a los miembros de tu familia. Describe también a algunos de tus amigos.

Ejemplo: *¿Cómo es tu madre?*
Mi madre es alta y delgada. Tiene el pelo largo y castaño y los ojos azules.

12 🎧 Carolina and Miguel are talking about their families. Answer the following questions in English.

1 In what way are both families similar?
2 How well does Carolina get on with her elder sister?
3 Explain Miguel's relationship with his sisters.
4 What does Miguel have to say about his mother?
5 What do they both have to say about their fathers?

LENGUA CLAVE

¿Cómo eres?	(no) soy	alto/a
	(no) es	bajo/a
¿Cómo es tu...?		de talla media
		ni alto/a ni bajo/a
¿Cómo es tu pelo?	tengo el pelo	corto
		largo
		rizado
		ondulado
		liso
		rubio
		castaño
		negro
	soy	calvo/a pelirrojo/a
¿De qué color son tus ojos?	tengo los ojos	azules
		marrones
		verdes
		grises
		negros
¿Llevas gafas?	llevo gafas	

Adjectives

Adjectives have to agree with the noun they describe and are generally positioned after
rather than before the noun as in English.

Masculine singular	Masculine plural	Feminine singular	Feminine plural
alto	altos	alta	altas
largo	largos	larga	largas
negro	negros	negra	negras

Ejemplo: Mi herman**a** es alt**a**, tiene el pel**o**
        larg**o** y negr**o**.

Adjectives that end in a consonant or with the letter
–e only change in the plural form.

Masculine singular	Masculine plural	Feminine singular	Feminine plural
azul	azules	azul	azules
verde	verdes	verde	verdes
gris	grises	gris	grises

Ejemplo: Mi madre tiene el pelo **gris** y los
        ojos **azules**.

Piensa bien en cómo terminan estos adjetivos
y completa las frases siguientes.

1 Me llamo Ana. Tengo los ojos azul…
  y soy pelirroj… . Soy alt… .

2 Soy Pepe. Mi pelo es cort… y negr…
  y mis ojos son marron… .

3 Mi hermana es baj… y gord… .
  Tiene el pelo larg… y rubi… .

4 Mi mejor amigo se llama Jaime.
  No es ni alt… ni baj… . Tiene el pelo
  castañ… y los ojos gris… .

5 Soy hija únic… . Tengo el pelo cort…
  y los ojos marron… .

6 Mi amiga Belén no es ni alt… ni baj… .
  Es una persona muy simpátic… .

7 Me llevo bien con mi tía Rosa porque
  es muy sincer… .

8 Tengo un gato grand… con pelo negr… .
  Desafortunadamente mi hermano
  es alérgic… al pelo de los gatos.

9 Mis padres están divorciad…, pero
  son supersimpátic… y me llevo bien
  con ellos.

10 Mi familia es bastante pequeñ… .

13 🎧 🏫 Escucha lo que dicen. Copia y completa la
tabla con los detalles que faltan.

Nombre	Talla	Ojos	Pelo	Otros
Ejemplo: Ana	baja	azules	negro largo	16 años española
Sandra				
Enrique				
Catalina				
José				
Sara				

14a 📖 ¿Cómo eres? Mira las imágenes. Emparéjalas
con las palabras del recuadro.

Ejemplo: **a** — deportivo

antipático   simpático   deportivo   inteligente

trabajador   un poco loco   amable   tonto

perezoso   divertido   tímido   aburrido

b 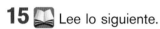 ¿Qué dicen estos jóvenes de sus amigos?
Copia y completa la tabla con los detalles que faltan.

Nombre	Carácter
Ejemplo: Marco	*simpático y divertido*
Yésica	
Juan	
Marta	
Paco	
Susi	

15 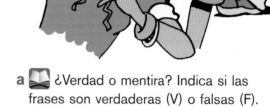 Lee lo siguiente.

¿Eres como tu nombre?

En los países hispanohablantes la mayoría de la
gente tiene uno o dos nombres y dos apellidos.
El primer apellido es en general el primer apellido
de la familia del padre, mientras el segundo es el
primer apellido de la madre. Las chicas normalmente
no cambian sus apellidos al casarse. Por ejemplo,
si Juan López García se casa con María Arollo Cruz,
los dos mantendrán sus apellidos. Entonces digamos
que tienen un hijo llamado Felipe, su nombre
completo sería Felipe López Arollo. Los nombres
de pila* son a menudo gracias a algún santo,
aunque también pueden ser de planetas o estaciones.
Si buscas los orígenes de los apellidos en tu familia,
es muy probable que tenga relación con el lugar
donde vivía o con la profesión que tenía la mayoría.
¿Pero sabías que hay conexiones entre nombres
españoles y la personalidad? ¡Además pasa con
los colores! Mira esto:

Nombre	Carácter		Color	Carácter
Ana	simpático		azul	valiente
Jorge	generoso		verde	animado
Dolores	triste		negro	obediente
Pilar	honesto		marrón	sencillo
Santi	hablador		rojo	romántico
Begoña	cariñoso		amarillo	extrovertido
Rosario	ambicioso		blanco	tranquilo
Antonio	inteligente		gris	tímido
Felipe	paciente		naranja	deportivo

*first name

a 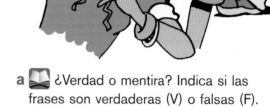 ¿Verdad o mentira? Indica si las
frases son verdaderas (V) o falsas (F).

1 Todos los españoles tienen cuatro nombres.
2 Los apellidos españoles vienen de los dos padres.
3 Las mujeres cambian sus apellidos cuando
se casan.
4 La mayoría de los nombres son nombres
de planetas.
5 Los apellidos a menudo tienen que ver con
un trabajo.

b 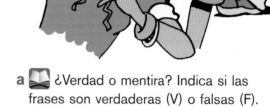 ¡A adivinar! Trabaja con tu pareja. ¿Cuántos
adjetivos conoces? Haz una lista. Usa un
diccionario para ayudarte.

16 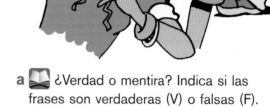 Trabaja con tu pareja. Haz preguntas sobre los
diferentes miembros de su familia. ¡No te olvides de
contestarlas!

Ejemplo:
A: *¿Cómo se llama tu hermano menor?*
B: *Mi hermano menor se llama Tomás.*
A: *¿Cuántos años tiene?*
B: *Tiene doce años.*
A: *¿Cuándo es su cumpleaños?*
B: *Su cumpleaños es el once de enero.*
A: *¿Cómo es?*
B: *Es alto y delgado. Tiene el pelo corto y negro
y los ojos azules.*
A: *¿Cómo es su carácter?*
B: *Es muy travieso, pero también es cariñoso.*

2 ¿Cómo es tu casa?

- ☑ Describe my home
- ☑ Describe my bedroom
- ☑ Use prepositions
- ☑ Talk about household chores
- ☑ Talk about pocket money
- ☑ Talk about daily routine
- ☑ Use reflexive verbs

1a 🎧 📖 Escucha y lee las descripciones para cada persona que habla. Apunta las letras que corresponden.

Ejemplo: **1** *Begoña — h, i*

1

¡Hola! Vivimos en un apartamento en la tercera planta, cerca del centro de la ciudad. Tenemos un balcón amplio detrás que da a unos jardines de la comunidad. Es muy agradable. ¡Hasta pronto!

Begoña

2

¿Qué tal? Nuestra casa nueva es fantástica! Tiene tres dormitorios grandes y ¡cada uno tiene su propio cuarto de baño! Hago mis deberes en el despacho.

Saludos de Juan.

3

¡Hola! Aquí Carlos.

Vivimos bastante cerca del mar que está muy bien, excepto que en verano hay demasiados turistas. Nuestra cocina es pequeña pero normalmente comemos afuera en el patio. Lo único que no me gusta es que no tenga mi propio dormitorio.

Abrazos

4

Siempre he vivido en una granja. Está en un pequeño pueblo donde no hay nada que hacer. La ciudad más cercana está a una hora en coche — cosa que no me gusta en absoluto. Sin embargo, tenemos mucho espacio. Arriba hay cuatro dormitorios y un cuarto de baño y abajo hay salón, comedor y al lado de la cocina una ducha y un retrete. Escríbeme para contarme cómo es tu casa.

Federico

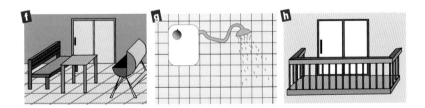

b 🎧 📖 ¿Qué dicen? Escribe el nombre de la persona correcta.

Ejemplo: **1** *— Juan*

1 Vive en una casa.
2 Vive en un piso.
3 Nació donde vive.
4 Vive en la costa.
5 Comparte su dormitorio.
6 Vive en un sitio tranquilo.
7 No tiene jardín.
8 Vive en el campo.
9 Acaba de mudarse.

Look at this address:
C/ Sepúlveda 28 1° B, 28045 Madrid.

C stands for *Calle* (road or street) and the number is always put after the street in Spain. B stands for the flat and the 1° indicates which floor it is on.

Most Spanish people live in flats or apartments — certainly in the cities. The postcode indicates in which part of the city the address is located, the same as in the UK. So, the above address shows that the property is a first floor flat (flat B), which is at number 28 Sepulveda Street in Madrid.

2a Escucha lo que dicen. Copia y rellena la tabla con los detalles que faltan.

	Ejemplo	1	2
Domicilio	*casa*		
Habitaciones	*5*		
Arriba	*2 dormitorios y baño*		
Abajo	*cocina/salón-comedor/aseo*		
Afuera	*nada*		
Otros detalles	*pequeño comparto con hermana*		

b Trabaja con tu pareja. Usa los apuntes de la actividad anterior. Haz preguntas y contéstalas.

1 ¿Vives en una casa o en un piso?
2 ¿Cuántas habitaciones tiene?
3 ¿Qué hay arriba/abajo/afuera?

c Usa esta tabla para ayudarte a escribir una descripción de tu casa. Intenta usar adjetivos y conectores para hacerla más interesante.

Ejemplo: Vivo en una casa grande en las afueras de Santander, cerca de la costa. Arriba tenemos cuatro dormitorios y un baño. Abajo hay salón, comedor y cocina. Afuera hay un jardín pequeño. También tenemos garaje.

GRAMÁTICA

How long?

To say you how long you have been doing something, use *desde hace* + a verb in the present tense.

Example: I've been living in my house for 2 years.
Vivo *en mi casa desde hace dos años.*

Write out the following sentences in Spanish.
1 I've been learning Spanish for 3 years. (*aprender*)
2 We've lived in Spain for 2 years. (*vivir*)
3 He's been doing his homework for 2 hours. (*hacer*)
4 I've been working in the hotel for 6 months. (*trabajar*)
5 She's been buying his CDs for 10 years now. (*comprar*)

vivo en	un piso un apartamento una casa una granja un chalet	grande pequeño/a	en el centro de en las afueras de cerca de en la primera/segunda planta de en el campo en la costa
arriba/abajo hay	… dormitorios un cuarto de baño un aseo una ducha un salón un comedor una cocina un despacho		
afuera hay	balcón patio terraza jardín garaje		

3a 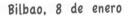 What do Carla and Rafael say about their dream home? Answer the questions in English.

1 Where would Carla like to live?
2 Why?
3 How does she describe her dream home?
4 Where would Rafael like to live?
5 Why?
6 Describe Rafael's dream home.

b Describe tu casa ideal.

Ejemplo: Mi casa ideal es una casa grande…

4 Read Javier's letter. Answer the questions in English.

Bilbao, 8 de enero

Querido amigo,

¿Qué tal? Como ya sabes, acabamos de mudarnos de casa. Antes vivía en el campo cerca de San Sebastián, pero desde el mes pasado, vivimos en un piso en el centro de la ciudad de Bilbao. El piso no es grande, así que tengo que compartir mi habitación con mi hermano menor. Éste me molesta mucho, sobre todo por la tarde cuando él quiere jugar con el ordenador mientras yo estoy estudiando. Sin embargo el piso es práctico y a solo diez minutos andando del instituto y del polideportivo.

Estamos en la tercera planta de un bloque moderno. Hay una entrada pequeña y a la izquierda una cocina. El salón-comedor es enorme. Está a la derecha, enfrente del cuarto de baño. Al final del pasillo hay tres dormitorios. También hay un balcón que da al jardín y es muy tranquilo. No tenemos animales. Las autoridades no los permiten. Además a mi padre le irritan mucho el ruido y el olor. ¿Y tú? ¿Cómo es donde vives? ¿Vives en una casa o en un piso?

Un saludo,

Javier

1 How long has Javier been living in Bilbao?
2 How does he feel about sharing a room with his brother?
3 What exactly is the reason?
4 Does Javier like his new home and how do you know? Mention four things he says.
5 Why doesn't Javier have any pets at home? Give two reasons.

5 📖 Mira la imagen. Indica si las frases son verdaderas (V) o falsas (F).

Ejemplo: En mi dormitorio hay dos camas — V

1 Hay una lámpara en la cama.
2 La estantería está encima de la mesa.
3 El armario está al lado de la puerta.
4 Hay una mesilla entre las camas.
5 Nuestra habitación está muy ordenada.
6 Hay una silla delante de la mesa.
7 En las paredes hay muchos pósters.

6 🎧 Añade los cuartos usando palabras del recuadro, según la descripción.

Ejemplo: 8 — la entrada

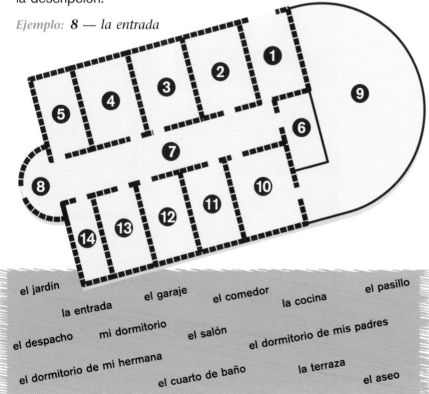

el jardín
la entrada
el garaje
el comedor
la cocina
el pasillo
el despacho
mi dormitorio
el salón
el dormitorio de mis padres
el dormitorio de mi hermana
el cuarto de baño
la terraza
el aseo

GRAMÁTICA

Using prepositions

Learn the following prepositions:

entre	between
sobre	on top of/above
encima de	on
detrás de	behind
delante de	in front of
a la derecha de	to the right of
al lado de	beside/next to
debajo de	under
enfrente de	opposite
contra	against
cerca de	near
a la izquierda de	to the left of

Some of these prepositions are followed by **de**. Remember that **de** + **el** = **del**

Example: La cama está al lado del armario.
The bed is beside the wardrobe.

Las tareas de casa

Escucha y empareja las imágenes con el texto.

Ejemplo: **1 — c**

7a
Busca estas palabras en el diccionario. ¿En qué habitación se encuentran? Copia y completa la tabla.

- el lavaplatos
- la cama
- el sofá
- la bañera
- la mesa
- el retrete
- el televisor
- la silla
- el armario
- la nevera
- el horno
- la estantería
- el sillón
- la lavadora
- la cómoda
- el aparador
- el congelador
- el fregadero

Habitación	
la sala de estar	*el sofá, el televisor...*
el comedor	
la cocina	
el cuarto de baño	
el dormitorio	

b
Trabaja con tu pareja. Describe y compara los cuartos en tu casa.

Ejemplo:

A: *Vivo en una casa grande y moderna.*
B: *Yo también vivo en una casa pero no es grande.*
A: *En mi dormitorio hay dos camas.*
B: *En mi dormitorio solo hay una cama.*
A: *El salón está al lado del comedor.*
B: *El salón de mi casa no está al lado del comedor. Está enfrente del comedor.*

8
Prepara una breve presentación sobre tu casa.

Usa estos apuntes para ayudarte:
- Dónde vives.
- Con quién vives.
- Cuánto tiempo llevas viviendo allí.
- Qué habitaciones hay en la casa.
- Dónde están las habitaciones.
- Cómo es tu dormitorio.

1. Friego los platos.
2. Pongo la mesa.
3. Paseo con el perro.
4. Lavo el coche.
5. Cocino un poco.
6. Hago mi cama.
7. Saco la basura.
8. Arreglo mi dormitorio.
9. Hago la compra.
10. Hago un poco de bricolaje.
11. Paso la aspiradora.
12. Plancho la ropa.
13. Hago de canguro.
14. Vacío el lavavajillas.

b
Trabaja con tu pareja. Averigua lo que hace y lo que no hace para ayudar en casa.

10 La familia de Maite tiene un hotel. ¿Qué dice de las tareas de casa? Copia y completa la tabla con los detalles que faltan.

Persona	Actividad 1	Frecuencia	Actividad 2	Frecuencia
Ejemplo: padre	*basura*	*cada mañana*	*bricolaje*	*de vez en cuando*
madre				
Juan (hermano)				
Maite				

11a Trabaja con tu pareja. Lee lo que dicen estos jóvenes ¿Estás de acuerdo con ellos? ¿Por qué (no)?

Ejemplo: *Estoy de acuerdo con Maribel. Su hermano debería ayudar.*

No sé porque Ramón no está contento. Tiene que arreglar su dormitorio, pero le gusta tener las cosas en su sitio.

Tengo que arreglar mi dormitorio todos los días. Me gusta tener las cosas en su sitio. Pero mi hermana menor deja sus cosas por todas partes y mis padres no dicen nada. No sé por qué. No estoy nada contento.

Ramón

Mis padres pagan a mi hermana por hacer tareas domésticas mientras que yo ayudo siempre sin cobrar. Hago mi cama y todo. No me dan nada y no estoy contento.

Alberto

Los sábados por la tarde mi padre y mi hermano mayor van al estadio de fútbol. Mi madre y yo tenemos que hacer las compras y limpiar la casa. No me gusta ayudar y estoy harta.

Carla

Mi hermana y yo tenemos que quitar la mesa y fregar los platos después de cada comida. No creo que sea justo porque mi hermano no hace nada. Sale del salón después de comer y se sienta enfrente del ordenador.

Maribel

b Escribe sobre lo que pasa en tu casa.

LENGUA CLAVE

Los adverbios siguientes te ayudarán a hacer tus respuestas más interesantes:

siempre	always
a menudo	often
mucho	a lot
muy poco	very little
nunca	never
a veces	sometimes
cada día/todos los días	each/every day
por la mañana/tarde	in the morning/afternoon
los fines de semana	at the weekends
el lunes	on Mondays

El dinero

12a 🎧 Mira las imágenes. Escucha lo que dicen los jóvenes. ¿En qué gastan su dinero?

Ejemplo: **1** — *c*

  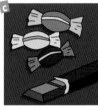 

CULTURA

1 ¿Qué países europeos tienen el euro (hay 17)? Entérate y haz una lista. Usa un diccionario para ayudarte con los países.

2 ¿Sabes cómo se llama el dinero que usan? Empareja el país con el dinero.

Inglaterra	bolívar
Chile	peso
India	rand
Venezuela	libra
Brasil	yen
Australia	rupee
China	real
Japón	dólar
África del Sur	yuan

b 📖 ✏️ ¿Cuánto dinero reciben? Lee el texto y completa la tabla con los detalles que faltan.

Según una encuesta hecha recientemente parece ser que no todos los jóvenes están contentos con la cantidad de dinero que reciben. Preguntamos a nuestros lectores. Debajo hay una selección de sus respuestas. ¿Qué piensas tú? Mándanos tus opiniones.

Mis padres no me dan nada de dinero. Así que tengo que trabajar en un bar los fines de semana, limpiando mesas y fregando. No es justo, pero por lo menos el dinero es mío para gastar como quiera.

Paco (17 años)

Mis padres me dan 8€ cada día y aparte de eso me pagan todo como mi ropa. El problema es que no siempre puedo hacer lo que quiero. Pero no está mal del todo.

Ana (15 años)

Recibo unos 20€ cada semana. Eso es mucho menos que mis amigos.

Eduardo (14 años)

A mí me dan 80€ al mes. Si necesito más para algo como salir con mis amigos o para comprar un regalo especial, le ayudo a mi padre en su empresa para ganar un poco de dinero extra. Eso me parece muy bien. Muchos de mis amigos trabajan cada fin de semana pero no quiero hacer eso porque tengo que estudiar también.

Conchita (16 años)

Mis padres me dan 25€ los sábados. No está mal porque trabajo también. Creo que los padres deberían pagar más a sus hijos, pero solo si hacen cosas en casa para ayudar.

Maite (15 años)

Nombre	Cantidad	Frecuencia	Opinión
Ejemplo: Eduardo	*20€*	*cada semana*	*menos que sus amigos*

c 💬 Trabaja con tu pareja. Contesta las preguntas.

1 ¿Te dan dinero tus padres?
2 ¿Cuánto dinero recibes?
3 ¿Cuándo recibes tu dinero?
4 ¿Trabajas para ganar dinero?
5 ¿En qué te gastas tu dinero?
6 ¿Estás contento con el dinero que recibes?
7 ¿Por qué (no)?

¡OJO!

Mi(s) padre/madre/padres me da(n)……? por día /semana /mes.

Mi(s) padre/madre/padres no me da(n)…… .

Trabajo los fines de semana/el sábado/durante las vacaciones.

Mi(s) padre/madre/padres paga(n) mi ropa

Gasto mi dinero en ……… .

En mi opinión (no) es suficiente.

La rutina diaria

13a  Según lo que oyes y lees, empareja las imágenes con las frases correctas.

Ejemplo: **1 — d**

1 Durante la semana siempre me despierto a las siete.

2 Normalmente regreso a casa a las cuatro y media.

3 Después de la cena me relajo enfrente de la televisión.

4 Siempre me ducho por la mañana.

5 Me peino y me lavo los dientes en el cuarto de baño.

6 Tomo la cena a las ocho.

7 A las seis de la tarde hago mis deberes. Tengo mucho que hacer.

8 Me visto.

9 Desayuno cereales y café.

10 Normalmente me acuesto a las diez y media.

11 A las ocho y media salgo de la casa para ir al instituto.

12 Me levanto a las siete y cuarto o así.

13 Antes de acostarme me baño.

b Trabaja con tu pareja. Haz preguntas como las de abajo y contesta. ¿Puedes añadir unas cuantas más?

1 ¿A qué hora te despiertas?

2 ¿Te duchas por la mañana?

3 ¿Desayunas?

4 ¿Cuándo regresas a casa por la tarde?

5 ¿Qué haces por la tarde?

6 ¿A qué hora te acuestas?

c Escucha a Mari Vi. Lee las frases e indica si son verdaderas (V) o falsas (F).

Ejemplo: **1 — F**

1 *Se levanta a las seis de la mañana.*

2 Le gusta bañarse por las mañanas.

3 No desayuna.

4 Vive bastante cerca de su colegio.

5 El día de colegio es bastante largo.

6 Normalmente se baña antes de cenar.

7 Se acuesta tarde los fines de semana.

d Escribe un pequeño párrafo para describir tu propia rutina.

Por la mañana, me despierto…

GRAMÁTICA

Reflexive verbs

In Spanish, most reflexive verbs are used to describe actions you do to yourself every day or that involve a change of some sort, for example getting up, sitting down or becoming angry. In Spanish, the 'self' word is a reflexive pronoun and appears in front of the verb, except in the infinitive. Here is an example:

levantar**se**	to get (**oneself**) up
me levanto	I get up
te levantas	you get up
se levanta	he/she/it gets up
nos levantamos	we get up
os levantáis	you get up
se levantan	they get up

Can you recognise these common reflexive verbs? If you are unsure, use a dictionary to help you.

acostarse	irse	ponerse
afeitarse	lavarse	quitarse
bañarse	levantarse	secarse
despertarse	llamarse	sentarse
dormirse	limpiarse	vestirse
ducharse	maquillarse	
enfadarse	pasearse	

A lot of the reflexive verbs in the activity above are not reflexive in English (i.e. they don't use the 'self' word), for example *acostarse* is 'to go to bed'. Can you find some others?

3 Mi barrio

- ✔ Talk about my local area
- ✔ Find my way around town
- ✔ Discuss advantages and disadvantages
- ✔ Use *ser*, *estar* and *hay*
- ✔ Use the imperfect tense

1 ¿Qué hay en tu barrio? Pon los dibujos en el orden correcto según la lista a la derecha.

Ejemplo: **1 — f**

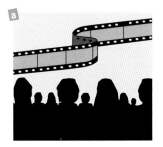

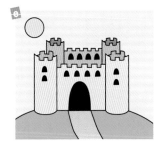

1. un banco
2. una discoteca
3. un instituto
4. una biblioteca
5. un teatro
6. un museo
7. correos
8. una tienda
9. una piscina
10. una playa
11. una pista de hielo
12. un castillo
13. un parque
14. un polideportivo
15. un mercado
16. un cine
17. una iglesia

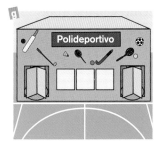

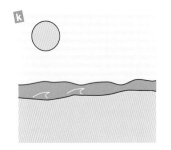

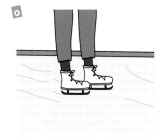

2 🎧 📖 Escucha y lee lo que dicen estos jóvenes. Indica si cada frase es verdadera (V) o falsa (F).

Ejemplo: Ana vive en el campo — V

1 Ana vive en un sitio grande.
2 Cree que es entretenido.
3 Enrique se ha mudado mucho.
4 Dice que donde vive es civilizado.
5 Donde vive Luci hay mucho que hacer para los jóvenes.
6 No es muy limpio.
7 Patrick está contento donde vive.
8 Vive en un sitio de vacaciones.
9 Su barrio es muy animado.

> ¡Hola! Me llamo Ana y vivo en un pequeño pueblo en el campo en el norte de España. Aquí no está mal. Es limpio y no hay mucho tráfico. Lo malo es que no hay mucho que hacer para los jóvenes, así que me aburro bastante.

Ana

> Me llamo Enrique. He vivido en varias ciudades pero ahora vivo en una ciudad pequeña y tranquila en el oeste de España. Creo que es mucho más agradable vivir aquí. Hay muchas diversiones como cines y discotecas. Sin embargo, no hay mucho vandalismo o graffiti como en otras ciudades más grandes. Prefiero ésta.

Enrique

> ¡Hola! Soy Luci. Vivo en una ciudad muy grande e industrial en el centro de España. Llevamos un mes viviendo aquí. Las atracciones son fantásticas y hay mucho para los jóvenes. Lo malo es que también hay muchos problemas. Por ejemplo, es una ciudad bastante ruidosa y con mucha polución y hay mucho tráfico. Además, hay basura por las calles. Cuando era joven vivíamos en un pueblo y lo prefería.

Luci

> Yo me llamo Patrick. Soy de Irlanda y me mudé aquí hace ocho años con mis padres. Vivimos en una ciudad pequeña, pero turística en el sur de España. Verdaderamente me encanta aquí. Hay mucho para los jóvenes pero a veces me parece que hay demasiados turistas en el verano.

Patrick

3 🎧 What do these people say about where they live? Answer the questions in English.

1 Why doesn't Antonio like his town? Give three reasons.
2 What is there for young people to do in Marisol's town? Give two ideas.
3 What does Yolanda see as the advantages of living in the country? Give three ideas.
4 Why is Carlos concerned about living in an industrial town?
5 What is the biggest advantage of living in Ana's town?

4a 💬 Habla con tu pareja. Describe tu pueblo.

Vivo en	Madrid Bilbao Londres Cardiff Bristol	una cuidad un pueblo una aldea	grande pequeño/a	y/e	industrial histórico/a turístico/a importante

Está situado/a en	el norte el sur el este el oeste	de España de Inglaterra de Escocia de Irlanda de Gales

Está cerca de…	
Está a…kilómetros de…	
Hay más o menos…habitantes.	

En…hay Cerca de…hay Para los jóvenes hay	un banco una discoteca un instituto una biblioteca un teatro un museo Correos una tienda una piscina una playa una pista de hielo un castillo un parque un polideportivo un mercado un cine una iglesia

b 💬 Trabaja con tu pareja. Pregúntale lo siguiente.

1 ¿Dónde vives?
2 ¿Dónde está tu cuidad/pueblo/aldea?
3 ¿Cómo es tu cuidad/pueblo/aldea?
4 ¿Qué hay en tu cuidad/pueblo/aldea?

c 📝 Escribe una descripción del lugar donde vives.

Vivo en…

Lo bueno y lo malo

5 📖 🏔 Lee lo que dice esta gente de donde viven. Escoge los adjetivos que mejor describan lo que piensan del recuadro de abajo. Escríbelos en la columna adecuada de la tabla.

Ejemplo: No hay ruido aquí, pero tampoco hay mucho que hacer.

3 El tiempo es fantástico pero ¡hay tanta basura!

1 Es un pueblo en la costa que está muy concurrido en el verano, pero cuesta mucho vivir.

4 Mi pueblo está en el norte. Hay muchas fábricas, lo que afecta el medio ambiente.

2 Hay mucho que hacer aquí, pero con todos los coches no te puedes entender.

5 Tenemos muchos castillos y museos aquí. Es de verdad pintoresco. Pero prefiero las ciudades grandes.
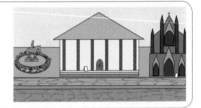

aburrido   animado   caluroso   caro
contaminado   histórico   industrial   pequeño
ruidoso   sucio   tranquilo   turístico

	Lo bueno	Lo malo
Ejemplo:	*tranquilo*	*aburrido*
1		

GRAMÁTICA

Ser, estar, hay

There are two verbs meaning 'to be': *ser* and *estar*. *Ser* is used when things are permanent and do not change, for example:

*Mi ciudad **es** grande.*   My town is large.

Estar is used for things that might change or to say where something is, for example:

*De momento la ciudad **está** sucia pero…*   At the moment the town is dirty but…

*Barcelona **está** en el noreste de España.*   Barcelona is in the northeast of Spain.

ser	estar
soy	estoy
eres	estás
es	está
somos	estamos
sois	estáis
son	están

To say '**there is**' or '**there are**', use **hay**. For example:

*En mi pueblo **hay** mucho tráfico.*   In my village there is a lot of traffic.

Completa las frases utilizando la forma correcta de **ser** o **estar**, o **hay**, según convenga.

1 En la capital _____ muchos edificios y monumentos.
2 Normalmente la plaza mayor _____ en el centro de la ciudad.
3 Mi familia y yo _____ de Barcelona.
4 En mi pueblo _____ un polideportivo nuevo.
5 Aquí las casas _____ muy bonitas.
6 Mi barrio _____ en el norte de la región.
7 Aquí _____ una pista de hielo donde puedes patinar.
8 Para ir al centro _____ mejor coger el metro.
9 En el verano _____ fiestas en el pueblo.
10 La primavera _____ una estación agradable.

6 Unos jóvenes están hablando de donde viven. ¿Qué piensan? Rellena la tabla con los detalles.

	Lo bueno	Lo malo
Ejemplo:	*bonita*	*aburrida/nada que hacer*
1		

7 Escucha esta entrevista. Llena los huecos añadiendo las palabras que faltan.

Entrevistador: *Hola Francina, ¿Me puedes contar algo sobre donde vives?*
Francina: Vivo en Mallorca — es la isla más ____ de España y está situada en el mar Mediterráneo. Es una de las Islas Baleares.

E: *¿Y cuánto tiempo has vivido allí?*
F: Llevo ____ años viviendo allí.

E: *¿Y dónde vivías antes?*
F: Antes vivía en Bilbao — una ciudad grande e ____ en el ____ de España.

E: *¿Y dónde exactamente vives en Mallorca?*
F: Vivo en Palma, la capital de la isla. También es la capital de las Islas Baleares.

E: *¿Y qué tipo de ciudad es Palma, Francina?*
F: Como puedes imaginar, la industria principal es el turismo. De hecho, ¡es casi la única industria!

E: *¿Y cómo es la isla?*
F: Es muy bonita con ____, una gran variedad de ____ y por supuesto el clima es ____ .

E: *¿Y cómo se llega a Mallorca?*
F: Eso es fácil. Hay un ____ grande en Palma y también se puede llegar en ____ .

E: *¿Qué es lo bueno de Mallorca?*
F: Hay mucho que hacer, incluso en invierno. Hay muchos clubs y restaurantes.

E: *¿Y lo malo?*
F: Lo malo es que la isla tiene demasiados turistas. Durante el verano, especialmente en ____ no es fácil encontrar un hotel o alquilar un ____ . También es difícil encontrar un sitio donde extender tu toalla en la ____ .

8 Trabaja con tu pareja. Habla de tu ciudad. Usa y adapta las preguntas de arriba.

LENGUA CLAVE

Lo bueno/malo es/son
 Lo bueno es/son… — the good thing(s) is/are…
 Lo malo es/son… — the bad thing(s) is/are…

These can be used with a noun:
 Lo bueno es la playa.
   The good thing is the beach.

Lo malo son los turistas.
The bad thing is the tourists.

They can also be used with another verb or *hay* by adding '*es que*':
 Lo bueno es que está cerca de las tiendas.
   The good thing is it's near the shops.

Lo bueno es que hay mucho que hacer.
The good thing is there's a lot to do.

Lo malo es que son caros.
The bad thing is they're expensive.

Lo malo es que no hay aparcamiento.
The bad thing is there isn't anywhere to park.

9a Escucha y pon los dibujos en el orden correcto. Indica la dirección con una de las señales.

Siga todo recto Tuerza a la izquierda

Tuerza a la derecha ⬇️

Ejemplo: ¿Por dónde se va a la estación, por favor?
Sigue todo recto — a ⬆️

la estación de trenes   la piscina

el mercado   el centro comercial

el ayuntamiento   el teatro

el hospital   la parada de autobús

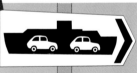

el puerto   la plaza mayor

el aparcamiento   la oficina de turismo

b 💬 Habla con tu pareja.
Haz preguntas y contéstalas.

¿Dónde está	el puerto? la iglesia?
¿Por dónde se va	al puerto? a la iglesia?
¿Está lejos/cerca?	

¡Atención! — a + el = al

Many shops in Spanish come from the name of the product they principally sell. While the addition of some other letters beforehand varies, generally the shop will end in *–ía*.

Mira estos sustantivos y conviértelos en tiendas. Usa un diccionario para ayudarte.

	Cosa	Tienda
	pan	*panadería*
	fruta	
	carne	
	pastel	
	flor	
	pescado	
	libro	
	zapato	
	papel	
	café	

Another way to make the name of a shop is to use the following: *tienda de…*

Mira estos sustantivos y conviértelos en tiendas. Usa un diccionario para ayudarte.

	Cosa	Tienda
	ropa	*tienda de ropa*
	discos	
	deportes	
	disfraces	
	caramelos	
	bricolaje	
	videojuegos	

¡Atención! — a book shop is **una librería** and a library is **una biblioteca**.

10a 📖 ¿Sabes orientarte por el laberinto?
Mira el plano. Lee las indicaciones.
Para cada persona indica su destino.

Ejemplo: **1** e — *tienda de discos*

Key:	**d** supermercado	**h** carnicería
a zapatería	**e** tienda de discos	**i** panadería
b pastelería	**f** papelería	**j** cine
c frutería	**g** tienda de ropa	**k** cafetería

Dentro del centro comercial

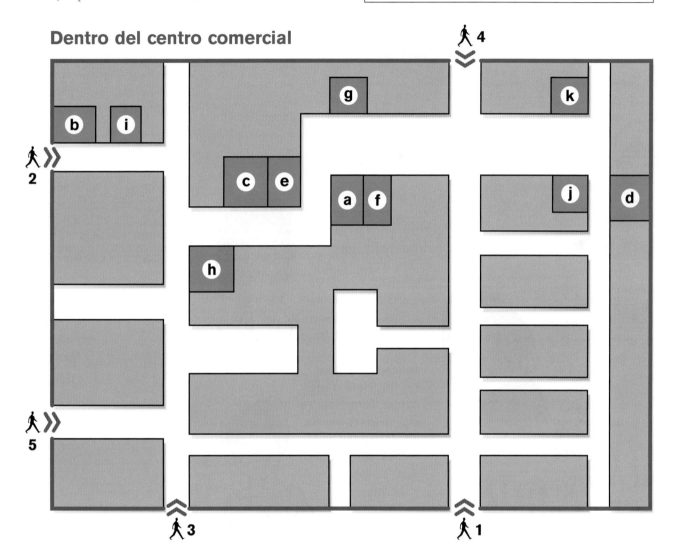

1 Cuando entres, tuerce en el primer pasillo a la izquierda. Sigue por él y coge el primero a la derecha. En la segunda esquina a la derecha verás la carnicería. Coge ese pasillo y es la tienda que hace esquina a la izquierda.

2 Sigue por este pasillo, gira a la derecha y a continuación a la izquierda. En este pasillo, al fondo está la tienda, en la esquina opuesta a la tienda de discos y enfrente de la tienda de ropa.

3 Si coges el primer pasillo a la derecha, sigues por él hasta que puedas girar a la izquierda. Una vez en ese pasillo tuerces la segunda esquina a la izquierda y en esa calle, en el lado izquierdo justo antes de la zapatería que hay en la esquina, tienes la tienda que buscas.

4 Es muy fácil. Tuerces ahí la primera a la izquierda, al fondo verás una cafetería en la esquina de la izquierda, en la de la derecha está lo que buscas, pero la entrada es por la otra calle, frente al supermercado.

5 Tuerces la primera a la izquierda, sigues hasta la segunda a la izquierda y en ese pasillo, a la derecha pasas la panadería y a ese mismo lado, justo antes de la salida, ahí tienes.

b 💬 Trabaja con tu pareja.
Practica orientándote alrededor del centro comercial.

Cuando era pequeño

11 🎧 📖 ¿Quién habla?
Escribe el nombre que corresponda con cada imágen.

Ejemplo: ***a*** *— Paco*

Cuando era joven vivía en el campo. Era precioso, muy tranquilo y bonito. Vivía con mis padres en una casa grande. Ahora vivimos en un piso pequeño en el centro de la ciudad.

Ana

Me encantaba jugar con mi hermana en el parque del barrio, pero ahora siendo mayor prefiero salir con mis amigos.

Isabel

Antes esta ciudad era una de las más importantes e industriales. Había mucho trabajo y era muy animada. Pero ahora se han cerrado muchas de las fábricas y hay mucho desempleo.

Paco

Siempre viajaba en coche o en autobús, pero ya no. Intento ir a todos los sitios a pie o en bicicleta. Pienso en el medio ambiente.

Iñes

Solíamos comprar en las tiendas del barrio pero hoy en día todo el mundo va al supermercado porque es mucho más cómodo y barato.

Federico

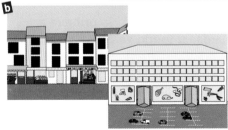
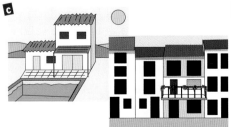

GRAMÁTICA

The imperfect tense

To describe what used to happen, what was happening or what happened habitually/ frequently at some time in the past, we use the imperfect tense. Some examples of imperfect tenses have been highlighted in the texts in Exercise 11.

To form the imperfect tense look at the box below.

-ar verbs	-er/-ir verbs
trabajaba	vivía
trabajabas	vivías
trabajaba	vivía
trabajábamos	vivíamos
trabajabais	vivíais
trabajaban	vivían

There are three irregular verbs in the imperfect tense

ser	ir	ver
era	iba	veía
eras	ibas	veías
era	iba	veía
éramos	íbamos	veíamos
erais	ibais	veíais
eran	iban	veían

The verb *soler* can also be used with the infinitive to replace the imperfect tense:

Solía ir a clase de baile todos los días.
I used to go to a dance class every day.

Copia y completa las frases.

1 Cuando (*ser*) joven mi familia y yo (*vivir*) en la costa.
2 (*ir*) al colegio a pie con mi hermano.
3 Antes mi madre (*ser*) profesora.
4 ¡Mis amigos (*ser*) todos españoles!
5 Mi padre (*trabajar*) en una fábrica.

24

12 🎧 Escucha a esta gente hablando de su juventud. ¿Qué hacían y con qué frecuencia? Rellena la tabla.

Actividad	Cuando
Ejemplo: deberes	*antes de salir con amigos*
1	

13 🗣 Habla con tus padres y con otra gente para acordarte de lo que hacías antes. Escribe un pequeño párrafo sobre ello. Indica con qué frecuencia hacías las cosas.

14a 📖🗣 Lee el texto sobre Guatemala. Copia las frases en negrita y encuentra sus significados entre las frases en inglés en la lista.

- it is worth a visit
- it is a unique product of indigenous customs
- everything is beginning to change now
- it is the third biggest nation in Central America
- half the population
- they don't have drinking water
- there is a great variety...
- there is a big difference between...
- they tend to wear traditional clothes
- they say that...

Ejemplo: es la tercera nación más grande de Centroamérica.
it is the third biggest nation in Central America.

b Answer the questions in English.

1 Name two physical features of Guatemala.
2 Who are the '*ladinos*'?
3 What is the main influence in the capital?
4 How do rural families generally earn a living?
5 How are parents described?
6 Why are they described in this way?
7 How are elderly people treated?
8 How does the city compare to rural parts?

Guatemala

Guatemala, una república de Centroamérica, es una tierra escabrosa de montañas y volcanes, lagos preciosos y fauna fértil. **Es la tercera nación más grande de Centroamérica.** Es muy bonita y desde luego **vale la pena visitarla.**

La cultura de Guatemala **es producto único de las costumbres indígenas** de los indios americanos y de la España colonial. **La mitad del pueblo** es mestiza (son conocidos en Guatemala como *ladinos*), lo que quiere decir que son una mezcla de sangre europea e indígena. Mucha gente guatemalteca todavía habla un idioma de los mayas.

Hay una gran variedad de modos de vivir en Guatemala. En la capital, por ejemplo, la cultura y la moda europea dominan. Cine, música, cultura y moda — incluso la comida rápida — han dejado su marca, lo cual ha hecho disminuir hasta cierto punto las costumbres tradicionales hispánicas.

Fuera de la capital — en el campo — siguen todavía las maneras antiguas. En los pueblos, por ejemplo, **tienden a llevar ropa tradicional** de colores vivos y destacados. La familia típica lleva una vida dura y trabajadora. Los hombres normalmente trabajan en el campo mientras las mujeres cuidan a los niños y tejen telas bonitas con imágenes únicas en cada comunidad.

Para la gente guatemalteca la familia es muy importante. **Dicen que** los padres son *espejos* y que a través de ellos aprendes quién eres y en qué te vas a convertir. Los niños reciben de sus padres consejos y ayuda a lo largo la vida.

Los miembros de las familias tienden a vivir el uno cerca del otro, y una familia típica consta de padres, hijos solteros y casados, y todos sus respectivos niños. La familia cuida bien a los mayores, y los padrinos son muy importantes en la vida de los pequeños. Sin embargo, **todo empieza a cambiar ahora** con la adopción de valores occidentales.

Tal diversidad hace que el país sea fascinante. Pero esa diversidad no es siempre positiva. En Guatemala **hay una diferencia enorme entre** los ricos y los pobres. Mientras la capital, que también se llama Guatemala, tiene edificios modernos, paseos arboleados y todos los servicios civilizados, hay muchas ciudades donde todavía hay pobreza y que **no tienen agua potable** a su alcance ni suficiente comida para sus habitantes.

Paper 1: listening

Some of the questions you meet in the examination are multiple-choice tasks. These questions normally target lower grades. If you are hoping to reach a high level of success, you should be able to select the correct answers without difficulty. Before you start, make sure you look closely at the title, the rubric and the specific questions that you are being asked to answer.

Work through the sample question below.

> **Exam tip**
>
> The title indicates the content of what you will hear. What vocabulary items will be key to finding the answers? Use the pause time to read carefully through all the questions.

Mi familia

¿Qué dice esta chica?

Pon una equis ⊠ en las casillas apropiadas.

What does this girl say?

Put a cross ⊠ in the correct boxes.

Ejemplo: Se llama…

| **A** María ☐ | **B** Mariana ☐ | **C** Maruja ⊠ |

The completed example is always obvious. It is included to help you to understand what you have to do.

1 Vive en…

| A ☐ | B ☐ | C ☐ |

Do you remember the Spanish for these three items of vocabulary? Listen out for what you know. If you are unsure it is always worth guessing the answer.

2 Tiene…

| A ⊠ | B ⊠ | C ⊠ |

Be careful. Is the key word masculine, feminine or plural?

3 También tiene…

| A ⊠ | B ⊠ | C ☐ |

One of these words is a cognate.

4 Se lleva bien con…

| A ☐ | B ☐ | C ☐ |

This question is key to finding the right answer. What does *se lleva bien con* mean?

5 Su padre es…

| A ☐ | B ☐ | C ☐ |

Make sure that the job you listen for is connected to Maruja's father.

(Total for Question: 5 marks)

Paper 2: reading

If you are aiming to reach a high level of success, you should expect to score well on this question. It requires:

- a good knowledge of vocabulary relating to the family: physical appearance, attitudes etc.

- the ability to link ideas in the statements made by the speakers with the sentences (i)–(v) below; in the example, you can deduce that Gloria has a big family by the number of brothers, sisters and cousins she has.

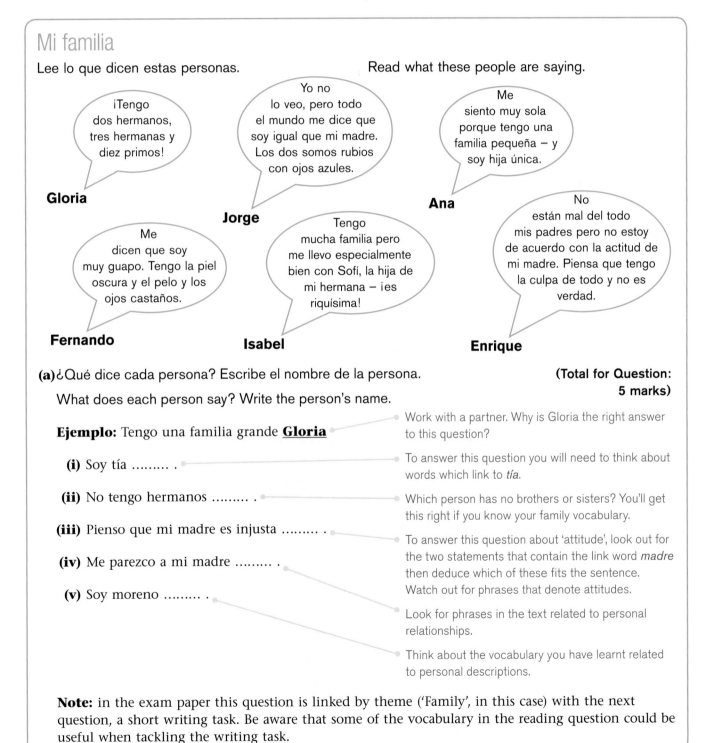

Mi familia

Lee lo que dicen estas personas.   Read what these people are saying.

Gloria: ¡Tengo dos hermanos, tres hermanas y diez primos!

Jorge: Yo no lo veo, pero todo el mundo me dice que soy igual que mi madre. Los dos somos rubios con ojos azules.

Ana: Me siento muy sola porque tengo una familia pequeña – y soy hija única.

Fernando: Me dicen que soy muy guapo. Tengo la piel oscura y el pelo y los ojos castaños.

Isabel: Tengo mucha familia pero me llevo especialmente bien con Sofí, la hija de mi hermana – ¡es riquísima!

Enrique: No están mal del todo mis padres pero no estoy de acuerdo con la actitud de mi madre. Piensa que tengo la culpa de todo y no es verdad.

(a) ¿Qué dice cada persona? Escribe el nombre de la persona.

What does each person say? Write the person's name.

(Total for Question: 5 marks)

Ejemplo: Tengo una familia grande **Gloria**

— Work with a partner. Why is Gloria the right answer to this question?

(i) Soy tía ....

— To answer this question you will need to think about words which link to *tía*.

(ii) No tengo hermanos ....

— Which person has no brothers or sisters? You'll get this right if you know your family vocabulary.

(iii) Pienso que mi madre es injusta ....

— To answer this question about 'attitude', look out for the two statements that contain the link word *madre* then deduce which of these fits the sentence. Watch out for phrases that denote attitudes.

(iv) Me parezco a mi madre ....

— Look for phrases in the text related to personal relationships.

(v) Soy moreno ....

— Think about the vocabulary you have learnt related to personal descriptions.

Note: in the exam paper this question is linked by theme ('Family', in this case) with the next question, a short writing task. Be aware that some of the vocabulary in the reading question could be useful when tackling the writing task.

Paper 2: writing

Question 3(b) is always a short writing task relating to the reading task in question 3(a). Question 3(a) will help you to think about the context of question 3(b), and perhaps give some vocabulary help. If you do use vocabulary to be found in question 3(a), it is important to make sure it fits the ideas and opinions that you put forward. **Do not copy out chunk of text from 3(a) or you will lose marks.**

Here is a sample question 3(b) that follows on from the previous reading question.

(b)¿Cuántas personas hay en tu familia? ¿Cómo te llevas con ellos?

Remember to answer *both* questions.

How many people are there in your family? How do you get on with them?

Escribe unas 50 palabras **en español**.
Write about 50 words **in Spanish**.

How many sentences can you include in 50 words?

(10)

Aquí tienes algunas ideas.
Here are some ideas.

Before beginning this task work with a partner. Can you think of two short statements relating to each of the ideas below? Use these as your draft content.

padres/parents   **hermanos/brothers and sisters**

apariencia/appearance   **mascotas/pets**   **relaciones/relationships**

Sample student answer

Read the question carefully. You need to answer **both** questions. Remember that you have only 50 words, so use them wisely. Keep the language you use simple, but try to include longer sentences by using connectives. Here is a sample student answer.

A good use of a subordinate clause to extend a short sentence and to add variety to the text.

This answers the second question well.

A good use of a connective to make the sentence more interesting.

The introduction of an opinion gives a reason for mentioning pets.

En mi familia hay cinco personas: mi padre que se llama Juan, mi madre, Ana, mis dos hermanos y yo. Me llevo muy bien con mis padres. No son estrictos y me tratan como a un adulto. Me parezco a mi madre, pero tengo el carácter de mi padre. Soy baja y tengo los ojos azules. Me encantan los animales. Tenemos un gato y un perro negro que se llama Fiesta.

This is a good answer but is longer than necessary (69 words). It shows that examiners do tolerate slightly longer answers. There is not a cut-off point, but you should be careful not to write answers that are too far over the limit. There is also limited space to write your answer on the question paper.

The first question has been answered clearly.

Commas are important. Use these well.

This extra detail explains the reference to good relationships at home and adds some interesting detail.

Use of the first person plural shows you can use verbs correctly.

Two tiny extra details also add interest to the response.

Now write your own answer to this question.

Paper 3: speaking (section A)

The format and marking of the speaking test is explained in *About Exam Corner* at the start of the book.

Section A is a presentation and follow-on discussion based on a picture that you choose. You may choose, for example, a family photograph, a holiday photo or a magazine picture relating to one of your interests. It is important to choose a photo or picture about which there is plenty to say and about which you can talk comfortably and with confidence. It must not contain any written text.

Exam tip

- The topic area chosen for the presentation is different from those chosen for the conversation part of the speaking test.
- You are assessed on the accuracy of your language as well as on the content of what you say. Make sure that you:
  - form verbs and their tenses correctly
  - pronounce accurately

Here is an example.

Work with a partner. Practise asking and answering the following questions related to photo 1.
- *¿Dónde fue sacada esta foto?*
- *¿Cuántas personas hay en la foto?*
- *Describe a las personas de la foto.*
- *¿Quién crees que son las personas de la foto?*
- *¿Quién es tu persona favorita en la foto? ¿Por qué?*
- *¿Por qué están sonriendo estas personas?*

To help you get started, here are some useful vocabulary and phrases that you could use:

Esta foto fue sacada en...	This picture was taken in...
Hay ... personas.	There are ... people.
La chica a la izquierda...	The girl on the left...
El señor de la derecha...	The man on the right...
La mujer que está en medio...	The woman in the middle...
La chica detrás de la mujer...	The girl behind the woman...
Se ve(n)...	You can see...
Yo estoy...	I am... (*position in the picture*).
En mi opinión...	In my opinion...
Pienso que...	I think that...

Now practise asking and answering questions using photo 2.

Vocabulario

Family

el **abuelo**   grandfather
la **abuela**   grandmother
el/la **bebé**   baby
el **bisabuelo**   great-grandfather
la **bisabuela**   great-grandmother
el **cuñado**   brother-in-law
la **cuñada**   sister-in-law
el **esposo**, el **marido**   husband
la **esposa**, la **mujer**   wife
el **hermano**   brother
la **hermana**   sister
el **hermanastro**   stepbrother
la **hermanastra**   stepsister
el **hijo**   son
la **hija**   daughter
el **hijastro**   stepson
la **hijastra**   stepdaughter
el/la **hijo**/a **único**/a   only child
la **madrastra**   stepmother
la **madre**   mother
el **nieto**   grandson
la **nieta**   granddaughter
el **novio**   boyfriend
la **novia**   girlfriend
el **padrastro**   stepfather
el **padre**   father
los **padres**   parents
los **parientes**   relatives
el/la **primo**/a   cousin
el **tío**   uncle
la **tía**   aunt
el **sobrino**   nephew
la **sobrina**   niece

Personal descriptions

¿Cómo eres/es?   What do/does you/he/she look like?
Soy/Es…   I am/He/She is…
  alto/a   tall
  bajo/a   short
  bonito/a   pretty
  calvo/a   bald
  delgado/a   slim
  feo/a   ugly
  gordo/a   fat
  guapo/a   good-looking
  ni alto/a ni bajo/a   neither tall nor short
  pelirrojo/a   red-haired
Tengo/Tiene…   I/He/She have/has….
  los ojos azules   blue eyes
  los ojos grises   grey eyes
  los ojos marrones   brown eyes
  los ojos negros   dark eyes
  los ojos verdes   green eyes
Llevo/Lleva gafas.   I/He/She wear/wears glasses.
Tengo/Tiene…   I/He/She have/has…
  el pelo castaño   light-brown hair
  el pelo corto   short hair
  el pelo largo   long hair
  el pelo liso   straight hair
  el pelo negro   black hair
  el pelo ondulado   wavy hair
  el pelo rubio   blond hair
  el pelo rizado   curly hair
Tengo/Tiene bigote.   I have/He has a moustache.
Tengo/Tiene barba.   I have/He has a beard.

Adjectives

activo/a   active
agradable   pleasant
alegre   cheerful
amable   nice
ambicioso/a   ambitious
antipático/a   unpleasant
cariñoso/a   affectionate
casado/a   married
comprensivo/a   understanding
contaminado/a   polluted
divorciado/a   divorced
egoísta   selfish
extrovertido/a   outgoing
generoso/a   generous
gracioso/a   funny
grande   big
hablador/a   talkative
histórico/a   historic
honrado/a   honest
impaciente   impatient
industrial   industrial
inteligente   intelligent
joven   young
jubilado/a   retired
limpio/a   clean
orgulloso/a   proud
paciente   patient
peligroso/a   dangerous
perezoso/a   lazy
pequeño/a   small
responsable   responsible
ruidoso/a   noisy
rural   rural
sensible   sensitive
separado/a   separated
serio/a   serious
severo/a   strict
simpático/a   nice, friendly
sincero/a   sincere
sucio/a   dirty
tímido/a   timid
tonto/a   stupid, crazy
trabajador/a   hardworking
tranquilo/a   quiet
triste   sad
turístico/a   tourist
viejo/a   old
viudo/a   widowed

My home

el **apartamento**   apartment
el **ático**   attic
el **balcón**   balcony
la **casa**   house
el **chalet**   bungalow, house, cottage
la **cocina**   kitchen
el **comedor**   dining room
el **cuarto** de **baño**   bathroom
el **despacho**   office, study
el **dormitorio**   bedroom
la **ducha**   shower
el **garaje**   garage
la **granja**   farm
el **jardín**   garden
el **piso**   flat
el **salón**   lounge, living room
el **sótano**   cellar
la **terraza**   terrace

Furniture

el **aparador**   sideboard
el **armario**   wardrobe; cupboard
la **bañera**   bath, bathtub
la **cama**   bed
la **cómoda**   chest of drawers
el **congelador**   freezer
la **estantería**   bookcase
el **fregadero**   kitchen sink
el **horno**   oven
la **lavadora**   washing machine
el **lavaplatos**   dishwasher
la **mesa**   table
el **microondas**   microwave
la **nevera**   fridge
el **retrete**   toilet
la **silla**   chair
el **sofá**   sofa
el **sillón**   armchair
el **televisor**   television

My town and my area

norte   north
sur   south
este   east
oeste   west
el **aeropuerto**   airport
la **aldea**   village
el **aparcamiento**   car park
el **ayuntamiento**   town hall
el **barrio**   neighbourhood
la **biblioteca**   library
la **cafetería**   café
el **castillo**   castle
la **catedral**   cathedral
el **centro**   centre
el **centro comercial**   shopping centre
el **cine**   cinema
la **ciudad**   town; city
Correos   post office

la **comisaría**   police station
la **discoteca**   disco
la **estación** de **trenes/autobuses**   train/bus station
el **estadio**   stadium
la **fábrica**   factory
la **fuente**   fountain
la **gente**   people
el **hospital**   hospital
el **hotel**   hotel
la **iglesia**   church
las **instalaciónes**   facilities
los **jardines**   gardens
el **lago**   lake
el **mercado**   market
el **museo**   museum
la **oficina de turismo**   tourist office
la **parada de autobús**   bus stop
el **parque de atracciones**   amusement park
la **piscina**   swimming pool
la **plaza**   square
la **plaza de toros**   bullring
el **polideportivo**   sports centre
el **pueblo**   small town; village
el **puerto**   port
el **restaurante**   restaurant
el **río**   river
el **supermercado**   supermarket
el **teatro**   theatre
el **valle**   valley
el **videoclub**   video-rental shop
el **zoo**   zoo

Jobs
el **empleo**   job
estar en el paro   to be unemployed
el/la **amo/a de casa**   housewife/husband
el/la **arqueólogo/a**   archaeologist
el/la **camarero/a**   waiter/waitress
el/la **canguro**   childminder, babysitter
el/la **cantante**   singer
el/la **carpintero/a**   carpenter, joiner
el/la **cocinero/a**   cook, chef
el/la **contable**   accountant
el/la **dependiente/a**   shop assistant
el/la **deportista**   sportsman/woman
el/la **diseñador/a**   designer
el/la **economista**   economist
el/la **electricista**   electrician
el/la **empleado/a**   employee
el/la **enfermero/a**   nurse
el/la **farmacéutico/a**   chemist, pharmacist
el/la **granjero/a**   farmer
el/la **hombre/mujer de negocios**   businessman/woman
el/la **jefe/a**   boss
el/la **peluquero/a**   hairdresser
el/la **recepcionista**   receptionist

la **oficina**   office
los **grandes almacenes**   department store
trabajar   to work
la **empresa**   company
la **compañía**   company
el **departamento**   department

Animals
la **araña**   spider
el **caballo**   horse
el **canario**   canary
la **chinchilla**   chinchilla
la **cobaya**   guinea pig
el **conejo**   rabbit
el **gato**   cat
el **jerbo**, el **gerbo**   gerbil
el **hámster**   hamster
el **lagarto**   lizard
la **lagartija**   small lizard
el **papagayo**, el **loro**   parrot
el **perico**   parakeet
el **perro**   dog
el **pez**   fish
la **rana**   frog
la **rata**   rat
el **ratón**   mouse
la **serpiente**   snake
la **tortuga**   tortoise

Daily routine
acostarse   to go to bed
afeitarse   to shave
bañarse   to bathe
despertarse   to wake up
desayunar   to have breakfast
dormirse   to go to sleep
ducharse   to shower
hacer los deberes   to do your homework
lavarse   to wash
levantarse   to get up
peinarse   to comb one's hair
regresar a casa   to go home
salir de casa   to leave the house
ver la televisión   to watch television
vestirse   to get dressed

Household chores
ayudar   to help
barrer el suelo   to sweep the floor
cocinar   to cook
dar de comer a las mascotas   to feed the pets
fregar los platos   to do the washing-up
hacer la cama   to make the bed
hacer la compra   to do the shopping
lavar el coche   to wash the car
lavar la ropa   to do the washing
limpiar los cristales   to clean the windows
limpiar el polvo   to do the dusting
pasar la aspiradora   to vacuum
pasear al perro   to walk the dog

planchar   to iron
poner la mesa   to lay the table
quitar la mesa   to clear the table
regar las plantas   to water the plants
sacar la basura   to take the rubbish out

Prepositions
a   to
al final de   at the end of
al lado de   next to
a la derecha de   to the right of
a la izquierda de   to the left of
alrededor de   around
antes de   before
bajo   below/under
cerca de   near
con   with
contra   against
debajo de   below, under, underneath
delante de   in front of
desde   since
después de   after
durante   during
en   in, on
encima de   on top of
entre   between
excepto   except
fuera de   outside (of)
lejos de   far from
por   by
sobre   on top of

Adverbs
abajo   downstairs; below
afuera   outside
antes   beforehand
arriba   upstairs, above
debajo   below
desde hace mucho tiempo   for a long time
después   afterwards
encima   on top, above
inmediatamente   immediately
luego   then
más   more
mucho   a lot
muy   very
muy poco   very little
nunca   never
recientemente   recently
siempre   always
sin embargo   however
sobre todo   above all

Conjunctions
o   or
pero   but
porque   because
y   and

Gente joven

1 El tiempo libre

2 ¿Cómo te enteras?

3 ¿A quién admiras?

☑ Say what I like to do in my free time

☑ Arrange to go out

☑ Use the present and past tenses

1 El tiempo libre

1a 📖 ✏️ Mira los dibujos y descifra las frases.

Ejemplo: **1** *jugar al fútbol*

garuj la túfobl

rev al veleótinsi

ri al a yalpa

hucersac scamúi

crato le napio

rele brilso

alibar

tramon a balacol

srali ocn gomsia

ri a la spicani

rujag al netis

chare teroped

rapinat

chear frundriws

ri ed scrampo

b 📖 ✏️ ¿Qué les gusta hacer? Copia y completa la tabla con los detalles que faltan.

Me gusta mucho salir con amigos, pero no me gusta nada bailar.

Cristina

Lo que más me gusta es ir al cine. No me gusta mucho hacer deporte.

Ana

En mi tiempo libre me gusta leer libros y revistas. No me gusta ver la televisión.

Pablo

Me divierte estar al aire libre así que me encanta ir de paseo en el campo. No me interesa tanto escuchar música.

Loli

En mi opinión los videojuegos son para niños. Prefiero ser activo. Soy aficionado a todos los deportes de equipo, el baloncesto por ejemplo. ¡Es fantástico!

Juan

Mis pasatiempos favoritos son la natación y la vela. Odio el fútbol.

Eduardo

	☺	☹
Ejemplo: Cristina	*salir con amigos*	*bailar*
Pablo		
Ana		
Eduardo		
Loli		
Juan		

The present tense

The present tense is use to describe actions that are happening now, usually happen or those which are true at the moment.

The present tense of regular verbs

Regular present tense verbs, as you already know, are formed as follows:

	escuchar	leer	escribir
yo	escucho	leo	escribo
tú	escuchas	lees	escribes
él/ella/usted	escucha	lee	escribe
nosotros/as	escuchamos	leemos	escribimos
vosotros/as	escucháis	leéis	escribís
ellos/as/ustedes	escuchan	leen	escriben

Look at these examples:
Escucho música todos los días.
I listen to music every day.

¿Lees mucho, Pablo? Sí, leo el periódico cada día.
Do you read much, Pablo? Yes, I read the paper every day.

María siempre escribe cartas por correo electrónico.
María always writes email letters.

The present tense of stem-changing or radical-changing verbs

Many verbs change their stem in the present when the stress is on the stem:

1 *e − ie*
2 *u − ue*
3 *o − ue*
4 (sometimes) *e − i*

You met some of these verbs in Module 1. You need to learn them. Look at the examples below.

1 *cerrar* (to close)
cierro
cierras
cierra
cerramos
cerráis
cierran

The following verbs follow the same pattern: *pensar* (to think), *empezar* (to begin/start), *entender* (to understand), *perder* (to lose), *preferir* (to prefer) and *querer* (to want to).

2 *jugar* (to play)
juego
juegas
juega
jugamos
jugáis
juegan

3 *encontrar* (to find)
encuentro
encuentras
encuentra
encontramos
encontráis
encuentran

The following verbs follow the same pattern: *recordar* (to remember), *contar* (to tell (a story)/to count), *poder* (to be able to), *dormir* (to sleep) and *volver* (to return/to come back).

4 *pedir* (to ask for)
pido
pides
pide
pedimos
pedís
piden

Servir (to serve) follows the same pattern.

Some radical-changing verbs are also reflexive. You met these verbs in Module 1.

- *despertarse* (to wake up):
  e → ie
- *acostarse* (to go to bed):
  o → ue
- *vestirse* (to get dressed):
  e → i

Pon un verbo en la forma correcta en cada espacio.

¡Hola amigo!

Te (**escribir**) sobre lo que hago en mi tiempo libre. Me gusta ir al club juvenil con mis amigos. Los lunes y los jueves (**jugar**) al fútbol pero en verano yo (**preferir**) ir a la playa. Mis padres no (**ser**) nada deportistas. En casa mi padre (**poner**) la televisión y luego (**dormirse**). Mi madre (**pasar**) todo su tiempo en la cocina. (**Cocinar**) y (**escuchar**) la radio. Mi hermana y yo (**ser**) miembros de la orquesta del colegio. Yo (**tocar**) el violín y mi hermana (**tocar**) el saxofón. Es muy divertido. Los sábados mis amigos y yo (**ir**) juntos a la discoteca del barrio. Siempre (**empezar**) a las nueve. (**Bailar**) y (**cantar**) hasta medianoche. Los domingos (**levantarse**) tarde. (**Leer**) o (**charlar**) con amigos por teléfono. Y tú, ¿Qué (**hacer**)? ¿(**Practicar**) algún deporte?

¡Hasta luego!

Teo

c ¿Qué te gusta hacer en tu tiempo libre? Completa las frases siguientes.

1 Para mí lo ideal es…
2 Me encanta…
3 Mi pasatiempo favorito es…

4 No me gusta tanto…
5 Lo que más me gusta es…
6 En mi opinión lo mejor es…

d Trabaja con tu pareja. Pregunta y contesta lo siguiente.

Ejemplo: **A:** *¿Qué es lo que más te gusta hacer en tu tiempo libre?*
B: *Lo que más me gusta hacer en mi tiempo libre es ir a la discoteca con mis amigos.*
A: *¿Cuál es tu pasatiempo favorito?*
B: *Mi pasatiempo favorito es hacer deporte — por ejemplo fútbol o baloncesto.*

2 Listen to the recording and read the text. Answer the questions in English.

Me encantan los deportes y mi favorito es el tenis. Llevo jugando desde los cinco años y entreno dos veces a la semana en el club de tenis de mi barrio. Tres veces al mes jugamos contra otros clubs del condado. También me gustan otras cosas — por ejemplo, los fines de semana me gusta salir con mis amigos. Me encantan el baloncesto y el fútbol, pero no aguanto la natación ni correr. Por las tardes me gusta escuchar música en mi ipod o leer. También tengo un ordenador en mi cuarto y con ése paso tiempo haciendo surf en Internet o mandando mensajes electrónicos. Me dan igual los videojuegos aunque tengo que admitir que son una pérdida de tiempo, así que no lo hago mucho. No suelo salir durante la semana porque tengo demasiados deberes, pero a veces veo la televisión — los programas de deporte son los que más me interesan.

Julián

¡OJO!

el tenis — jugar al tenis
el cine — ir al cine

1 What sport does Julián prefer?
2 What other sports does he enjoy?
3 What things does he not enjoy doing?
4 What else does he like to do in his free time?
5 What does he say about his computer?
6 What does he have to say about computer games?

3 Escribe un breve párrafo en español explicando lo que te gusta y lo que no te gusta hacer.

4 Escucha la grabación. Copia y completa la tabla con los detalles que faltan.

Nombre	Lo que le gusta hacer	Razones	Lo que no le gusta hacer	Razones
Ejemplo: Juanita	*salir con amigos*	*divertido*	*ir de compras*	*aburrido*
Federico				
Emma				
Pablo				
Isabel				

LENGUA CLAVE

Saying what you like or do not like doing

Use for example, *me gusta* + the infinitive of the verb. Use the table below to help you.

(no) me gusta me encanta prefiero detesto	bailar escuchar hacer jugar ir leer montar salir tocar ver	la televisión música deporte al fútbol la guitarra en la discoteca a caballo revistas al cine con amigos

En el club juvenil

5 Lee esta información. Apunta los detalles.

a Algunas palabras del texto están en negrita.
Escríbelas y lo que significan en inglés.
Usa un diccionario para ayudarte.

b Indica si las frases siguientes son
verdaderas (V) o falsas (F).

Ejemplo: *El club se llama Campamento*
La Hermita. — V

1 Solo hay dos sesiones cada semana para
los niños de ocho años.
2 Hay clases de baile para todas las edades.
3 El club cuesta más para gente joven.
4 Hay clases cada tarde de la semana.
5 Se puede ir de excursión.
6 La cafetería sirve solo comida rápida.
7 Solo hay cierta cantidad de plazas
en excursiones.

c Busca la palabra intrusa.
Explica por qué en inglés.

1 me gusta   me divierto   prefiero   odio
2 lunes   martes   jueves   domingo
3 fútbol   tenis   badminton   squash
4 karate   natación   judo   baloncesto
5 playa   campo   parque   piscina

Campamento La Hermita
Programación mes de julio

Los martes: 8–15 años (de 17:30 a 19:30)
Por solo 10€: natación, snooker, gimnasia, ping pong,
club de ajedrez, acceso internet, **esgrima**.

Los miércoles: 13 años+ (de 19:00 a 21:00)
Por 12€: snooker, natación, ping pong, club de
dibujo, actividades deportivas (fútbol, **tiro con
arco** o baloncesto).

Los jueves: 8 a 12 años (de 18:00 a 20:00)
Por 12€: **juegos de equipo**; futbolín, tenis de
mesa, natación, snooker, clases de baile, tarde de cine, **pesas**, club de música,
clases de baile, tarde de cine, **artesanía y bricolaje**,
judo, fútbol, atletismo.

Camping
Cafetería (con amplia gama de raciones sanas)
Horario fin de semana: sábados de 9:00 a 17:00

Parque de atracciones:
• 26€ sin límite de atracciones
• 19€ con tres atracciones
• 15€ con dos atracciones
Excursión marítima 21€ comida incluida.
• Paintball
• Escalona libre 10€ • **Vela** 25€
Plazas limitadas — no te lo pierdas! • Windsurf 20€

6a ¿A qué hora? Empareja lo que oyes
con la hora correcta.

Ejemplo: **1 — c**

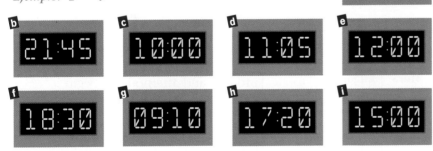

a 14:15
b 21:45
c 10:00
d 11:05
e 12:00
f 18:30
g 09:10
h 17:20
i 15:00

b Mira los relojes del ejercicio de arriba. Trabaja con tu
pareja. ¿Cuándo quedáis?

Ejemplo: **A:** *¿A qué hora nos vemos?*
B: *Nos vemos mañana a las dos y cuarto.*

¡OJO!

Spelling changes affect nouns
as well as verbs. For example:

e → ie: *ventana* (window)
— *viento* (wind)

o → ue: *volar* (to fly)
— *vuelo* (flight)

u → ue: *jugar* (to play)
— *juego* (game)

The stems of verbs and their
endings can help you to work
out the meaning of nouns.
For example:

comer (to eat) — *comida* (food/meal)

beber (to drink) — *bebida* (drink)

7a 📖 Mira las imágenes. Emparéjalas con las frases.

Ejemplo: a — en el bar

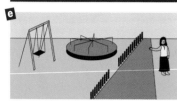

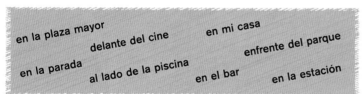

en la plaza mayor

delante del cine

en mi casa

enfrente del parque

en la parada

al lado de la piscina

en el bar

en la estación

b 💬 Observa las imágenes de la actividad anterior. Trabaja con tu pareja. ¿Dónde vais a quedar?

Ejemplo: A: ¿Dónde nos vemos?
B: Nos vemos en el bar.

8a 🎧 Escucha la grabación. Copia y completa la tabla con los detalles que faltan.

	Actividad	Día	Hora	Lugar
Ejemplo:	*tenis*	*mañana*	*2:30*	*en el parque*
1				
2				
3				
4				

b 💬 Trabaja con tu pareja. Usa la información en la tabla arriba para ayudarte con tu propio diálogo.

9a 🎧 📖 Escucha la grabación y sigue la conversación. Elige las palabras del recuadro que faltan y llena los huecos.

> te apetece
> estoy segura
> a las ocho   bien   ponen
> tu casa   hasta luego   me interesan

A: ¡Hola! Soy Adelina ¿_____ ir al cine conmigo esta tarde?

B: ¡Quizás! ¿Qué _____?

A: No _____ de los títulos, pero sé que echan una comedia romántica.

B: No _____ las películas románticas, incluso si son graciosas. ¿Por qué simplemente no vemos una película en la tele?

A: Si quieres. Me parece _____ ¿Qué echan?

B: Hay una película de ciencia-ficción _____ esta tarde si te apetece.

A: ¡Guay! Me encantan las películas de ciencia-ficción. Llegaré a _____ a las siete y media.

B: Vale ¡_____!

b 💬 Trabaja con tu pareja y adapta el diálogo según las imágenes abajo.

A: *Hola Javier, soy Adelina. ¿Te apetece ir al cine conmigo esta noche?*

B: *Depende. ¿Qué echan?*

A: *Echan dibujos animados esta tarde.*

B: *¡No seas boba! Odio los dibujos animados. Son muy aburridos.*

10a 🎧 📖 Escucha a estos jóvenes hacer planes para el fin de semana. Lee la conversación.

Paco:	¡Hola Sonia! ¿Tienes las entradas para el sábado?
Sonia:	¡Todavía no! ¡Ahora llamo! (*Saca su móvil*)
Paco:	Vale.
Recepcionista:	¡Dígame!
Sonia:	¡Oiga! Sí. Hola. Quisiera reservar unas entradas para el concierto el sábado.
Recepcionista:	¿Qué fecha?
Sonia:	El veinticuatro de noviembre.
Recepcionista:	¿Y para qué concierto?
Sonia:	El concierto de Nacen de las Cenizas.
Recepcionista:	¿De pie o sentado?
Sonia:	De pie, por favor.
Recepcionista:	¿Cuántas entradas quiere?
Sonia:	Seis.
Recepcionista:	Sí, quedan entradas.
Sonia:	¿Cuánto cuesta?
Recepcionista:	Son trescientos euros. Le puedo guardar las entradas hasta las ocho esta tarde. ¿Cuál es su nombre?
Sonia:	Sonia Delgado.
Recepcionista:	De acuerdo. Le esperamos hasta las ocho.
Sonia:	Muchas gracias. Adiós. (*Cuelga*) ¡Ya está! ¡Hay que ir al teatro antes de las ocho!

b 🗨 Ahora practica el juego de rol con tu compañero, sustituyendo la información según las imágenes.

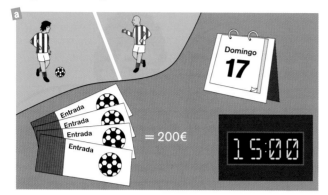

11 📖 ✏️ ¿Qué actividades son? Completa las definiciones eligiendo la palabra adecuada del recuadro de abajo.

Ejemplo: **1** — *nadar*

ir de compras	jugar al ping pong
jugar al tenis	ir al cine
esquiar	nadar
jugar al ajedrez	ir a un concierto
hacer equitación	ir a la discoteca

1 Esto se hace en el agua.
2 Esto se puede hacer en el centro de la ciudad.
3 Para hacer esto necesitas una raqueta.
4 Para hacer esto, ¡hace falta un caballo!
5 Esto se juega en una mesa.
6 Se va la gente aquí para ver todo tipo de películas.
7 Se hace esta actividad en la nieve.
8 Esto es un juego de tabla.
9 Se va aquí para bailar.
10 Aquí es adonde se va para escuchar música en vivo.

12 🎧 ¿Qué haces? Escucha lo que dicen estos jóvenes de qué hacen en su tiempo libre y apunta las actividades que nombran.

Ejemplo: **1** — *b*

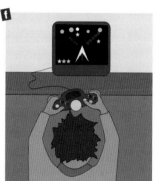

13a Escucha otra vez el texto 12 y léelo. Haz una lista de todos los verbos mencionados por los chicos. ¿Puedes identificar todos?

Entrevistador: Carmen, ¿qué haces en tu tiempo libre?

Carmen: Yo veo bastante la tele. Me relaja mucho.

E: ¿Y tú, Carlos? ¿Ves la tele?

Carlos: Sí, a veces, pero normalmente juego con mi PSP u otros juegos electrónicos.

E: ¿Y qué haces tú, Leticia?

Leticia: En mi tiempo libre salgo con mis amigos y paseo al perro. ¡Es guay!

E: ¿Qué dices, Nacho?

Nacho: Yo no salgo mucho y ¡no tengo perro! Sin embargo, practico mi guitarra y la trompeta. ¡Quiero ser famoso!

E: Y tú, ¿practicas la guitarra, Alberto?

Alberto: Sí. Todo el rato. Soy miembro de un grupo y ensayamos tres veces a la semana.

E: ¿Qué haces tú en tu tiempo libre, Susana?

Susana: Yo soy muy deportista y juego al fútbol o al baloncesto. A veces juego al tenis también. También escucho música.

E: ¿Practicas algún deporte, Luis?

Luis: Vivo en una granja en las afueras de la ciudad y tenemos muchos caballos. Así que durante la mayoría de mi tiempo libre hago equitación. Me encanta y es buen ejercicio para mí y para el caballo.

E: ¿Y tú, Leonor? ¿Qué haces?

Leonor: ¿Yo? Err. Normalmente en mi tiempo libre hago natación. Me gusta mucho nadar y soy bastante fuerte. También hago dibujos animados y tal. ¡Soy artista!

b Discuss with your classmate what the verbs have in common. Think about the tense and person of the verbs.

c Pon un verbo en la forma correcta en cada espacio. Escoge entre los verbos del recuadro de abajo.

La ciudad de Méjico ____ una de las ciudades más grandes del mundo y se ____ considerar la ciudad más rica y poblada del país. En el centro de la ciudad ____ la catedral Metropolitana y el palacio Nacional. ____ unos de los monumentos más importantes de toda América. La ciudad ____ también una gran variedad de museos, actividades y diversiones. Si ____ hacer algo diferente, solo ____ que alquilar alguno de los barcos en los canales de Xochimilco. La aventura ____ cada día a las once. Conocer todos los rincones de la Ciudad de Méjico es una tarea imposible. Si ____ a ir a Méjico de vacaciones, ¿por qué no ____ unos días en la capital? ¡ ____ la pena visitar!

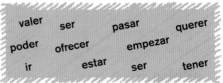

valer   ser   pasar   querer
poder   ofrecer   empezar
ir   estar   ser   tener

GRAMÁTICA

The present tense of irregular verbs

Some common verbs are irregular in the *yo* form only, as follows:
dar (to give) – *doy* (I give)
decir (to say) – *digo* (I say)
hacer (to do/make) – *hago* (I do/make)
poner (to put) – *pongo* (I put)
salir (to go out) – *salgo* (I go out)
ver (to see/watch) – *veo* (I see/watch)

Look at these examples:

***Salgo** de casa a las ocho.*	I leave home at 8.
*Siempre **hago** mis deberes en la cocina.*	I always do my homework in the kitchen.

The following verbs are very irregular and need to be learned carefully. You met some of these verbs in Module 1.

	estar	ir	ser	tener	venir
yo	estoy	voy	soy	tengo	vengo
tú	estás	vas	eres	tienes	vienes
él/ella/usted	está	va	es	tiene	viene
nosotros/as	estamos	vamos	somos	tenemos	venimos
vosotros/as	estáis	vais	sois	tenéis	venís
ellos/as/ustedes	están	van	son	tienen	vienen

Look at these examples:

***Vamos** a la piscina los domingos.*	We go to the swimming pool on Sundays.
*¿**Vienes** a la playa con nosotros?*	Are you coming to the beach with us?

¿Qué hiciste el fin de semana pasado?

14a 🎧📖 Escucha y lee lo que dicen estos jóvenes.

> ¡Hola, Marta! ¿Qué tal tu fin de semana?

> ¡Muy bien! Salí con mis amigos. Y tú, Alberto, ¿qué tal te lo pasaste?

> ¡Muy aburrido! Me quedé en casa como siempre.

> ¿Qué hiciste el sábado?

> Hice mis deberes y vi la televisión. ¿Y tú?

> Por la mañana jugué al tenis y por la tarde fui a la discoteca con Ángel y Raquel.

> ¿Y el domingo?

Marta

> El domingo tomé el sol en la playa y por la tarde fui a una fiesta. Fue muy agradable. Y tú, Alberto?

> Leí una revista en el jardín. Por la tarde navegué por Internet.

Alberto

b ✏️ Mira los dibujos. ¿Quién dice cada frase? Escribe 'Alberto' o 'Marta' y escribe la frase.

Ejemplo: **a** *Alberto — vi la television*

40

The preterite tense

When talking about free time, it is important to use a variety of tenses. To talk about what you did yesterday, last week, last month, last year etc., use the preterite tense. Look at the tables below. They represent the most common verbs you will want to use. Learn these carefully.

The preterite tense of **regular** verbs

Regular present tense verbs are formed as follows:

	hablar	comer	vivir
yo	hablé	comí	viví
tú	hablaste	comiste	viviste
él/ella/usted	habló	comió	vivió
nosotros/as	hablamos	comimos	vivimos
vosotros/as	hablasteis	comisteis	vivisteis
ellos/as/ustedes	hablaron	comieron	vivieron

Look at these examples:
- ***Hablé** con Andrés por teléfono*
  I spoke to Andrés on the telephone.

- *¿Dónde **comiste** anoche, Juan?*
  Where did you eat last night, Juan?

- ***Comí** en un restaurante italiano.*
  I ate at an Italian restaurant.

Be very careful with the *yo* part of the following two verbs:
jugar: jugué (I played) but: *jugó* (he played)

navegar: Navegué por Internet toda la noche but: *María navegó por Internet ayer.*

The preterite tense of the three most frequently used **irregular** verbs:

	ir	ser	hacer
yo	fui	fui	hice
tú	fuiste	fuiste	hiciste
él/ella/usted	fue	fue	hizo
nosotros/as	fuimos	fuimos	hicimos
vosotros/as	fuisteis	fuisteis	hicisteis
ellos/as/ustedes	fueron	fueron	hicieron

You will notice that *ir* and *ser* share the same preterite form. Look at this example:
- ***Fui** al colegio a las ocho. El día **fue** muy aburrido*
  I went to school at 8. It was a very boring day.

The preterite form of *hay* (there is/are) is *hubo*:
- ***Hubo** tormenta anoche.*
  There was a storm last night.

15 Los sábados, Raúl siempre hace las mismas cosas. ¿Qué hizo el sábado pasado? Cambia los verbos al pretérito.

Ejemplo: Se levantó a las ocho…

Me levanto a las ocho, **me ducho**, **desayuno** y entonces **salgo** de casa a las diez. **Llego** a casa de mi amigo Martín a las diez y media. **Jugamos** con los videojuegos hasta mediodía, luego **vamos** al polideportivo donde **nadamos** en la piscina y **vamos** al gimnasio. Yo **hago** una sesión con el entrenador y Martín **hace** las pesas. A las dos, **volvemos** al centro donde **tomamos** algo de comida en una cafetería. Por la tarde **nos reunimos** con otros amigos y entonces **compramos** las entradas para ir al cine. A las diez, **vuelvo** a casa. **Veo** la televisión y **escucho** música. Por fin, **me acuesto** a las once.

16 Ana is talking about her weekend. Listen to what she says. Answer the questions in English.

1 Where did Ana go last weekend and why?
2 What did she have to say about the journey?
3 Where did she stay?
4 What did she do during her time there?
5 Did she enjoy herself?
6 How do you know?

LENGUA CLAVE

Frases útiles
Match the Spanish words with the English ones.

hoy	in the evening
esta mañana	last night
esta tarde	last week
por la noche	today
ayer	this morning
anoche	a week ago
anteayer	this afternoon
hace una semana	the day before yesterday
la semana pasada	yesterday

17 Usando lo que sabes ya de como se habla del tiempo libre, haz la pareja adecuada español–inglés.

*Ejemplo: **a — 1***

Español
a Cada tarde escucho música.
b Ayer jugué al tenis con mi hermano.
c Los lunes veo la tele o escucho música.
d El sábado pasado salí con mis amigos.
e Jugué al fútbol el viernes.
f El verano pasado practiqué la natación todos los días.
g Normalmente voy al cine los martes.
h El miércoles paseé el perro de mi vecina.
i A veces hago equitación.

Inglés
1 I listen to music each afternoon
2 I usually go to the cinema on Tuesdays.
3 Sometimes I go horseriding.
4 Yesterday I played tennis with my brother.
5 On Mondays I watch TV or listen to music.
6 Last Saturday I went out with my friends.
7 I played football on Friday.
8 Last summer I went swimming every day.
9 On Wednesday I took my neighbour's dog for a walk.

18 Ahora escribe por lo menos seis frases sobre lo que haces tú en tu tiempo libre. Incluye alguna información en el pasado. Explícaselo a tu pareja.

Ejemplo: Me gusta mucho nadar y siempre voy a la piscina el martes y el jueves. Ayer fui a la playa por la tarde y nadé en el mar.

19 Copia estas preguntas y prepara tus respuestas. Pregunta a tres personas lo que hacen en su tiempo libre. ¡No te olvides del pasado!

1 ¿Qué haces normalmente en tu tiempo libre después del colegio?
2 ¿Qué haces los fines de semana?
3 ¿Qué hiciste ayer?
4 ¿Qué hiciste el sábado pasado?
5 ¿Qué hiciste el verano pasado?

2 ¿Cómo te enteras?

☑ Say what types of media I prefer

☑ Give opinions and reasons

☑ Use impersonal verbs and infinitives

1a 📖✏️ Escribe la palabra adecuada al lado de cada imagen.

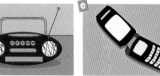
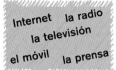

Internet   la radio
la televisión
el móvil   la prensa

b 📖✏️ Lee las palabras en el recuadro abajo. Empareja cada palabra con la imagen que corresponde. Haz una lista.

*Ejemplo: correo electrónico — **a***

correo electrónico	cadena	antena	oyente
noticias	periódico	documental	ring tone
película	dibujo animado	presentador	teclado
mensaje	lector	periodista	espectador
carta	página web	chat room	artículo

2 🎧📖 Escucha y lee. Copia y completa el cuadro con las palabras adecuadas.

1 Me gusta Internet porque es bastante fácil e interesante. Sin embargo creo que la televisión es un rollo.

2 A mí, me encantan los documentales porque son muy informativos y divertidos. Yo odio las noticias.

3 Pienso que las películas son geniales. Me encantan los anuncios también; son educativos. No me gustan los periódicos porque creo que son inútiles.

4 Me entusiasman las revistas porque me inspiran. Además la radio me parece muy útil.

	Medio de comunicación	☺	☹	Razones
Ejemplo: **1**	Internet	✓		fácil/interesante
	televisión		✓	un rollo
2				
3				
4				

GRAMÁTICA

Expressing an opinion

Pay special attention when expressing an opinion. It is what you have an opinion about that tells you the ending to use. Look at the table below:

me	gusta/n
te	chifla/n
le	gusta/n mucho
a usted le	encanta/n
nos	inspira/n
os	entusiasma/n
les	
a ustedes les	

Look at these examples:
- *Me encanta ver la televisión. Pienso que los anuncios son muy divertidos.*
- *A Manuel le encantan las películas de acción.*
- *A mis padres les gustan los documentales.*

Adapta las frases siguientes. Usa algunos de los verbos en la tabla arriba.

Ejemplo: Mi amigo Juan compra muchas revistas.
A Juan le gusta mucho leer revistas.

1 Marta siempre surfea Internet.
2 Escuchamos la radio a veces.
3 Mis hermanos no leen los periódicos.
4 ¿Qué opinas de los anuncios?
5 Creo que ir al cine es muy aburrido.

3 💬 Habla con tu pareja de los medios de comunicación.

Ejemplo: **A:** *¿Qué te parece Internet?*
　　　　　　　B: *Me entusiasma Internet porque es divertido.*

4 👥 Escribe un pequeño párrafo explicando qué medio(s) prefieres y por qué.

5 📖 Empareja los verbos con las imágenes. ¿Qué tienen las frases en común? Explícaselo a tu pareja.

Ejemplo: **1 — e**

1 No entiendo muy bien. ¿Me puedes **explicar**?

2 ¿Cuál es el número? Quiero **telefonear**.

3 Mis amigos acaban de **llegar**.

4 ¿Te gusta **viajar** en tren? Yo prefiero **viajar** en coche.

5 A mi hermano le encanta **leer** tebeos.

6 Hay que **estudiar** para **sacar** buenas notas.

7 No puedo **salir** esta noche. Tengo que **ayudar** a mis padres.

8 Voy a **jugar** al baloncesto esta tarde.

9 No deseo **tener** más hermanos.

10 ¿Sabes **esquiar**?

LENGUA CLAVE

Preguntas	Positivos/negativos	¿Por qué?
¿Te gusta…/¿Qué te parece… …la televisión? …la radio? …Internet? …el cine?	A mí me gusta… Me chifla… Me gusta mucho… Me encanta… Me inspira… Me entusiasma… No me gusta (nada)… Lo/la odio… Lo/la detesto…	porque es/creo que es/pienso que es… …importante. …interesante. …educativo/a. …divertido/a. …fácil. …genial. …útil. …un rollo. …inútil. …aburrido/a. …una pérdida de tiempo.
¿Te gustan…/¿Qué te parecen… …las películas? …los periódicos? …las revistas? …las noticias? …los anuncios? …los documentales? …las cartas?	A mi me gustan… Me chiflan… Me gustan mucho… Me encantan… Me inspiran… Me entusiasman… No me gustan (nada)… Los/las odio… Los/las detesto…	Creo que son/pienso que son… …importantes. …interesantes. …educativos/as. …divertidos/as. …fáciles. …geniales. …útiles. …inútiles. …aburridos/as.

GRAMÁTICA

Using infinitives

The infinitive is the form of the verb that hasn't had any ending added to it. It is the only form of the verb you will find listed in a dictionary.

In English, the infinitive is usually shown with the word **to**:
● *cantar* – to sing

Be careful when translating the English *–ing* form. This is often an infinitive in Spanish:
● *Me encanta **comer** pizza.* I love **eating** pizza.

The second verb used in any sentence is always in the infinitive form:
● *Me encanta **hablar** con mis amigos* I love talking to my friends.

● *Prefiero **escuchar** música pop.* I prefer listening to pop music

Escribe la forma del infinitivo de estos verbos. Usa un diccionario para ayudarte.
● dibujó
● salgo
● anduviste
● saltamos
● se sienta
● corrieron
● pongan
● pagué
● volvió
● abren
● compramos
● cae
● venimos
● recuerde
● evitamos
● decidieron

6 📖 Read the article. Answer the questions in English.

¿Qué es Facebook?

Facebook es un sitio web de redes sociales. Fue creado originalmente para estudiantes de la Universidad de Harvard, pero ha sido abierto a cualquier persona que tenga una cuenta de correo electrónico. Los usuarios pueden participar en una o más redes sociales en relación con su situación académica, su lugar de trabajo o región geográfica.

¿Por qué utilizar las redes sociales?

La vida es más alegre si se puede compartir y los problemas parecen más sencillos contados a otra persona. Por eso principalmente se ha hecho tan popular el uso de redes sociales como Facebook o su equivalente español, Tuenti. Ofrecen contactos que también sirven en los negocios y es un foro excelente para anunciarse y así, vender. Además, para muchas organizaciones y empresas, es una manera de encontrar información sobre ti – así que ¡ojo! ¡Nunca sabes quién te está observando!

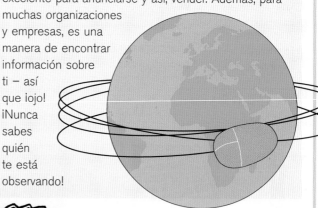

¿Y qué piensan nuestros lectores?

A mi madre le encanta Facebook porque es una forma de localizar a amigos con quienes perdió el contacto.

Idoya

Para mí es la mejor manera de hacer nuevos amigos con quienes puedo intercambiar fotos y mensajes. También se pueden reunir personas con intereses comunes.

Héctor

No me interesa mucho la vida de otra gente — en realidad hay demasiado de ese tipo en la tele. No sé si quiero que cualquiera sepa algo sobre mi vida privada.

Antolín

Sé que a la gente las redes sociales le parecen una maravilla, pero yo creo que son una pérdida de tiempo. Prefiero leer periódicos y revistas y sobre todo, ¡mi Kindle!

Olinda

Oí de alguien que perdió su trabajo por usar Facebook en la oficina. Eso es lógico. La gente debería ser responsable y usar esos medios en su propio tiempo. ¡No se puede usar Facebook en mi cole!

Óscar

1 What exactly is Facebook?
2 Who is Facebook for?
3 Name two advantages of social networking sites.
4 Name two advantages of Facebook mentioned.

5 What is the majority opinion of the readers? Are they for or against social networking sites?
6 From what these young people say, how should Facebook and equivalents be used responsibly?

7 Lee esta información. Empareja las imágenes con la hora de los programas.

Ejemplo: **a — 11.30**

Programación televisiva	
Lunes el 24 de mayo	
TVE 1	
06:00	Noticias 24 horas
11:30	Entrevista con Carlos Moya
14:00	Oliver y Benji (dibujo animado)
15:00	Piratas y corsarios (ciencia-ficción)
15:55	El tiempo
16:00	La naturaleza en África (documental)
16:50	Destilando amor (telenovela)
17:50	La viuda de blanco (Película de suspense)
18:20	Millonario (concurso)
20:00	Fútbol: Copa del Mundo
22:00	Siete vidas (comedia)
23:00	Ópera con Plácido Domingo

8a ¿Qué deciden ver estos jóvenes? ¿Por qué razones? Pon una X en la casilla adecuada.

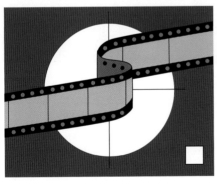

b ¿Por qué eligen esa idea? Da cuatro razones en español.

9 Trabaja con tu pareja. Habla de lo que te gustaría ver en la tele.

Ejemplo: **A:** *Me gustaría ver una película esta tarde.*
B: *¿Qué tipo de película?*
A: *Es una película de risa. Se llama* Los Simpsons. *Lo echan a las cuatro.*
B: *La verdad es que no me apetece ésa. Prefiero ver un programa de música. MTV internacional, por ejemplo.*
A: *Vale. ¿A qué hora es?*
B: *Empieza a las cinco de la tarde.*

¿Qué opinas?

10 Lee lo siguiente. Decide si las frases son positivas o negativas. Escribe tus respuestas en la tabla.

> No me gustó la película porque...

> Me gustó la película porque...

Anoche fui a ver *El caballero oscuro: La leyenda renace*. La verdad es que no me gustó mucho la película y había gente que hablaba todo el rato — ¡cosa que me molesta un montón! Para mí no era nada interesante. En realidad no es mi tipo de entretenimiento, ¡aunque tengo que admitir que el protagonista era superguapo! No sé qué pasaba en el cine, pero no se oía bien, ni siquiera la música. ¡Creo que tenían algún problema! En fin, la verdad es que no creo que valga la pena.

1 La historia era increíblemente aburrida.
2 El actor principal era muy guapo.
3 La música era demasiado alta.
4 Fue bastante entretenida.
5 Valía la pena verla.
6 Había muchas distracciones.
7 Las entradas eran muy caras.
8 Había mucha acción.
9 Daba demasiado miedo para mi gusto.
10 Los efectos especiales eran fantásticos.
11 El paisaje era alucinante.
12 No era mi tipo de película.

Positivas	Negativas
Ejemplo: **2** El actor principal era muy guapo.	*Ejemplo:* **1** La historia era increíblemente aburrida.

11 Recibes este mensaje electrónico. Escribe una respuesta.

¡Hola!

¿Qué te pareció la peli de anoche? Estoy deseando saber lo que piensas.

Hasta pronto.

Óscar.

¡ojo!

With adjectives ending in *–o* or *–a* an easy way to add emphasis in Spanish is to take off the final vowel and add *–ísimo/–ísima*, as appropriate. For example, *bueno* (good) becomes *buenísimo* (very good); *mala* (bad) becomes *malísima* (very bad) etc. Most adjectives ending in other vowels, or consonants, have to rely on the use of *muy* or *mucho* before them, e.g. *trabajador — muy trabajador* (hardworking — very hardworking) or *emocionante — muy emocionante* (moving/exciting — very moving/exciting).

Use some in your writing to make it more authentic.

12a 📖🖋 Lee estas palabras y después lee la carta. Decide en cada caso qué palabra falta. Usa un diccionario para ayudarte.

Ejemplo: **1** — *historia*

acaba   vender

problemas   mejor

historia

película

emocionantes

encanta   famoso

desafortunadamente

equipo   maravillosos

b 🖋 Usa la carta para ayudarte a escribir tu propia carta a un amigo contándole sobre una película que has visto últimamente.

¡Qué hay?

¡Hola David!

Acabo de ver una película fantástica llamada Flying Start y como me impresionó muchísimo, decidí escribirte para contártelo.

Es la _____(1)_____ de un mecánico de coches de carrera. Le _____(2)_____ conducir y un día le hace caso el director del equipo – un tal Nerón.

Nerón es celoso y le da envidia el talento de Sabi así que le mete en un _____(3)_____ malo para impedir su éxito. Pero Sabi es tan bueno que gana de todas formas. Se hace _____(4)_____ y gana todo. Se enamora de una azafata guapísima y se casa con ella.

Más que nada es un hombre casado y contento. Tiene una casa preciosa, dos hijos _____(5)_____ y una carerra de ensueño.

_____(6)_____ su vida ideal se transforma cuando tiene un accidente grave que le deja sin poder conducir más. No tiene más remedio que _____(7)_____ todo y mudarse a un barrio pobre.

La película trata principalmente de su pelea para conseguir de nuevo todo lo que perdió. ¡No te voy a contar cómo _____(8)_____!

Es una _____(9)_____ magnífica que desde luego vale la pena ver. Tiene música preciosa y las escenas de las carreras de coches son verdaderamente _____(10)_____. Me hizo reir y llorar.

Flying Start demuestra como es mejor enfrentarse a sus _____(11)_____ y no hay que ignorar las cosas esperando que se mejoren sin ningún esfuerzo.

Esa es la _____(12)_____ película que he visto este año.

Por favor, escríbeme para contarme sobre la última peli que has visto.

Besos,

Luis

CULTURA

¿Ya sabes?

Álex de la Iglesia es uno de los cineastas más celebres de España.

Álex de la Iglesia nació el 4 de diciembre de 1965. Es un director de cine y guionista español. Su trayectoria cinematográfica tras las cámaras ha crecido de una manera asombrosa desde sus comienzos en el mundo del cortometraje a principios de los años noventa. Se ha hecho respetar internacionalmente. De hecho, se está estableciendo como uno de los cineastas españoles más famosos fuera de su país de origen y ya ha recibido numerosos premios. Tras varias nominaciones, recibió en 1995 el premio Goya por su película *El día de la bestia*. Conocido por su afición a las películas de suspense, Álex de la Iglesia es sin duda, una personalidad imprescindible en el panorama cultural español e internacional.

¿Conoces otras de sus películas ¿Cómo se llaman? ¡Haz una investigación!

Visitando Correos

13  Empareja lo que oyes con la imagen apropiada.

Ejemplo: **1 — d**

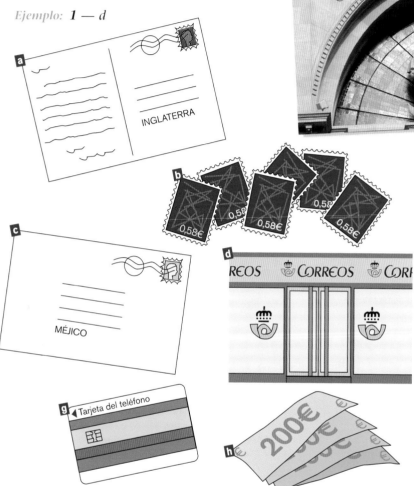

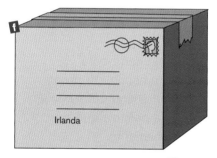

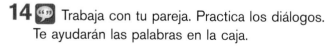

14 Trabaja con tu pareja. Practica los diálogos. Te ayudarán las palabras en la caja.

Ejemplo: **A:** *Buenos días señor. ¿Qué desea?*
B: *¿Cuánto cuesta enviar una carta de Inglaterra, por favor?*
A: *Cuesta 58 céntimos*
B: *Gracias. Quisiera dos sellos de 58 céntimos por favor.*
A: *Aquí tiene. ¿Algo más?*
B: *Sí, un billete de la lotería de la Cruz Roja, por favor.*

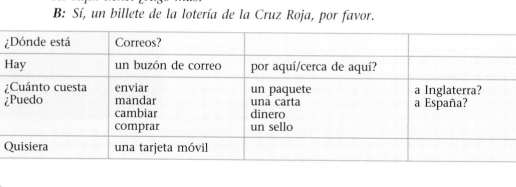

¿Dónde está	Correos?		
Hay	un buzón de correo	por aquí/cerca de aquí?	
¿Cuánto cuesta ¿Puedo	enviar mandar cambiar comprar	un paquete una carta dinero un sello	a Inglaterra? a España?
Quisiera	una tarjeta móvil		

15a 📖 Read this article from a Spanish magazine and answer the questions in English.

¿Estás enchufado?

¿Sabías que hoy en día cinco de cada seis jóvenes tienen teléfono móvil? ¡Y que la mayoría de ellos mandan unos 100 mensajes de texto por día!

Los que venden los móviles justifican esa cifra diciendo que con la tecnología de ahora nuestra juventud disfruta también del acceso a Internet, con lo cual pueden recibir todo tipo de información y enterarse de lo que está pasando en el mundo. Los que están en contra piensan que son peligrosos — dañan la salud, y también provocan atracos. Sin hablar de como distraen a los chicos de sus estudios y de lo que les cuestan a sus padres.

Marta, una joven entusiasta de Valladolid dice:- 'iYo soy adicta! No puedo sobrevivir ahora sin mi móvil. Me hace sentirme segura y así mantengo contacto con mi familia y mis amigos. ¿Por qué estar sola?'

Hicimos una encuesta para saber cómo los jóvenes prefieren enterarse de las noticias. Como se ve en el gráfico, la mayoría escucha las noticias en la tele, mientras 224 consiguen esa información de Internet. Sorprendentemente, más de 300 personas escuchan la radio. ¿Quién ha dicho que la generación de la radio ya no existe?

Pie chart labels: Otros medios, Libros electrónicos, Periódicos, Radio, Internet, Televisión

Muy pocos compran y leen periódicos. Dicen que son incómodos y sucios y que otros medios son preferibles. Una cifra pequeña usa otros medios de comunicación, como hablar con el móvil y usarlo. Graciosamente, ninguno admitió que no lee ni escucha las noticias en absoluto.

Muchos de los chicos con quienes hablamos afirman que saber lo que pasa es importante, pero que quieren un método rápido y fácil — como hoy en día no hay tiempo para nada — y en este respecto la tecnología es una maravilla.

Un porcentaje muy pequeño cree que hay demasiada tecnología y que se sienten controlados por el Gran Hermano de Orwell. No importa si los odias o los crees imprescindibles, los medios de comunicación siguen desarrollándose y ya no hay excusa para no saber lo que pasa en el mundo. Muchos están de acuerdo con que el mundo ahora es mucho más pequeño y asequible gracias a los logros de la tecnología.

¿Y tú? Tienes móvil? ¿Cuántas horas pasas al día hablando por teléfono o mandando mensajes? ¿Y usas Internet? ¿Para qué?

Queremos oír lo que opinas tú. Mándanos un correo electrónico explicándonos todo.

1 According to the article, what are two advantages of using mobile phones?
2 What, if any, are the disadvantages?
3 Why do so few young people read newspapers?
4 Why is there no excuse these days for not knowing what is going on in the world?
5 What does the journalist want you to do?

b Ahora escribe un correo electrónico a la revista contestando todas las preguntas del recuadro. No te olvides de dar razones de tus opiniones y hábitos.

Señor,
He leído su artículo en la revista *Prima* y quisiera comunicarle lo que pienso yo de los medios de comunicación…

3 ¿A quién admiras?

☑ Practise using *ser* and *tener* to describe people

☑ Practise talking about people I admire

☑ Practise extended writing

☑ Use adverbs and adjectives

☑ Use the superlative

1  Mira la lista de adjetivos siguientes. Pon cada uno en la categoría apropiada.

interesante	feo	horrible	trabajador	feliz
aburrido	bueno	estupendo	nervioso	cortés
antipático	bonito	tímido	contento	agradable
divertido	emocionante	simpático		
perezoso	malo	abierto		
orgulloso	inteligente	honesto		

Positivo	Regular	Negativo
trabajador		

2 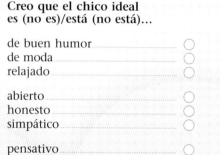 Trabaja en pareja. ¿Cómo es tu media naranja?

¿Cómo es tu media naranja?	¿Cómo es tu media naranja?
Creo que el chico ideal es (no es)/está (no está)...	**Creo que la chica ideal es (no es)/está (no está)...**
de buen humor ○	de buen humor ○
de moda ○	de moda ○
relajado ○	relajada ○
abierto ○	abierta ○
honesto ○	honesta ○
simpático ○	simpática ○
pensativo ○	pensativa ○
cariñoso ○	cariñosa ○
bien educado ○	bien educada ○
perezoso ○	perezosa ○
egoísta ○	egoísta ○
tranquilo ○	tranquila ○
un poco loco ○	un poco loca ○
menos hablador que yo ○	menos habladora que yo ○
tan inteligente como yo ○	tan inteligente como yo ○
Odio a los chicos	**Odio a las chicas**
tontos ○	tontas ○
exagerados ○	exageradas ○
creídos ○	creídas ○
groseros ○	groseras ○
ensimismados ○	ensimismadas ○

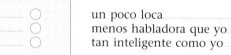

3 🎧 👥 Escucha a Ana y Jorge hablar de su pareja ideal.
Haz apuntes sobre lo que dicen utilizando los rasgos siguientes.

	Ana	Jorge
pelo		
ojos		
altura		
edad		
rasgos positivos		
lo que no tiene que ser		

4 💬 Trabaja con tu pareja. Pregunta y contesta las preguntas siguientes
sobre la encuesta.

1 ¿Cómo es tu media naranja?
2 Mi media naranja es un(a) chico/a...
3 ¿Qué rasgos no te gustan para un chico/a?
4 No me gustan los chicos/las chicas que sean...

5 🏰 Escribe un pequeño párrafo para describir a tu pareja ideal. Usa estas
frases para ayudarte. Lee primero los apuntes sobre la gramática.

Para mí la pareja ideal sería...
Prefiero un chico/una chica que sea...
Lo que no me gusta de un chico/una chica es...
Me gustan los chicos/las chicas...
Me gustan los chicos/las chicas con el pelo... y ojos...

Está **muy** contento.

Está **poco** contenta.

Es **bastante** perezoso.

Es **más** perezosa que...

6 💬 Trabaja con tu pareja. Describe a alguien de tu clase.
¿Puedes adivinar quién es?

---

7 🎧 📖 Which celebrity is each person describing? Match the opinions with the right person. Use a dictionary if necessary.

Ejemplo: **1** *an English actress — Óscar*

1 an English actress
2 a charismatic person
3 a sporty person
4 a kind person
5 someone with long blond hair
6 a song writer
7 a writer
8 a hardworking person
9 a small slim person with green eyes
10 a clever person

Keira Knightley

Usain Bolt

J. K. Rowling

Bruno Mars

> Es mi cantante estadounidense preferido. Es carismático y tiene mérito porque escribe muchas canciones para sí mismo y para otros artistas famosos como Flo Rida. Hasta escribió la canción del último Mundial de fútbol — Wavin' Flag. Tiene 27 años y es bastante alto y delgado. Tiene la piel morena y el pelo y los ojos castaños. Ha ganado muchos premios y le admiro mucho. Me encanta su música.
>
> **Eduardo**

> Es maja y abierta y es mi actriz inglesa favorita. Tiene unos 28 años y es famosa, gracias a varias películas. Pero lo mejor de ella es su papel de Elizabeth Bennet en Pride and Prejudice. Es bastante baja y delgada. Tiene ojos verdes y la piel clara. De momento tiene mucho éxito.
>
> **Óscar**

> Es muy lista y tiene mucho éxito como escritora. La admiro cantidad porque sus novelas son divertidísimas. Tiene algo más de 40 años y es alta y delgada con el pelo largo y rubio. Es británica.
>
> **Esther**

> Es un deportista guay. Es un corredor jamaicano. Tiene 26 años. Es superrápido y está muy en forma. Es alto, fuerte y delgado. Tiene la piel negra y los ojos y el pelo muy oscuros. Es simpático y muy exitoso. Ha ganado seis medallas olímpicas de oro y tiene el récord del mundo en los 100 y 200 metros. Me gusta porque es trabajador y dedicado.
>
> **Beatriz**

LENGUA CLAVE

¿A quién admiras?	Admiro a...	¿Cómo es?
		Es muy/bastante/un poco/poco... ...alto(a). ...delgado(a). ...guapo(a). ...británico(a). ...español(a). ...irlandés/esa. ...norteamericano(a).
	Tiene...	...la piel oscura/clara/morena. ...pecas. ...cara redonda/ancha/alargada. ...ojos azules/verdes/castaños. ...barba. ...bigote.
¿Cómo es su personalidad?	Es...	...simpático(a). ...cariñoso(a). ...divertido(a). ...gracioso(a). ...listo(a). ...abierto(a). ...rápido(a). ...majo(a). ...trabajador(a).
	Tiene...	...éxito. ...mérito.
¿Qué hace?	Es...	...cantante. ...escritor(a). ...deportista. ...futbolista. ...actor/actriz.

8 💬 Habla con tu pareja de una persona a quien admiras.

Ejemplo:
A: ¿A quién admiras?
B: Admiro a David Beckham.
A: ¿Cómo es?
B: Es alto y fuerte. Tiene el pelo rubio y corto, la cara alargada y la piel clara.
A: ¿Cómo es su personalidad?
B: Es majo y cariñoso y en el campo es rápido y trabajador.
A: ¿Qué hace?
B: Es futbolista.

9a 🏔 Escribe una lista de todos los adjetivos que conoces para describir a una persona y encuentra el contrario. Usa un diccionario si es necesario.

Adjetivo	Contrario
alto	bajo
majo	insoportable

¡OJO!

Make your writing more interesting

For example, if you are writing about somebody famous, you could write:

La princesa Kate es miembro de la familia real británica (profession). *Es bastante alta, delgada, muy guapa y rica. Tiene los ojos castaños y el pelo largo y moreno* (looks). *Es simpática, sonriente y muy trabajadora* (personality). *Es inglesa* (nationality). *Le encanta el deporte y le parece divertido salir con sus amigos* (likes and dislikes).

This will be the 'bones' of your description. Then make up longer, more complex sentences. Use connectives such as:

pero (but) — *Es grande, pero no es gordo.* (He is big but not fat.)

porque (because) — *Me gusta porque es muy buen cantante.* (I like him/her because he/she is a very good singer.)

como (since/as) — *Como es muy fuerte, mete muchos goles.* (As he/she is very strong, he/she scores lots of goals.)

Lo mejor de él/ella es… (the best thing about him/her is…)
— *Lo mejor de ella es que es muy tranquila y simpática.* (The best thing about her is that she is very calm and kind.)

b 🏔 Escribe cinco frases sobre una persona famosa e inglesa a quien admiras.

Ejemplo: Admiro a Kim Kardashian porque es…

c 🏔 Escribe cinco frases sobre una persona famosa e inglesa que no te guste.

Ejemplo: No me gusta X porque es…

10 🏔 Escribe un artículo sobre gente famosa que te guste.

GRAMÁTICA

More about using adjectives

Adjectives agree in number and gender with the noun they are describing:

masculine singular	*un chico majo* (a lovely boy)
masculine plural	*ojos negros* (black eyes)
feminine singular	*una piel oscura* (a dark complexion)
feminine plural	*unas personas divertidas* (fun people)

In Spanish some adjectives are used with the verb *ser* while others are used with *tener*:

Es guapo.	He is good looking.
Es bastante alto.	He is quite tall.
Tiene el pelo rubio.	He/she has blond hair.
Tiene éxito.	He/She is successful.

Ser is used with nationality:

Soy inglés/esa.	I am English.
Es irlandés/esa.	He/She is Irish.
Son americanos/as.	They are American.

Completa las frases siguientes con el verbo correcto:
1 J. R. R. Tolkein _____ inglés.
2 Mi novio _____ fuerte y delgado y _____ los ojos morenos.
3 Mi amigo _____ suerte. Ya tiene bigote y se afeita cada día.
4 Ana Kornikova _____ una tenista muy famosa.
5 Bill Gates _____ listo y _____ mucho éxito.
6 Los chicos de Green Day _____ éxito porque _____ simpáticos.
7 Los Kaiser Chiefs _____ majos y graciosos.
8 Yo _____ alto y un poco gordo.

11 🎧📖 Escucha y lee lo siguiente. ¿Quién es? ¿María, Suzi, Pili, Juan, Anabel o Pablo?

Ejemplo: **1** — *María*

1 Le gusta la misma comida.
2 Tiene novia.
3 Está triste.
4 Tiene la misma edad que su amiga.
5 Se lleva muy bien con la persona que vive al lado.
6 Le gusta hacer deporte.
7 Comparte muchas cosas.
8 Cree que su amigo le ayuda.

Mi mejor amigo se llama Ángel. Es el chico más simpático de mi clase. Tiene un sentido del humor fantástico y siempre se está riendo. A los dos nos gustan las mismas cosas. Nos encanta salir, la música rock y hamburguesa con patatas fritas. Ángel me escucha y yo le escucho a él. Lo más importante es que te puedes fiar de Ángel. Tener un amigo con quien puedes contar es esencial para mí.

María

Mi mejor amiga se llama Bárbara. Es más que una amiga porque es mi gemela. Compartimos la mayoría de las cosas — yo le dejo mi ropa y ella me deja su maquillaje. Barbara es estupenda. Es la persona más lista que conozco, pero también es la más maja. Es una amiga de verdad. Para mí eso es lo más importante. Te puedes llevar bien con la gente pero eso no significa que sean amigos de verdad. Con Barbara no es así.

Suzi

Mi mejor amiga se llama Marta. Desafortunadamente de momento no nos llevamos demasiado bien. Es porque se ha enamorado de un chico de nuestra clase y ahora no tiene tanto tiempo para mí. Apenas me habla, como siempre está con el novio. Me siento muy mal. No sé qué hacer.

Pili

No me llevo bien con Pili, la mejor amiga de mi novia. Es muy egoísta y no nos deja solos nunca. Es muy pesada y creo que me tiene celos.

Juan

Mi mejor amiga es mi madre. Es la persona más maja que conozco. Me encanta su sentido del humor y tenemos los mismos gustos en todo. Pasamos mucho tiempo juntas — por ejemplo, cada semana jugamos al tenis y montamos en bici. Tengo muchos amigos, pero mi madre es la única que me entiende de verdad.

Anabel

La persona que mejor me cae es mi mejor amigo Max. Es mi vecino y siempre estamos juntos. Me encanta salir y siempre puedo contar con él para acompañarme. Nunca estoy solo. Es muy listo y me ayuda mucho con mis deberes.

Pablo

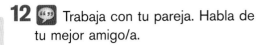

GRAMÁTICA

The superlative

The superlative is used to compare the most or the least. In English, we add -est to the adjective, for example the kind*est*, the rich*est*, the happi*est*, or we add the word 'most', for example the *most* beautiful.

In Spanish, you use the following construction:
el/la/los
+ más/menos
+ noun + adjective.

For example:
- *El chico más simpático de mi clase.*
  The nicest boy in my class.

- *La persona menos inteligente que conozco.*
  The least intelligent person I know.

NB: *mejor* – best; *peor* – worst.

Write two sentences using the superlative for the following set of pictures.

Ana   María   Suzi

---

12 🗣 Trabaja con tu pareja. Habla de tu mejor amigo/a.

Mi mejor amigo/a se llama…
Es el chico/la chica más…
Me encanta su…
Tenemos los mismos gustos en…
Puedo fiarme de él/ella…
Para mí lo más importante es…

13 📖 Lee lo que dice Francisco de su hermano.

Admiro mucho a mi hermano mayor porque es un experto de la informática. Si tengo un problema con mi ordenador o si se estropea, Andrés no tarda nada en recuperar los archivos o vencer a un pirata de informática.

Solo tiene 18 años, pero es superlisto y repara cualquier fallo.

Tiene cuatro ordenadores en total, pero no me deja usarlos porque no tengo éxito con los ordenadores. ¡Con solo mirarlos consigo borrar los archivos! ¡Siempre se me olvida mi contraseña! Lo mejor de Andrés es que es muy tranquilo y explica bien las cosas. ¡También me quema muchos CDs de música guay!

Uso el ordenador para los estudios y es muy importante entender del 'disco duro', 'lector de disquettes' etc., pero soy un poco tonto porque siempre tengo algún problema. ¡Andrés es mi héroe!

a ✏ ¿Cuáles de estos adjetivos describen Andrés y Francisco? Rellena la tabla.

> inteligente   divertido   perezoso   generoso
> antipático   antiguo   rápido   agradecido
> trabajador   nervioso   alto   despistado
> aburrido   egoísta   despistado

Andrés	Francisco
inteligente	*agradecido*

b ✏ Haz una lista de los usos diferentes de *ser* y *tener* en este artículo.

Ejemplo: ser — Es un experto.
tener — Tengo un problema.

---

14 📖 ¿Qué dice Ángel de la gente a quien admira?

La persona más importante en mi vida es mi madre. Sin ella no sería quien soy. Es cariñosa, simpática y perdona muy fácilmente. Le quiero porque me ha enseñado como ser una persona honrada. También está mi padre. Dicen que me parezco a él, pero prefiero pensar que quieren decir que me parezco con respecto a mi personalidad. Es trabajador y honesto. Siempre dice algo majo de los demás.

Creo que los amigos son muy importantes. Conozco a mucha gente pero solo tengo una a quien le considero una amiga de verdad. A Ana le conozco de toda la vida y es la única persona con quien puedo hablar porque ella escucha. Es discreta y muy lista, pero modesta. Con Ana puedes ser serio o relajado. Salimos juntos bastante pero no importa si no nos vemos durante un tiempo. Al juntarnos de nuevo todo sigue como antes.

a ✏ Answer the questions in English.

1 Name two things Ángel says about his mother.
2 What has his mother taught him?
3 How does he describe his father?
4 What does he say about Ana?
5 Why doesn't it matter if they don't see each other for a while?

Paper 1: listening

Exam tip

- Don't forget that you are not allowed to use a dictionary during the listening exam.
- There is often more than one correct answer to choose from, so if you don't understand everything you hear, try to work out an answer from the question and from what you do understand of the text.
- After the recording has been played the first time, if you have already written some answers, remember to check them as well as find the missing ones during the second playing.

Try this listening task, which is aimed at the higher grades.

Los medios de comunicación

Unos jóvenes hablan de los medios de comunicación.
Some young people are talking about communication.

¿Qué medio de comunicación prefieren?
Which method do they prefer?

A la televisión

B los móviles

C las revistas

D Internet

E la radio

F las cartas

G el correo electrónico

H los periódicos

This is the example answer. You can rule it out as a possible answer since no item is used twice.

Think about all the items on this list. What do you think you will hear?

Pon la letra adecuada en cada casilla.
Put the correct letter in each box.

The answer will be obvious. It is there to show you what to do. It is a good opportunity as well to get used to the speed of delivery.

Ejemplo:	Pablo	D
(i)	Susana	
(ii)	Jorge	
(iii)	María	
(iv)	Arturo	
(v)	Inés	
(vi)	Juan	

(Total for Question: 6 marks)

Paper 2: reading

This section looks at Paper 2: reading and
writing. Try to answer this reading task, which
is in the style of question 3(a) on paper 2.

Exam tip

Look carefully at the example. This shows you what you
have to do to answer the question. It also shows you
how to find the answer. In this case the link is made
between *fútbol* in the text and *deportes de equipo* (team
games) in the answer. When you work through this task
be prepared to explain how and why you arrived at your
answers. What are the links you made?

Mi tiempo libre

Lee estas frases. Read these comments.

(a) ¿Qué dicen? Escribe el nombre de la persona.

What do they say? Write the person's name.

> Me
> encanta estar al aire
> libre. Por eso mis padres y yo
> vamos al campo muy a menudo
> y andamos mucho.

Rocío

> Me
> dan la paga el
> viernes y después la gasto
> en las tiendas el sábado.

Isabel

> Los
> sábados juego al
> fútbol con mis amigos.

Juan

> Lo que
> más me gusta hacer
> es leer. En mi opinión es
> relajado.

Ana

> Soy
> miembro de un
> club de ajedrez. Lo juego
> en el ordenador.

María

> Paso
> todo mi tiempo en
> la piscina del barrio. Es mi
> actividad preferida.

Leonardo

> Vivimos
> al lado del mar. Los
> fines de semana salgo con mis
> amigos en nuestro barco. Es
> muy divertido.

Yolanda

Ejemplo: Me gustan los deportes de equipo. **Juan**

Be careful. There will always be one piece of
text you do not need for the answers.

 (i) Me gusta la vela. ....

 (ii) Voy de compras. ....

 (iii) Me encanta nadar. ....

 (iv) Salgo de paseo. ....

 (v) Leo libros. ....

**(Total for Question:
5 marks)**

Hints to answer the question

- When preparing for this type of task, it is useful to think about linking words and phrases.
- The context of this reading text, leisure activities, is similar to that of the writing task that follows it.
  Bear in mind that some of the vocabulary might be useful in you in answering the writing task.

Paper 2: writing

Exam tip

Remember that question 3(b) is always a short writing task related to reading task 3(a) before it. Be careful, however, as you will not get any marks for copying chunks of text.

The question below follows on from the content of the reading task above.

(b) ¿Cómo es tu fin de semana? Escribe unas 50 palabras **en español**.

What is your weekend like? Write about 50 words **in Spanish**. **(10)**

Aquí tienes algunas ideas.

Here are some ideas.

horas/times   **actividades/activities**   **rutina/routine**

comidas/meals   **ejercicio/exercise**

Sample student answer

This first writing task is marked both for communication and content. Ask yourself the following questions:
- Have I answered the question asked? Is my Spanish accurate?
- The ideas give you some clues about what to write. How can you use them?

Here is a sample student answer. This answer is longer than required (67 words) but shows that examiners do tolerate slightly longer answers and that there is no cut-off point.

This opening sentence answers the question well.

A change to the subject of the verb and use of the past tense adds variety to this text.

Using a question at the end adds interest and authenticity to the text.

Siempre me lo paso muy bien los fines de semana y me gusta hacer muchas cosas distintas. El viernes salí a cenar con mis amigos. Fuimos a un restaurante en el centro para celebrar mi cumpleaños. ¡Qué divertido! El sábado me levanté a las diez y fui al polideportivo. Es importante hacer ejercicio, creo yo. El domingo voy a hacer mis deberes. ¡Qué aburrido! ¿Qué tal tu fin de semana?

This is a clever way of covering the content in a limited word count.

This covers two of the guidance notes: routine and time.

This is a good reply to the question asked. Two tenses have been used and the future is implied in the response. There are many opinions expressed. The writer has addressed all the points suggested in the notes, and the sentences are interesting and varied.

Hints to answer the question

Now write your answer to this question. Remember the following key points.
- You can re-use items of vocabulary from the reading text, but be careful not to copy whole chunks of text. If you do this, you will lose marks.
- Try to use at least one past or future tense.
- When you have completed the task, check carefully that you have:
  - covered each of the five aspects listed in the notes
  - given an opinion
  - written the correct number of words

» Paper 3: speaking

Section A is a presentation and discussion based on a picture and lasts a maximum of 4 minutes.

These are the sorts of questions you are likely to be asked. Remember that you need to refer to the picture in your answers.

(i) Questions that relate to the picture might include:
- *¿Qué hacen las personas de la foto?*
- *¿Qué llevan?*
- *¿Qué tiempo hace?*
- *¿Cómo son las personas?*
- *¿Qué persona te parece más interesante? ¿Por qué?*

(ii) Questions indirectly related to the picture might include:
- *¿Qué crees que...ha(n) hecho antes?*
- *¿Qué van a hacer después?*
- *¿Qué persona de la foto va a...?*
- *¿Qué tipo de...?*
- *¿Por qué?*

(iii) Other questions will relate to the wider topic area. These are listed in the Edexcel specification.

Look at the pictures on the right. Can you think of appropriate questions that might be asked about them — first in English and then in Spanish. Use the examples above to help you.

Now prepare some questions of your own. Practise with a friend. Use the picture below.

Topic area E: Social activities, fitness and health

Hints to answer the question

- Some of your questions will need to relate to content of the picture you have chosen. Think WHO? WHAT? WHERE?
- Some of the questions need to be about the picture and the topic it relates to. Think about FILMS. What type of films do you like? Who is your favourite actor? What film have you seen recently?
- The rest of the conversation will be about the GENERAL topic area. In this case leisure/keeping fit and healthy lifestyles.
- Remember, if you are to achieve a high mark, you need to include tenses other than the present.

Vocabulario

Sports and hobbies

el **ajedrez**   chess
el **alpinismo**   mountain/rock climbing
las **artes marciales**   martial arts
el **atletismo**   athletics
el **bádminton**   badminton
el **baile**   dance
el **baloncesto**   basketball
el **balonmano**   handball
el **béisbol**   baseball
el **billar**   billiards
el **boxeo**   boxing
el **bricolaje**   do-it-yourself (DIY)
el **buceo**   (scuba)diving
la **caza**   hunting
el **ciclismo**   cycling
la **cocina**   cooking
correr   running
la **corrida de toros**   bullfighting
el **críquet**   cricket
los **dardos**   darts
el **deporte**   sport
el **entrenamiento**   exercise, training
la **equitación**   horse riding
la **esgrima**   fencing
el **esquí**   skiing
el **esquí acuático**   water-skiing
el **footing**   jogging
el **fútbol**   football
la **gimnasia**   gymnastics
el **golf**   golf
la **halterofilia**   weightlifting
el **hockey**   hockey
la **informática**   ICT
la **jardinería**   gardening
el **kárate**   karate
la **lectura**   reading
la **lucha**   wrestling
ir en **monopatín**   skateboarding
la **música**   music
la **natación**   swimming
el **patinaje**   skating
la **pesca**   fishing
el **piragüismo**   canoeing
el **rugby**   rugby
la **televisión**   television
el **tenis**   tennis
el **tenis de mesa**   ping pong
el **tiro con arco**   archery
la **vela**   sailing
el **voleibol**   volleyball
el **windsurf**   windsurfing

Verbs

abrir   to open
aburrirse   to get bored
acompañar   to accompany
cerrar   to close
chatear   to chat
coger   to catch; to take
crear   to create
dar   to give
decidir   to decide
encontrar   to find
entrar   to enter
escapar   to escape
escribir   to write
escuchar   to listen (to)
esperar   to wait
estar   to be
hablar   to speak, to talk
hacer   to do/to make
interesarse por/en   to be interested in
invitar   to invite
ir   to go
ir al cine/teatro   to go to the cinema/
    theatre
ir de excursión   to go hiking; to go on a
    trip
ir de paseo   to go for a walk
jugar (a)   to play (a game)
leer   to read
mandar   to send
navegar por/en Internet   to surf the
    internet
poner   to put
practicar   to practise
reír   to laugh
salir   to go out
saltar   to jump
ser   to be
tener   to have
terminar   to finish
tirar   to throw
tocar   to touch; to play an instrument
utilizar   to use
visitar   to visit

Musical instruments

el **arpa**   harp
la **batería**   drumkit
la **corneta**   cornet
la **flauta**   flute
la **guitarra**   guitar
el **piano**   piano
los **platillos**   cymbals
el **saxofón**   saxophone
el **tambor**   drum
el **teclado**   keyboard
el **trombón**   trombone
la **trompeta**   trumpet
el **violín**   violin
la **voz**   voice

Media and communication

los **anuncios**   advertisements
el **artículo**   article
los **correos electrónicos**   e-mails
la **entrevista**   interview
el **informativo**   news programme
(el/la) **Internet**   internet
los **mensajes de texto**   sms
las **noticias**   news
el **ordenador**   computer
el **periódico**   newspaper
la **prensa**   press
el **presentador**   presenter
la **programación**   viewing guide
la **publicidad**   advertising
la **radio**   radio
el **reportaje**   report
la **revista**   magazine
el **tebeo**   comic
el **(teléfono) móvil**   mobile phone
los **titulares**   headlines

Televison, radio and cinema

el **actor**   actor
el **actor secundario**   supporting actor
la **actriz**   actress
la **banda sonora**   soundtrack
la **comedia**   comedy
los **concursos**   game shows
los **créditos**   credits
la **crítica de cine**   film review
el **director**   director
el **documental**   documentary
el **drama**   drama
la **escena**   scene
los **efectos especiales**   special effects
la **estrella de cine**   film star
los **extras**   extras
el **papel (de cine)**   role
las **películas de acción**   action films
las **películas de amor/románticas**
    romantic films
las **películas de aventuras**   adventure
    films
las **películas de ciencia ficción**   science
    fiction films
las **películas de espionaje**   spy films
las **películas de guerra**   war films
las **películas de terror**   horror films
las **películas del Oeste**   Westerns
las **películas históricas**   historical films
las **películas musicales**   musicals
las **películas policíacas**   detective films
el **productor**   producer
el **programa**   programme
los **programas de deportes**   sports shows
el **reparto**   cast

los **subtítulos** subtitles
el **telediario** news
la **telenovela** soap opera
el **tiempo** weather

Opinions

(No) Me gusta(n) I (don't) like
Admiro a I admire
En mi opinión In my opinion
Lo que más me gusta es The thing I like best is
Me da(n) miedo I'm afraid of
Me entusiasma(n) I'm keen on
Me fascina(n) I'm fascinated by
Me hace(n) reír It/They make(s) me laugh
Me impresiona(n) I'm impressed by
Me interesa(n) I'm interested in
Me encanta(n) I love
No aguanto I can't stand
Odio I hate
Prefiero I prefer

Adjectives

abierto/a open
aburrido/a boring
agradable agreeable
anticuado/a old-fashioned
antipático/a unkind
bello/a beautiful
bien educado/a well-brought-up
bueno/a good
cariñoso/a loving
carismático/a charismatic
contento/a content
corto/a short
de buen humor in a good mood
de moda fashionable
deportivo/a sporty
divertido/a fun, amusing
egoísta selfish
elegante smart
exitoso/a successful

famoso/a famous
feliz happy
feo/a ugly
gracioso/a funny
grosero/a rude
hablador/a chatty/talkative
honesto/a honest
inteligente intelligent
interesante interesting
joven young
largo/a long
listo/a clever
loco/a mad
majo/a lovely
malo/a bad
nervioso/a nervous
orgulloso/a proud
pensativo/a thoughtful
perezoso/a lazy
relajado/a relaxed
simpático/a kind
tonto/a stupid
tranquilo/a quiet
viejo/a old

Places to go

la **bolera** bowling alley
el **centro** town centre
el **cine** cinema
el **club** club
el **concierto** concert
la **discoteca** club; disco
la **entrada** entrance
el **estadio** stadium
el **gimnasio** gym
la **parada de autobús** bus stop
el **parque** park
el **parque de atracciones** amusement/ theme park
la **piscina** swimming pool
la **pista de patinaje** ice rink
la **pista de tenis** tennis court

la **playa** beach
el **polideportivo** sports centre
el **restaurante** restaurant
la **taquilla** ticket office
el **teatro** theatre
las **tiendas** shops

Asking questions

¿A qué hora nos vemos? At what time shall we meet?
¿A qué hora empieza(n)/ termina(n)...? At what time does/do... start/finish?
¿A quién admiras? Who do you admire?
¿Cómo es? What is he/she/it like?
¿Cómo pasas tu tiempo libre? How do you spend your free time?
¿Cuál es tu pasatiempo favorito? What is your favourite hobby?
¿Cuánto cuesta(n)? How much does it/ do they cost?
¿Dónde está? Where is (it)?
¿Dónde quedamos? Where shall we meet?
¿Practicas algún deporte? Do you do any sports?
¿Por qué? Why?
¿Qué echan en el cine? What's on at the cinema?
¿Qué opinas? What's your opinion?
¿Qué ponen esta noche? What's on this evening?
¿Qué te apetece hacer? What do you feel like doing?
¿Qué quieres hacer? What do you want to do?
¿Te gusta(n)...? Do you like...?

Adverbs

bastante quite
más more
menos less
muy very
tan as
un poco a bit

El mundo del trabajo

1 ¿Qué tal tu cole?

2 Las prácticas de trabajo

3 El futuro

1 ¿Qué tal tu cole?

1a ¿Qué estudias? Pon los dibujos en el orden correcto según la lista siguiente.

Ejemplo: **1 — d**

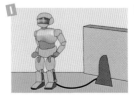

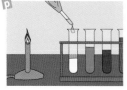

1 el español
2 el diseño
3 las matemáticas
4 la música
5 el inglés
6 el arte dramático
7 la historia
8 la tecnología
9 el alemán
10 las ciencias
11 la religión
12 el dibujo
13 el francés
14 la geografía
15 la informática
16 la educación física
17 la educación civil

b Habla con tu pareja.
¿Qué asignaturas te gustan más?

c Cada una de las palabras siguientes es una asignatura. Adivina cuál es cada una.

Ejemplo: **1 — *español***

1 pasleoñ	9 jubdio
2 narfséc	10 gtaeíconlo
3 lenaám	11 cacdenóiu safíic
4 ticámsameta	12 cacdenóiu licvi
5 rosaitih	13 lerinóig
6 grefogaaí	14 sienacci
7 samúci	15 ficátamrino
8 rate tamárdcoi	16 sediño

2 🎧 ⛪ Copia el horario. Rellena los huecos 1–10 con las asignaturas que faltan.

Ejemplo: 1 — dibujo

	lunes	martes	miércoles	jueves	viernes
8:00	inglés	geografía	informática	tecnología	español
9:00	ciencias	(2)	(5)	historia	(9)
10:00	(1)	ciencias	(6)	(8)	matemáticas
11:00					
11:30	español	(3)	ciencias	informática	inglés
12:30	matemáticas	deporte	geografía	inglés	dibujo
1:30					
3:00	historia	deporte	(7)	francés	deporte
4:00	geografía	(4)	español	matemáticas	(10)

3 📖 Lee lo que dicen estos jóvenes.
Mira el horario. ¿A qué día se refieren?

1 *Me encanta estudiar idiomas y hoy ¡tengo la oportunidad de estudiar dos! Es mi día preferido, ¡por supuesto!*

2 *Me gusta trabajar con ordenadores y como hoy estudiamos esa asignatura dos veces ¡es genial!*

3 *De veras no me gustan las ciencias así que el único día que no las tenemos es mi preferido.*

4 *Soy muy deportista y por eso el día que tenemos dos clases de esta asignatura es mi favorito.*

5 *La verdad es que no me gusta el colegio en absoluto. Pero, como es el día que no hay geografía — ¡la que odio! — tiene que ser mi preferido.*

4 💬 Trabaja con tu pareja. Habla de los días escolares que más te gustan y cuáles no.
¿Sabes explicar por qué?

Mi día preferido es…
Hoy tengo…
Una vez a la semana/dos veces a la semana
    tenemos…
Porque se me da(n) bien…
Aunque no me gusta/n…

5a 🎧 📖 Escucha a dos jóvenes hablando de sus colegios y horarios. Lee las frases y decide si son verdaderas (V) o falsas (F).

Ejemplo: 1 David tiene seis horas de clase al día. — F

1 David tiene seis horas de clase al día.
2 María va a casa para comer.
3 A David le gusta la informática.
4 David y María están en el mismo año de cole.
5 El recreo de María dura veinte minutos.
6 Las clases de David terminan a las cinco.
7 María no tiene clases el jueves.
8 David no hace ninguna actividad después del colegio.

b ⛪ Ahora para cada frase que pienses que es falsa, escribe la frase correcta en tu cuaderno.

c 🎧 ⛪ Escucha otra vez. Copia y rellena el cuadro siguiente con la información adecuada.

	María	David
Hora de empezar el colegio	9:00	8:45
Hora de terminar el colegio		
Número de recreos		
Número de clases por día		
Actividades extracurriculares		
Dónde pasa la hora de comer		
Lo que hace durante los recreos y las comidas		
Curso/año del cole		
Opinión del cole		

6a Mira la tabla en la página anterior. Escribe una pregunta para cada frase y tu propia respuesta.

Ejemplo: ¿A qué hora empieza el colegio?
Mi colegio empieza a las nueve menos cinco.

b Trabaja con tu pareja. Hazle una entrevista sobre su colegio.

7a Yésica y Martín están hablando de su colegio. Encuentra lo que significan las frases en negrita. Usa un diccionario para ayudarte.

1 ¿Qué opinas tú de las ciencias, Yésica?

No las aguanto. Son muy difíciles y **el profesor no hace más que gritar.**

2 ¿Martín, tienes una asignatura preferida — o un profesor preferido?

Me encantan los idiomas. **Saco buenas notas** porque **mi profesor explica muy bien las cosas. Me ayuda mucho.**

3 ¿Qué piensas de la historia y la geografía, Yésica?

No están mal. El Señor Montoya **enseña bien,** pero **nos pone demasiados deberes.**

4 ¿ Y tu qué opinas, Martín?

Estoy de acuerdo con Yésica. Considero que estas asignaturas están bien, pero que el profesor **nos hace escribir demasiado** y es en realidad bastante aburrido.

5 ¿Entonces crees tú Yésica que nuestro cole es bueno?

Pues sí. **Nos hacen trabajar mucho** y así **aprobaremos los exámenes**, que es lo importante. Creo que **tienes razón**.

b Trabaja con tu pareja. Haz preguntas sobre lo que estudia en el cole. Contesta las preguntas de tu pareja.

¿Te gusta(n) ¿Qué te parece(n)	el inglés? la historia? las matemáticas? el dibujo?	(No) me gusta(n)... Odio... Me encanta(n) Detesto... No aguanto... Se me da(n) bien/mal/muy mal
	el(la) profesor(a) de ciencias/español/física?	Grita mucho Me ayuda Enseña/explica muy bien Nos hace trabajar demasiado Nos pone demasiados deberes

8a ¿Cuáles son las reglas del cole? Pon los dibujos en el orden correcto.

Ejemplo: **1 — b**

b Escribe una lista de reglas para tu colegio. ¡Usa tu imaginación!

GRAMÁTICA

Verbs expressing necessity and obligation

To express obligation or necessity **tener que + infinitive** can be used. For example:

Para mantenerme en forma tengo que comer las verduras.
To keep in shape I have to eat vegetables.

Amparo tiene que hacer sus deberes.
Amparo has to do her homework.

Ellos tienen que comprar un regalo.
They have to buy a present.

María tiene un examen el lunes. Ella tiene que estudiar.
María has a test on Monday. She has to study.

Hay que + infinitive is an alternative. There is no subject, so the verb form **hay** is always used:

Hay que coger un autobús.
It's necessary to take a bus.

Hay que estudiar mucho.
One must study a lot.

No es fácil aprender español. Hay que practicar mucho.
It isn't easy to learn Spanish. It's necessary to practise a lot.

9 📖 **Lee la lista de reglas de colegio.**

Colegio Arturo Soria

Los alumnos tienen la responsabilidad de conocer las reglas del colegio. Tienen que entender su importancia y deben seguirlas todo el tiempo. Se aplican a todas las horas del colegio e incluso durante visitas escolares. Además, deben ser seguidas durante actividades extraescolares.

Para disminuir y quizás eliminar acontecimientos desagradables la seguridad de alumnos y profesores es imprescindible. Por eso se pide todo tipo de cooperación.

Reglas generales

Cada alumno tiene que llevar consigo identificación.
Deben tener un bloc para apuntes, bolígrafos, lápices y libros de texto apropiados para cada clase.
Hay que llevar el uniforme adecuado.
No se permite llevar gorra o zapatillas — ni cascos ni MP3 etcétera.
El colegio no reconoce ninguna responsabilidad por objetos perdidos en el colegio.
No se permiten cerillas o mecheros.
Demostrar respeto.
Hay que ser cortés a toda hora. Los alumnos tienen que tratar a otros alumnos y a adultos con respeto.
Hay que parar e identificarse en cualquier momento si se lo pide un adulto.

Se prohíbe

■ Mentir, hacer trampa, copiar y hacer plagio.
■ Vender objetos dentro del colegio sin el permiso del director.
■ Juegos de azar — con o sin recompensa monetaria.
■ Chantaje.
■ El uso de MP3, televisores, teléfonos móviles, radios, ipods, juegos electrónicos y todo tipo de cosas semejantes.
■ Sacar comida de la cantina — solo se permite comer y beber dentro de la cantina.
■ El chicle.
■ Tirar misiles sólidos — incluyendo bolas de nieve.
■ El uso de patines o monopatines.
■ Traer y usar pistolas de agua.
■ Actividades ilegales.
■ El uso de teléfonos durante el horario escolar sin el permiso explícito de un adulto.

a ✏️ Escribe una lista de las reglas que existen en tu colegio.

b 💬 Trabaja con tu pareja para decir lo que, en tu opinión, se debe y lo que no se debe permitir en el cole.

Ejemplo: En mi opinión es importante…
No creo que sea razonable…

10a 📖 Mira los uniformes. Escribe las palabras en el orden correcto.

*Ejemplo: **a** — unas botas*

unas botas
una chaqueta
una camisa
una falda
unos calcetines
una corbata
una camiseta
unas zapatillas
una blusa
un pantalón
unas medias

b  ¿Puedes describir los uniformes con más detalles?

Ejemplo: *Este chico lleva un pantalón largo y gris.*

c ¡Ahora a ti! Describe tu uniforme a tu pareja y escribe unas frases sobre él.

GRAMÁTICA

Agreement of adjectives

Remember that nouns in Spanish are masculine or feminine and adjectives must agree in number and gender with the noun they are describing:

un pantalón blanco
but *una corbata blanca*

unos calcetines blancos
but *unas zapatillas blancas*

Adjectives of colour come after the noun in Spanish. They have to agree with the noun they are describing:

una camiseta negra
a black t-shirt

unos pantalones azules
some blue trousers

Make sure you change the adjective endings where necessary!

---

11 a Lee el diálogo siguiente y ponlo en el orden correcto.

A: Muy bien. ¿Qué talla usa?
A: ¿Y qué color prefiere?
A: A ver…un momento…aquí tiene.
B: Talla 38.
B: Gracias.
A: Buenos días. ¿En qué puedo servirle?
B: ¿Cuánto cuestan?
B: Creo que azul marino.
A: En la caja que está allí al fondo.
B: ¿Dónde se paga?
B: Quisiera unos pantalones por favor.
A: Cuestan 38.

b Ahora escucha y corrige.

12 a Escucha esta información. Empareja cada artículo con el precio adecuado.

Ejemplo: **1 a — 65€**

12€   56€   28€

65€   15€   44€

b Trabaja con tu pareja. Usa el diálogo de arriba. Practica comprando las cosas en los dibujos.

La tienda del colegio

13a  Mira el dibujo. ¿Qué compran? ¿Cuánto pagan?

Ejemplo: 1 a — 2€

b Trabaja con tu pareja. Empareja los nombres de todos los artículos con la imagen adecuada.

Ejemplo: boli — a

boli   lápiz   regla   goma   cuaderno
diccionario   libro   carpeta   agenda   grapadora
paquete de papel   tijeras   sacapuntas   estuche
rotuladores   compás   papel líquido   cola
pluma

c Lee estas conversaciones y practica con tu pareja para comprar algo de la lista.

A: ¡Hola! ¿Qué desea?
B: Quisiera un bolígrafo azul, por favor.
A: ¡Aquí tiene! ¿Algo más?
B: No, nada más, gracias. ¿Cuánto es?
A: Son 2€, por favor.

A: ¡Hola! ¿Qué quiere, señorita?
B: Quisiera unos rotuladores, por favor.
A: ¡Aquí tiene! ¿Algo más?
B: No, nada más, gracias. ¿Cuánto es?
A: Son 15€, por favor.

A: ¡Buenos días! ¿Qué desea?
B: Quisiera un diccionario, por favor.
A: ¿De qué idioma?
B: Español–inglés, por favor
A: Toma. ¿Algo más?
B: No, gracias ¿Cuánto es?
A: Son 22€, por favor.

GRAMÁTICA

Pronouns

Pronouns are words that replace nouns.

Subject pronouns generally appear before the verb. They explain who is doing the action.

Singular		Plural	
I	yo	we	nosotros/as
you (informal)	tú	you (informal)	vosotros/as
he/it	él	they	ellos
she/it	ella	they	ellas
you (formal)	usted	you (formal)	ustedes

Spanish uses a different word for 'you' according to whether the relationship is:
informal (talking to a young person or child or an adult you know well), or
formal (talking to an adult you don't know well or a person who is in authority)

You do not always need to use the subject pronouns, as the ending of the verb tells you who is speaking. Always use them, however, to make things clear. For example:

Él tiene un gato. Yo tengo un perro.
He has a cat. I have a dog.

Direct object pronouns replace nouns that 'receive' the verb. They answer the question 'what?' or 'who(m)?' with regard to what the subject of the sentence is doing. They are often used to avoid repetition. For example:

Pedro compró un helado y se lo regaló a su madre.
Pedro bought an ice cream and gave it to his mother.

Singular		Plural	
me	me	us	nos
you (informal)	te	you (informal)	os
him/it	le/lo	them	les/los
her/it	la	them	las
you (formal)	le/lo/la	you (formal)	les/los/las

Indirect object pronouns also replace nouns that 'receive' the verb, but answer the question 'to what?' or 'to whom?' with regard to what the subject of the sentence is doing. For example:

Voy a traer una taza de café a mi madre.
Le voy a traer una taza de café.

I'm going to bring **my mother** a cup of coffee.
I'm going to bring a cup of coffee **to her**.

Singular		Plural	
to me	me	to us	nos
to you (informal)	te	to you (informal)	os
to him/to her/to it	le	to them	les
to you (formal)	le	to you (formal)	les

Object pronouns generally come before the verb but can also be placed at the end of some forms of the verb, e.g. the infinitive. For example:

Tienes que enviarme una carta.
or *Me tienes que enviar una carta.*
You have to send **me** a letter.

14 Sustituye las palabras subrayadas con el pronombre adecuado.

Ejemplo: Quiero comprar <u>estos bolígrafos</u>. — Quiero comprarlos.

1 Voy a ver <u>a mi madre</u> esta tarde.
2 Hoy es el día de los exámenes. Voy a llamar <u>a mi profesor</u>.
3 He perdido mis gafas. ¿Has visto <u>mis gafas</u>?
4 Detesto <u>la geografía</u>.
5 Quiero ver <u>el partido de fútbol</u> mañana.
6 Juan prefiere hablar <u>español</u>.

15a  Empareja las frases y los dibujos.

Ejemplo: **1 — d**

1
He perdido mi teléfono móvil. Creo que lo perdí en el patio hace media hora.

2
He perdido mi cartera. La dejé en la cantina ayer. Es roja y contenía cuatro billetes de diez euros.

3
Dejé mis llaves en el laboratorio esta mañana. ¿Las has encontrado?

4
He perdido mi bolsa de deportes. Contiene mi pantalón corto, una camiseta y unas zapatillas. Creo que la dejé en el autobús.

5
¿Has encontrado un estuche rojo? Contiene dos bolis, un lápiz y una goma. No lo he visto desde esta mañana. Creo que lo dejé en el aula de matemáticas.

6
Busco mi bicicleta. Estaba en el almacén durante el recreo, pero ¡ahora no está! Creo que me la han robado.

a

b

c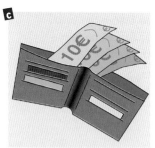

d

e

f

b Escucha las conversaciones.
¿Qué han perdido? ¿Cuándo y dónde? Copia y completa las casillas con la información adecuada.

¿Qué?	¿Cuándo?	¿Dónde?
Ejemplo: mochila	esta mañana	el gimnasio
1		

c  Trabaja con tu pareja.
Practica estos dos diálogos, a y b.

A: ¿En qué puedo ayudarle?
B: He perdido mi…

a  **b**

A: ¿Dónde la perdió?
B: La perdí…

a  **b**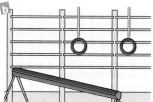

A: ¿Cuándo la perdió?
B: La perdí…

a  Hoy **b**  Ayer

A: ¿Qué contenía?
B: Contenía…

a  **b**

A: ¿Cómo se llama?
B: Me llamo…..
A: Le informaremos si la encontremos.
B: Gracias.

2 Las prácticas de trabajo

- ☑ Apply for a job
- ☑ Learn about workplace activities
- ☑ Use the imperfect and preterite tenses
- ☑ Give opinions

1a 🎧 ✏️ Copia estos títulos en tu cuaderno. Escucha lo que dice la chica. Rellena los detalles que faltan.

Apellido: **Belén**

Nombre:

Fecha de nacimiento:

Edad:

Nacionalidad:

Mejores asignaturas:

Pasatiempos favoritos:

Dónde quiere trabajar:

Por qué:

Cualidades:

Ambiciones:

b 💬 Trabaja con tu pareja. Haz las siguientes preguntas y contéstalas.

1 ¡Hola! ¿Cómo te llamas?
2 ¿Y cuál es tu fecha de nacimiento?
3 ¿Y cuántos años tienes?
4 Muy bien, y ¿de dónde eres?
5 Y ¿cuáles son tus mejores asignaturas en el colegio?
6 ¿Tienes algunos pasatiempos o actividades?
7 ¿Dónde quieres hacer tus prácticas de trabajo?
8 ¿Por qué?
9 Háblame de tus cualidades personales.
10 ¿Me puedes dar otra razón por tu elección?

c ✏️ Completa la solicitud de arriba para ti mismo.

2 📖 Quieres hacer prácticas de trabajo. Lee los anuncios.

Anuncios de trabajo

a ¿Te interesa la educación? Hay puestos en colegios de primaria y secundaria por esta región.

b ¿Estás buscando un trabajo en informática? Empresa de informática en centro ciudad busca empleados temporales.

c ¿Te gustan los idiomas y viajar? Considera hacer tus prácticas de trabajo en una agencia de viajes. Hay muchas oportunidades.

d Si te interesa trabajar en el mundo de la hostelería no busques más. Hay puestos en hoteles y pensiones de este barrio.

e Si estás interesado en asuntos sociales te ofrecemos la oportunidad de trabajar en hospitales y residencias de ancianos.

f Si te interesan los medios de comunicación Radio X tiene el puesto que buscas. Escribe inmediatamente.

a 📖 Qué anuncio te interesará si…

1 Eres bueno con los ordenadores.
2 Quieres ser recepcionista.
3 Quieres ser profesor(a).
4 Se te da bien la música.
5 Quieres ser médico.
6 Hablas francés y español.

b 📖 Lee la carta siguiente. ¿A qué anuncio se refiere?

Fecha

Muy señor mío,

Vi su anuncio en la revista de febrero del colegio ofreciendo puestos para las prácticas de trabajo. Me interesa mucho una carrera en medicina y un puesto con ustedes me vendría muy bien. Sería una gran oportunidad.

En el colegio mis mejores asignaturas son las ciencias y la informática. También se me dan bien los idiomas.

Soy un alumno honesto y trabajador. Tengo buen sentido del humor y trabajo bien en equipo.

Creo que tengo las cualidades que busca y le agradecería que me considerara para un puesto.

Le mando adjunto mi currículum y una carta de mi profesor.

Muchas gracias.

Le saluda atentamente,
Angélica Dorado.

c ✏️ Escribe una carta parecida solicitando un puesto de los anunciados en la página 71. Si prefieres, prepárala para otro trabajo de tu elección.

3a 🎧 📖 Escucha y lee. ¿Quién habla? Empareja los nombres con los dibujos.

Ejemplo: Luci — b

Hice mis prácticas de trabajo en un banco.
Luci

Hice mis prácticas de trabajo en una tienda de animales domésticos.
Pablo

Trabajé en una fábrica de galletas del barrio. ¡Un rollo!
Juan

Pasé mis prácticas en una oficina del centro.
Marta

Trabajé en un colegio. Fue genial.
Suzi

Trabajé en una agencia de viajes. No fue muy interesante que digamos.
Javier

b 🎧 ✏️ ¿Qué más dicen estos jóvenes? Copia y completa la tabla con los detalles que faltan.

	¿Cuándo?	¿Cuánto tiempo?	Horario	Transporte
Ejemplo: Luci	*marzo*	*tres semanas*	*9–5*	*coche*
Pablo				
Suzi				
Juan				
Marta				
Javier				

c 💬 Trabaja con tu pareja. Usa la información de arriba. Practica preguntas y contéstalas.

Ejemplo: Luci

A: *¿Dónde hiciste tus prácticas de trabajo?*
B: *Trabajé en un banco.*
A: *¿Cuándo hiciste tus prácticas de trabajo?*
B: *Hice mis prácticas de trabajo en marzo*
A: *¿Cuánto tiempo duraron las prácticas?*
B: *Duraron tres semanas en total.*
A: *¿Cuál era tu horario?*
B: *Empezaba a las nueve y terminaba a las cinco.*
A: *¿Cómo ibas al banco?*
B: *Iba en coche con mi madre.*

4a Mira el ejemplo. Sigue el código. Usa las imágenes para ayudarte a escribir frases acerca de tus prácticas de trabajo.

Ejemplo:

1 g *Mis prácticas de trabajo duraron quince días.*
    j *Trabajé en una tienda de recuerdos.*
    a *Cada día iba en autobús.*
    o *Empezaba a las diez de la mañana y terminaba a las dos de la tarde.*
    s *En mi opinión el trabajo era aburrido y no me gustaba nada.*

2 e, k, c, m, r
3 h, l, b, p, q
4 f, i, d, n, q

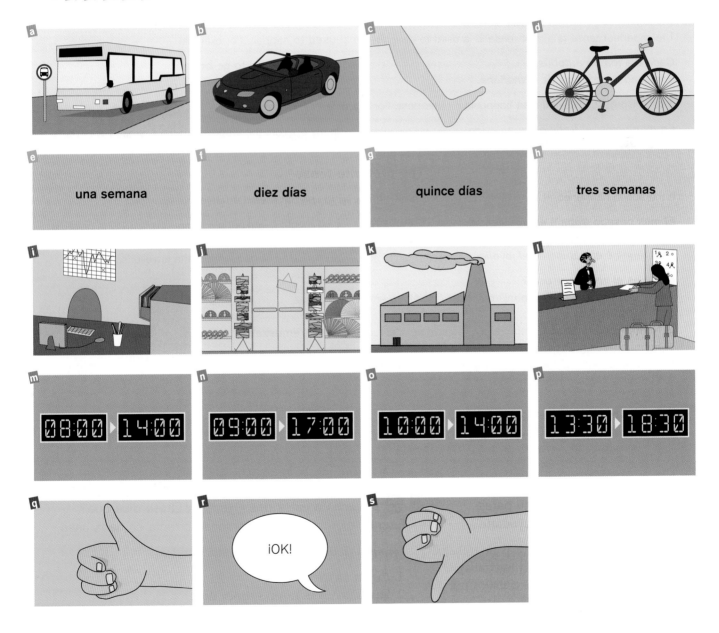

una semana   diez días   quince días   tres semanas

¡OK!

b Ahora escribe un pequeño párrafo o una serie de frases sobre tus propias prácticas de trabajo.

The imperfect and preterite tenses
The imperfect tense

*Mis prácticas de trabajo duraron una semana. Trabajé en un supermercado y cada día **iba** a pie. **Empezaba** a las nueve de la mañana y **terminaba** a las cinco de la tarde con un descanso al mediodía. En mi opinión el trabajo **era** poco interesante y no me **gustaba** mucho.*

*Mis prácticas de trabajo duraron dos semanas. Trabajé en una fábrica y cada día **iba** en bicicleta. **Empezaba** a las ocho de la mañana y **terminaba** a las tres de la tarde con dos descansos al día. En mi opinión el trabajo **era** muy fácil y me **gustaba** mucho.*

The highlighted verbs in the text above are in the imperfect tense. You met this tense in Module 1.

The imperfect tense is a past tense. It is used to describe what **used to** happen. For example:

Cada día iba en autobús.	Every day I **used to** go by bus.
Empezaba a las diez de la mañana.	I **used to** start at 10 a.m.

It can also describe what **was** happening in the past. For example:

En mi opinión, el trabajo era aburrido.	In my opinion, the work was boring (**while I was there**).

The preterite tense

If the action happened at a particular time in the past, you need to use the preterite tense. For example:

El mes pasado trabajé en una tienda.	Last month I worked in a shop. (the activity is **finished**)
En junio del año pasado empecé a trabajar en el restaurante.	In June last year I began to work in the restaurant.
Ayer terminé el trabajo en el joyería.	Yesterday I finished work in the jeweller's.

¿Cuál es el verbo correcto?

1 El mes pasado **hice/hacía** mis prácticas de trabajo en un restaurante.
2 Cada día **fui/iba** en metro.
3 Normalmente **empecé/empezaba** a las seis pero el lunes **empecé/empezaba** a las siete.
4 En mi opinión, trabajar en un hospital **fue/era** poco interesante.
5 La visita al hospital **fue/era** una experiencia inolvidable.
6 El trabajo **fue/era** repetitivo y no muy variado.
7 **Trabajé/trabajaba** en la cantina de un hospital.
8 El primer día **olvidé/olvidaba** traer dinero para comprar comida.
9 Lo peor **fue/era** hacer el café.
10 El trabajo **fue/era** variado y no **estuvo/estaba** mal.

5 💬 Haz un diálogo con tu pareja. Usa las preguntas para ayudarte.

¿Dónde hiciste tus prácticas de trabajo?
¿Cuánto tiempo duraron los trabajos?
¿Cuándo empezabas los trabajos por la mañana?
¿Cuándo terminabas por la tarde?
¿Cómo ibas al trabajo?
¿Cómo era el trabajo?

6 🎧 Escucha a estos dos jóvenes. ¿Quién dice qué? Escribe el nombre de la persona correcta en cada caso.

Ejemplo: 1 Iba en bicicleta. Mari Carmen.

1 *Iba en bicicleta.*
2 Sus trabajos duraron quince días.
3 El trabajo era muy aburrido.
4 Trabajó en una tienda.
5 El día era demasiado largo.
6 Le gustó el trabajo.

7a 📖 ✏️ Lee en el recuadro de al lado lo que dice alguna genta sobre sus experiencias de trabajo. Decide cuáles son negativas, cuáles son positivas y cuáles no estaban mal.

b Busca más comentarios que puedas dar sobre tus prácticas de trabajo. Usa un diccionario para ayudarte. Escríbelos en la tabla también.

era aburrido	había mucha variedad
era interesante	mi jefe era antipático
era fácil	me llevaba bien con todos los demás
era útil	el día era demasiado largo
era insoportable	el trabajo era un poco repetitivo

Me gustaba	No estaba mal	No me gustaba
Ejemplo: era interesante		

8 📖 ✏️ Lee los siguientes párrafos. Mira la lista de abajo y escribe las palabras que faltan en cada hueco.

1 Pasé dos semanas trabajando en una peluquería en el centro de la cuidad. Era muy interesante pero el trabajo era un poco repetitivo. Cada día tenía que

para los clientes,

y también

.

2 Trabajar en una oficina estaba bastante bien. Tenía que

, y , lo que no me gustaba mucho. Pero la oportunidad de y era, en mi opinión, una experiencia muy útil.

3 Hice mis prácticas de trabajo en una agencia de viajes. Tenía muchas oportunidades. Por ejemplo:

, y mucho más. Lo único que no me gustaba era mi jefe: era un poco frío y yo tenía que

cada día.

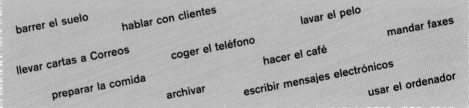

barrer el suelo   hablar con clientes   lavar el pelo   mandar faxes
llevar cartas a Correos   coger el teléfono   hacer el café   usar el ordenador
preparar la comida   archivar   escribir mensajes electrónicos

9 🗨️ Haz una encuesta entre tus compañeros de clase. Averigua dónde hicieron sus prácticas de trabajo, qué horario tenían que hacer, y qué opinan de sus experiencias. Usa las siguientes preguntas.

* ¿Dónde hiciste tus prácticas de trabajo?
* ¿Qué tenías que hacer?
* ¿Te gustó? ¿Por qué (no)?

10 ✏️ Escribe una carta a tu corresponsal acerca de tus prácticas de trabajo. ¡No te olvides de dar tus opiniones! Menciona lo siguiente.

dónde trabajaste
durante cuánto tiempo
cómo llegabas al trabajo
las horas que trabajabas
lo que tenías que hacer

Al teléfono

11 📖 Lee el texto.

Llamando por teléfono

A pesar de que muchísima gente hoy en día tiene teléfono móvil, una gran cantidad de personas tienen problemas con usar el teléfono convencional en su lugar de trabajo. A mucha gente le causa ansiedad ¡e incluso trauma! Cada empleado tiene que vencer sus temores y encontrar una manera de superar esas preocupaciones. Si tienes problema con usar el teléfono, a lo mejor te ayudan los consejos siguientes.

Haciendo la llamada

Hacer una llamada se puede dividir en tres fases principales:
la preparación
la llamada
la evaluación

La preparación

Asegúrate de a quién estás llamando. Apunta la razón de la llamada y de lo que te quieres enterar y ten eso delante de ti antes de llamar. Antes de hacer una llamada superimportante practica con un colega. Eso te ayudará a relajarte y a saber cuáles pueden ser los problemas que surgen. Si tienes una lista de llamadas ponlas en orden de dificultad con la que te parece la más fácil primero. Así ganarás confianza antes de hacer la que más te asusta. No dejes para luego llamadas difíciles — eso solo servirá para hacerlo más estresante todavía.

La llamada

A menudo lo más difícil es conseguir comunicar con la persona a quien llamas. Si contesta una operadora, por ejemplo, ten a mano el número de extensión de la persona y su nombre. Si hace falta, explícale brevemente por qué llamas. Sé flexible con lo que dices y ante todo muéstrate tranquilo y bien educado y habla despacio — sobre todo si estás llamando al extranjero.

La evaluación

Apunta lo que pasa durante la llamada para tener un archivo de los hechos. Si una llamada no ha sido demasiado exitosa, intenta decidir por qué para evitarlo en el futuro. Mantén una actitud positiva y acuérdate de que con la práctica las llamadas se hacen más fáciles.

Recibiendo llamadas

Solo contesta las llamadas cuando estás preparado. Aprende frases apropiadas que puedas usar al contestar. Saluda a la persona que llama; da el nombre de tu empresa y tu nombre y pregunta en qué puedes ayudarle. Si recibes la llamada en un sitio donde hay mucha gente o ruido no te distraigas — concéntrate en la llamada. No te preocupes por los silencios — es bastante común. La persona que te llama a lo mejor puede estar nerviosa también.

a Answer the following questions in English.

1 In the article, what three stages are identified when making a telephone call?

2 During preparation, what is it a good idea to have written down?

3 Why is it inadvisable to put off difficult calls?

4 Which three adjectives are used to describe how you should ideally sound during your call?

5 What are you advised to do if calling abroad?

6 Why is it important to analyse why a call might not have been successful?

7 How can you improve your telephone skills?

8 What information should you give when you answer a call?

9 What might silences indicate?

12a 🎧 📖 Escucha y lee lo que dicen estas personas.

b 📖 Empareja el inglés con el español.

¡Diga! ¡Dígame!	Thank you very much.
¿Puedo hablar con …..?	Hello!
Quisiera…	Can I take a message?
De parte de…	He/She isn't here.
Lo siento…	Don't mention it/You're welcome.
Está ocupado/a…	Would you like to wait/hold on?
No está.	I would like to…
¿Puedo coger un recado?	Goodbye.
¿Puedo dejar un recado?	Can I leave a message?
Muchas gracias.	On behalf of…
De nada.	He/She is on the phone.
Está al teléfono.	I'm sorry…
¿Quiere esperar?	Can I speak to…?
Adiós.	He/She is busy.

13 💬 Trabaja con tu pareja. Practica esta conversación. Úsala como ejemplo para practicar tus propias conversaciones.

Ejemplo:

A: *Dígame. Arquitectos López. ¿En qué puedo servirle?*

B: *Oiga. Quisiera hablar con el señor Albani, por favor.*

A: *¿De parte de quién?*

B: *Soy Conchita González.*

A: *Desafortunadamente no está aquí.*

B: *¿Cuándo volverá?*

A: *No estoy seguro. ¿Quiere dejar un mensaje?*

B: *Sí. Pídele al señor Albani que me llame a las cuatro.*

A: *Por supuesto.*

B: *Muchas gracias. Hasta luego.*

14 📖 Lee el texto.

Las prácticas de trabajo

Las prácticas de trabajo ofrecen amplias oportunidades.

Hoy en día no es suficiente con el título para conseguir el trabajo de tus sueños. Hace falta tener experiencia y habilidades más allá de lo académico.

Habrás estudiado mucho y habrás aguantado mucho estrés y cantidad de preocupación para lograr tu plaza en la universidad. **Querrás descansar un poco**, disfrutar de la vida con tus nuevos amigos además de estudiar para la carrera. ¿Pero qué pasa después de terminarla?

Ser licenciado no es todo. Cada vez más los empresarios quieren más. Quieren a individuos con experiencia, y que sepan tratar con la gente. Quieren a personas que estén dispuestas a seguir mejorando su nivel profesional. **Tendrás que convencerles** que tú eres la persona a quien buscan y que tienes las cualidades adecuadas. Así que **nunca es demasiado temprano** para conseguir experiencia en el mundo del trabajo. ¡Nunca es temprano para empezar tu currículum! Hoy no es extraño empezar un pequeño trabajo durante los fines de semana o las vacaciones a la edad de catorce años.

¿Qué piensa la gente?

Preguntamos a unos jóvenes acerca de su experiencia de trabajo. Lee lo que dijeron:

Silvia, 14 años

'Trabajé en el departamento de pediatría de un hospital cerca de donde vivo. Fue una experiencia verdaderamente positiva para mí. Aprendí mucho. Cada día fue diferente. Ayudaba a preparar las comidas y jugaba con los niños. Los empleados eran majos y nos llevábamos muy bien. **Creo que me gustaría ser** enfermera cuando deje el colegio y esta experiencia me ha ayudado a entender de lo que trata este trabajo.'

Enrique, 15 años.

'**Siempre he querido ser** mecánico así que tuve mucha suerte conseguir hacer mis prácticas en un garaje del barrio. **Sin embargo** la verdad es que me desilusioné un poco porque no me dejaron trabajar en los vehículos. **La mayoría del tiempo** tenía que preparar el café o lavar los coches. A veces acompañaba a un mecánico si había una avería, lo cual me gustaba mucho. El horario estaba bien. Empezaba a las nueve y terminaba a las cuatro. Creo que haré otra cosa cuando deje el colegio. Ser mecánico es bastante duro.'

Pablo, 16 años

'Pasé tres semanas trabajando en una peluquería. Fue una experiencia valiosa y **es lo que de verdad quiero hacer** cuando termine el colegio. **Antes de hacer mis prácticas** pensaba que era un trabajo fácil, pero no lo es. Hay que estar de pie todo el día, lo que cansa mucho. Algunos de los clientes son desagradables y hay que estar sonriente todo el rato — cosa que no encuentro fácil. De todos modos ahora sé mucho más y tengo una buena idea de lo que tengo que hacer **para tener éxito** en esta profesión.'

¿Has hecho ya las prácticas de trabajo? Dónde las hiciste? ¿Qué hiciste? ¿Cómo fue? Escríbenos para contar tus experiencias y opiniones.

a 📖 ✏️ Match the phrases in bold with their equivalent in English listed below. Use a dictionary to help you.

Ejemplo: hoy en día — nowadays

nevertheless
it's never too early
I think I'd like to be
being a graduate isn't the be all and end all
I've always wanted to be
most of the time
before doing my work experience
to be successful
you'll have to convince them
you'll want to rest a little
it's what I really want to do

b 📖 Según lo que dice el artículo, indica si las frases siguientes son verdaderas (V) o falsas (F).

1 Todos los chicos quieren trabajar en lo que hicieron en sus prácticas.
2 Todos piensan que la experiencia fue útil.
3 A veces es difícil tratar con el público.
4 Sus experiencias les han ayudado a tomar decisiones con respecto a su futuro.
5 Les dejaban hacer todo tipo de tareas.
6 Han aprendido mucho.

c ✏️ Escribe una contestación a la revista dando tus ideas y opiniones sobre tus propias prácticas de trabajo. Menciona:

dónde trabajaste
durante cuánto tiempo
qué hiciste exactamente cada día
si era una experiencia positiva o negativa y por qué
tu opinión sobre las prácticas de trabajo en…

3 El futuro

- ☑ **Talk about future plans**
- ☑ **Use the future and conditional tenses**
- ☑ **Use adverbs**

1 🎧 📖 Escucha y lee lo que piensa hacer esta gente y pon las letras en el orden en que se mencionan.

Ejemplo: **1 — b**

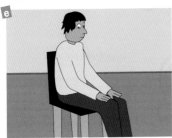

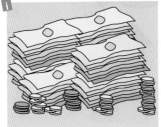

1 *Voy a buscar trabajo.*
2 Me voy a casar.
3 Voy a trabajar como voluntaria.
4 Voy a ir a otro colegio.
5 Voy a trabajar en un banco.
6 No voy a hacer nada.
7 Voy a hacer un aprendizaje.
8 Voy a dejar el colegio.
9 Voy a viajar.
10 Voy a ganar mucho dinero.
11 Voy a seguir estudiando.

GRAMÁTICA

The immediate future

To form the immediate future tense use *ir + a*.

The verb *ir* (to go) is formed as follows:

voy
vas
va
vamos
vais
van

2 👥 ¿Qué quieren hacer? Empareja las personas con las frases correctas. Piensa en qué persona del verbo es apropiada en cada caso.

1 Ana	¿qué vas a hacer el año que viene?
2 Pablo y Marta	voy a trabajar en el banco.
3 Iñigo,	va a seguir estudiando.
4 Conchi y yo	van a ir a Inglaterrra.
5 Yo	¿vais a hacer algo?
6 Juan y Susana,	vamos a buscar un empleo.

3 💬 Pregunta a tus compañeros de clase lo que van a hacer el año que viene.

Ejemplo: ¿Qué vas a hacer el año que viene?
El año que viene voy a…

4 Escucha a estos jóvenes hablando de su futuro. Rellena los huecos en las frases siguientes con los verbos correctos.

Ejemplo: **1** — *Buscaré un trabajo.*

1 _____ un trabajo.
2 _____ más. Quiero estudiar ciencias y diseño.
3 _____ un año y luego _____ a estudiar.
4 _____ un poco antes de empezar a trabajar.
5 _____ como voluntaria en el extranjero.
6 _____ un aprendizaje. Quiero ser mecánico.

trabajaré   haré   buscaré
viajaré   descansaré
estudiaré   volveré

¡ojo!

Todas estas palabras son verbos.
¿Qué tienen en común?

5 Ahora escucha otra vez. Empareja cada persona con la frase adecuada abajo.

Quiere un puesto pagado.   *Ejemplo:* **1**
Quiere aprender mientras trabaje.
Quiere conocer el mundo.
Seguirá con sus estudios.
Quiere unas vacaciones antes de estudiar.
No le importa el dinero.

6a 🎧 📖 Escucha y lee lo que dicen estos jóvenes sobre sus planes futuros. Haz una lista de todos los verbos en el futuro que encuentras.

> Tengo planes y sueños. Hay una diferencia entre los dos, pero el futuro no siempre es seguro. Primero, lo que sí es seguro, es que me iré del colegio. Me gusta estar aquí, pero creo que la gama de asignaturas es aburrida. Seguiré estudiando y quiero ser ingeniero. Después de mis estudios cogeré un año de descanso y me iré de viaje. Haré algún trabajo voluntario — construyendo carreteras y pozos en África o algo así. Más tarde buscaré un trabajo mejor pagado. En mis sueños, el futuro ideal para mí es así: compraré una casa grande y me casaré. Pero el tiempo decidirá. Ya veremos.

Toni, 17 años

> El año que viene me quedaré en el cole para terminar mis estudios. Luego me iré a la universidad y estudiaré idiomas. Si es posible, trabajaré en el extranjero, en Estados Unidos o en China. No estoy segura. Dentro de diez años, en el mundo de mis sueños, tendré mi propia empresa. Seré rica y famosa. ¿Casarme? Sé que no me casaré — por lo menos dentro de los próximos diez años.

Ana, 16 años

b Decide cuáles de estas frases son verdaderas (V) y cuáles son falsas (V).

Ejemplo: Toni va a seguir estudiando en el cole. F

1 Toni quiere estudiar asignaturas más interesantes que las del cole.
2 Toni quiere visitar otras partes del mundo.
3 A Toni no le importa ayudar a los demás.
4 Ana se va inmediatamente del cole.
5 Ana quiere viajar.
6 Para Ana un matrimonio es más importante que su carrera.

Verbs with irregular stems in the future

Note that some verbs have *irregular* stems. For example:

hacer: haré, harás, hará, haremos, haréis, harán

Can you find the future stem for the following verbs?

decir	*querer*	*tener*
poder	*saber*	*valer*
poner	*salir*	*venir*

7a 📖 ✏️ Lee lo que dice Alberto de sus planes para el futuro. Apunta todos los verbos en el futuro.

Alberto

¿Qué pienso hacer en el futuro? Pues, seguiré estudiando hasta terminar la universidad y buscaré un trabajo. Por supuesto, cuando tenga éxito mi grupo, viajaré con ellos por todo el mundo. Me haré famoso y ¡tendré mucho dinero! Entonces ayudaré a la gente pobre en, por ejemplo, África. Veré todos los sitios que me han interesado durante muchos años, como África o Cuba. Más adelante me imagino que conoceré a mi media naranja. No me casaré porque no creo en ello, pero a lo mejor tendré algunos hijos. Si Dios quiere, disfrutaré de buena salud y ¡seré feliz! ¡Y esto es todo!

b 👥 Ahora usa lo que dice Alberto para escribir sobre lo que harás en el futuro.

8a 📖 La mayoría de la gente no consigue cumplir sus sueños. Lee con lo que soñaban estas personas y lo que les pasó.

¡ojo!

All the verbs in bold are in the conditional tense. What do they mean?

1

Inés, 6 años
Me gustaría ser conductor de trenes. **Viviría** en una casa pequeña cerca de la estación y **sería** muy feliz.

Inés, 40 años
Soy dentista. Vivo en un pequeño piso en el centro de la ciudad con mi marido y mis dos hijos.

2

Marisol, 16 años
Me gustaría ser azafata. **Viajaría** por todo el mundo y **hablaría** muchos idiomas diferentes.

Marisol, 22 años
Trabajo en una agencia de viajes. Sueño con vacaciones exóticos pero no gano suficiente dinero de momento.

3

Adalia, 12 años
En mi mundo ideal **tendría** dos hijos — un chico y una chica. No **trabajaría**. **Viviría** en una casa del campo.

Adalia, 35 años
Tengo dos hijos. Trabajo en una oficina en la ciudad. Estoy muy contenta pero no es lo que pensaba.

4

Ico, 15 años
Me encanta cantar y bailar. **Me encantaría** ser famoso. **Actuaría** en el teatro y bailaría en todos los mejores espectáculos.

Ico, 50 años
Soy profesor de música en un colegio secundario. Me encanta mi trabajo, pero ¡no es exactamente lo que tenía planeado! ¡Quizás un día uno de mis estudiantes será famoso!

5

Moisés, 7 años
Me encantaría ser piloto o quizás piloto de un coche de carreras. **Sería** famoso y muy rico.

Moisés, 26 años
Soy mecánico. Trabajo para mi padre en un garaje y ¡es genial! No es el futuro con que soñaba, pero la verdad es que es el mejor trabajo del mundo para mí y ¡eso me gusta!

b Empareja el español con el inglés.

Ejemplo: 1 — b

1 Me gustaría ser…	a I would be
2 Viviría	b I would like to be…
3 Estaría	c I would be
4 Viajaría	d I would live
5 Hablaría	e I would act
6 Tendría	f I would love to
7 No trabajaría	g I would have
8 Actuaría	h I would speak
9 Me encantaría	i I would not work
10 Sería	j I would travel

9a 🎧 Escucha los sueños de estos jóvenes.
Pon las actividades en el orden en que se mencionan.

Ejemplo: **1 — f**

Edexcel International GCSE Spanish ● Edexcel Certificate in Spanish

GRAMÁTICA

The conditional tense

This tense is used when talking about events that *would* happen. For example:

Buscaría un trabajo.	**I would look** for a job.
Compraríamos una casa en las montañas.	**We would buy** a house in the mountains.

The conditional tense of regular verbs is formed by adding the following endings to the infinitive (the part found in the dictionary):

-ía	*-íamos*
-ías	*-íais*
-ía	*-ían*

For example: *estudiar* **(to study)**

estudiaría	I **would** study
estudiarías	you **would** study
estudiaría	he/she **would** study
estudiaríamos	we **would** study
estudiaríais	you **would** study
estudiarían	they **would** study

b 💬 Mira la lista de actividades de ensueño. Trabaja en pareja. Decide lo que te gustaría o lo que no te gustaría hacer.

Ejemplo: comprar un coche de lujo
Compraría un coche de lujo./
No compraría un coche de lujo.

comprar un coche de lujo
visitar América del Sur
tocar un instrumento
bailar en un escenario
cantar en público
escribir una obra maestra
hablar un idioma nuevo
aprender a cocinar
montar a caballo
conocer a alguien famoso

c 🧑 Escribe tu lista. Empieza con lo más importante para ti.

10 🎧 📖 Escucha y lee lo que dice Manolo sobre un mundo perfecto.

Mi vida ideal

Durante mi vida ideal tendría muchas experiencias emocionantes para contar a mis nietos. Querría seguir estudiando, así por fin sabría mucho más que ahora acerca de mis asignaturas favoritas – la historia y la literatura. Como tendría un trabajo interesante, bien remunerado y que valdría la pena, podría permitirme el lujo de viajar mucho y conocer otras culturas. Saldría con mis amigos todos los fines de semana o les invitaría a mi casa, que sería grande y bonita – muy lejos de los vecinos. ¡Pondría mi música favorita a todo volumen sin que nadie se quejara! Habría un cine y una piscina en el jardín. Vendría mi familia a visitarme también. Me gustaría tener suficiente dinero para ayudarles. ¡Mucho más tarde diría la gente que yo había sido una persona inteligente, generosa, simpática y divertida! No pido mucho, ¿verdad!?

Manolo Montoso-Sánchez, 16 años

✏️ Escribe una lista de todos los verbos condicionales en el texto y lo que significan en inglés. Lee otra vez la gramática que explica cómo formar el condicional e identifica cuáles de los verbos en tu lista son regulares y cuáles no. Practica deletrearlos.

¡OJO!

Remember there are many cognates. These are words which sound, mean or are spelt similarly to English words. For example:

fotógrafo — photographer
veterinario — vet
ingeniero — engineer
parque — park
garaje — garage
león — lion
cebra — zebra

How many other examples do you know?

11 ✏️ ¿Cómo sería tu vida ideal? Escribe tu propio párrafo.

12 ✏️ ¿Cuántos trabajos, profesiones y lugares de trabajo conoces en español? Haz una lista así:

Profesión/ trabajo	Inglés	Lugar de trabajo	Inglés
profesor	teacher	colegio	school

13 📖 Lee este artículo sobre las cualidades necesarias para realizar las ambiciones.

¿Qué es lo que hace falta para lograr tus sueños? Preguntamos a unos alumnos que se están preparando para sus exámenes qué es lo que les parece esencial para realizar sus ambiciones. Aquí están los resultados:

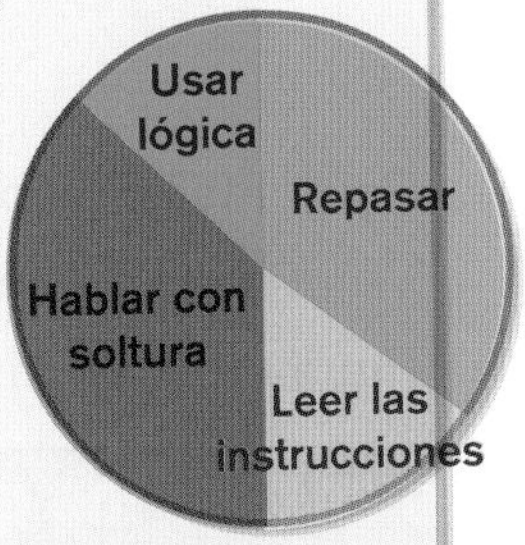

- Un 35% dice que lo importante es estudiar y repasar **cuidadosamente** para aprobar los exámenes.
- Un 15% habla de cómo hay que leer **exactamente** las instrucciones para contestar **bien** las preguntas en los exámenes.
- La mayoría de los alumnos creen que al escribir es imprescindible expresarse **claramente**.
- Con respecto a los exámenes orales, un 37% dice que lo más importante es hablar con **soltura**.
- Un 13% da importancia a tratar los problemas de matemáticas **lógicamente**.

(Diagram labels: Usar lógica, Repasar, Hablar con soltura, Leer las instrucciones)

📐 How do students best achieve their goals as far as exams are concerned? What skills are necessary? Answer the following questions in English.

1 How should they revise?
2 How should they read instructions?
3 How should they write?
4 How should they speak?
5 How should they solve mathematical problems?

14 📖📐 ¿Qué adverbios conoces en español? Haz una lista.

Ejemplo: cuidadosamente, con cuidado;
hábilmente, con habilidad

15a 📖📐 Cambia estos adjetivos a adverbios añadiendo '–mente'. ¿Qué significan en inglés? ¡Se permite usar un diccionario!

Ejemplo: afortunado, afortunadamente — fortunately

- afortunado
- agradable
- alegre
- claro
- correcto
- cortés
- falso
- feliz
- furioso
- igual
- lento
- normal
- nuevo
- perfecto
- primero
- reciente
- útil
- verdadero

GRAMÁTICA

Adverbs

The words highlighted in the article are all adverbs. Adverbs tell you how something is done. They often end in –ly in English. For example: carefully, exactly, well, clearly, fluently, logically.

To form most adverbs in Spanish, first choose the adjective, make it feminine and then add **–mente**.

Adjective	Feminine form	Adverb	English
ciudadoso	*cuidadosa*	*ciudadosamente*	carefully
tranquilo	*tranquila*	*tranquilamente*	quietly
fácil	*fácil*	*fácilmente*	easily

Remember that some adjectives do not change in the feminine form.

When two adverbs appear together, the first one you use does **not** have **–mente**. For example:

Para aprobar mis exámenes estudié cuidadosa y tranquilamente.
To pass my exams I worked **carefully** and **calmly**.

The following adverbs do not end in **–mente**:

bien	***Mi profesora de inglés es muy buena, enseña muy bien.*** My English teacher is very good, she teaches very well.
mal	***El trabajo está muy mal escrito.*** The work is very badly written.
despacio	***No entiendo. ¡Habla más despacio, por favor!*** I don't understand. Speak more slowly, please!

The adverb 'quickly/fast' has two forms: ***rápido*** and ***rápidamente***.

b 💬 Trabaja con una pareja. Usando adverbios, busca maneras de hacer estas acciones.

Ejemplo: ¿Cómo se puede hablar bien español?
Se puede hablar claramente.

hablar bien español
trabajar
aprobar exámenes
jugar al fútbol

Paper 1: listening

Las prácticas

Raúl habla de sus prácticas de trabajo.

¿Qué dice?

Pon una equis ☒ en las 4 casillas apropiadas.

Raúl is talking about his work experience.

What does he say?

Put a cross ☒ in the 4 correct boxes.

☒	**Ejemplo:** Tiene todo preparado.
☒	**A** Va a trabajar en una granja.
☒	**B** Va a trabajar con gente.
☒	**C** Tiene que vender.
☒	**D** Tiene que limpiar.
☒	**E** Sabe el trabajo que quiere.
☒	**F** Tiene ganas de hacerlo.
☒	**G** Quiere ser piloto
☒	**H** No aprenderá nada.

Hints to answer the question

- During reading time think about the possible answers to questions and jot down key words in Spanish you might be listening for – or a little sketch – to help you focus while listening to the recordings.

- Like this sample task, some exam questions ask you to select correct statements from a number of possible answers. Understanding the structure of these questions can save you time when looking to make the correct choices.

- Statements are often contrasting ideas. For example, two different jobs may be listed. If one is correct, the other will *not* be correct. Look at statements A and G.

- Some statements may focus on verbs. Look at statements C and D. Is there a link to these activities and the jobs mentioned as possible answers?

- When reading the options think logically through all the possible answers. Ask yourself: if X is correct then can Y also be correct?

- Have a go at this task. Once you have made your selections and checked the answers, ask your teacher for the transcript so you can link the text to each of the correct statements.

(Total for Question = 4 marks)

Paper 2: reading

Paper 2 always includes a reading question that requires you to answer the questions in Spanish. Look at the question below. Consider the sample student answers and discuss them with a partner as you work through the text.

Lee este artículo.

Read this article.

Make sure you do this before you look at the questions. Remember that you are not expected to understand every word. Try picking out key points. What strategies can you use to work out the meanings of less familiar words and phrases? Some items have been highlighted in the text. Can you explain what they mean?

En el cole colombiano

The heading is important because it gives you your first clue about the content. This text is about schools in Colombia.

A pesar de ser el cuarto país más grande de Sudamérica, con sus grandes reservas de petróleo, oro, plata, esmeraldas y carbón, en Colombia la calidad de la educación varía mucho. Se podría decir que muchos países sudamericanos son así, pero en Colombia esa variedad es mucho más destacada debido a los efectos de décadas de conflicto y violencia internos. Y como siempre, las víctimas son los más pobres.

Si tienes la buena fortuna de tener dinero suficiente para asistir a un colegio privado, no tienes problema porque suelen ser buenísimos y los alumnos salen con las mejores calificaciones. En zonas rurales, sin embargo, hay menos consistencia y en realidad es cuestión de suerte. Desafortunadamente, Colombia tiene partes muy pobres, principalmente en regiones rurales, donde todavía hay niños que no asisten al cole porque no pueden viajar hasta allí. Por supuesto, los que viven en las calles, no asisten nunca. Los pobres que sí van al colegio de su barrio, suelen recibir una educación inferior y menos sólida, con menos recursos y peores perspectivas.

El gobierno está introduciendo algunas medidas para intentar mejorar la situación, siguiendo los consejos que han recibido de expertos estadounidenses. Quieren que no haya nadie que no reciba una educación adecuada.

Contesta las preguntas **en español** basándote en el texto.

Answer the questions **in Spanish** based on the text.

No necesitas escribir frases completas.

You do not need to write in full sentences.

Exam tip

The skimming and scanning techniques you have just used are an effective way to help you to find key information you need to answer the questions.

Exam tip

Read through *all* the questions before you begin. Remember that they follow a logical sequence so the answer to the first question is at the start of the text.

Sample student answer

(a) ¿Qué grandes reservas de energía tiene Colombia?
Petróleo, oro (2)

This student's answer is only partially correct. Which of the two items is not correct? What should the other right answer be? Discuss this with a partner.

(b) ¿Por qué varía más la educación en Colombia que en otros países sudamericanos?
Porque han sufrido décadas de conflicto (1)

Although *violencia* could have been included in this response, this answer is correct.
Tip: remember you do not need to write complete sentences. Keep your answers short.

(c) ¿Quiénes van a colegios privados?
Los que tienen suficiente dinero (1)

This is a good answer. Can you provide an alternative? Think of a synonym for a person who has plenty of money.

(d) ¿Cómo son los colegios privados en Colombia?
Los alumnos salen con las mejores calificaciones (1)

This answer is not quite correct and would not gain any marks. What is missing? Discuss it with a partner.

(e) ¿Qué suelen conseguir los que van a colegios privados?
.... (1)

Answer this question by yourself. Share your response with a partner. Is yours the right answer? Tip: part of the text for your answer could come from the question you were asked.

(f) ¿Cómo son los colegios normalmente en las zonas rurales?

Menos consistencia .... (1)

This student has identified where the correct answer is in the text. However, the answer is not correct. Can you say why? What would be a correct answer? Tip: use the verb from the question to start your answer. You need to compare the two types of schools.

(g) ¿Qué niños no van nunca al cole?

.... (1)

Answer this question by yourself. Tip: you could begin your answer with Los que....

(h) ¿Qué país está ayudando al gobierno?

.... (1)

Think carefully about countries and nationalities to answer this question.

(i) ¿Quiénes van a beneficiarse?

.... (1)

Discuss the answer to this question with a partner. The key is in No haya nadie que no reciba....

(Total for Question = 10 marks)

Paper 2: writing

Exam tip

- Use the sample speaking question on page 89 to help you — look especially at the good features identified.
- Remember to cover each of the four points more or less equally. This gives you the best chance of gaining top marks. If you neglect one or more of the four points, you will lose marks.

Here is an example of the longer writing task for you to try. Remember that in the exam you are given a choice of three tasks. This question is worth 20 marks, 10 of which are for communication and content, so it is essential that you address *all* the bullet points listed.

Escribe unas 150 palabras **en español**.   Write about 150 words **in Spanish**.

Escribe una carta a tu amigo/a español/a explicando cuáles son tus planes para el futuro. Menciona:
- lo que vas a hacer después de tus exámenes
- lo que vas a hacer cuando termines el colegio
- cuáles son tus ambiciones
- qué cualidades tienes para tener éxito

(20)

Hints to answer the question

Follow this recipe for success:
- Start with a general greeting to your friend. You can begin an informal letter with *Querido/a...* or simply *¡Hola...!*
- Set the context. For example, *acabo de terminar mis exámenes.*
- To cover bullet point 1 you could refer to your plans for the summer. Make sure you use the immediate future tense *voy a....*
- Link bullet points 2 and 3 together. Your plans for when you leave school will clearly be linked to your ambitions.
- Use bullet point 4 as your conclusion. Remember to ask questions as well. For example, ask your friend what he/she plans to do.
- End the letter with the appropriate informal ending, such as *Un abrazo* or *Besos.*

Exam tip

- If you are asked to write a letter, make sure it is set out appropriately, as in this example of a short formal letter. Beware of making the kinds of error explained in some of the marginal comments.

Paper 3: speaking (section B)

Here are some sample questions that could be asked about two Edexcel topic areas. Do you understand the questions?

Topic area A: Home and abroad

- *¿Dónde vives?*
- *¿Cómo es tu casa?*
- *¿Cómo es tu ciudad/pueblo?*
- *Describe tu casa.*
- *¿Has estado en el extranjero?*
- *¿Cómo era?*
- *¿Adónde vas normalmente de vacaciones?*
- *¿Adónde fuiste el año pasado?*

Topic area B: Education and employment

- *¿Cómo es tu colegio?*
- *¿Qué asignaturas estudias?*
- *¿Cómo es un día típico?*
- *¿Has hecho tus prácticas de trabajo?*
- *¿Cómo fueron?*
- *¿Tienes un trabajillo?*
- *¿Qué vas a hacer después de los exámenes?*
- *¿Qué quieres hacer en el futuro?*

Listen to the following sample student answers and note why they score higher marks.

Sample student answer

¿Tienes un trabajillo?

Como estoy ahorrando para ir a la universidad, tengo un trabajo guay cerca de mi casa. Llevo casi toda la vida nadando y lo hago muy bien, así que hice el examen para hacerme socorrista. Me encanta porque trabajo en el polideportivo de mi barrio los fines de semana, y en verano, como vivo en la costa, lo hago en la playa. Me pagan bastante bien y es un horario flexible, lo que me deja tiempo para estudiar tranquilamente. También. Me llevo bien con la gente y ya he ahorrado ¡200 euros!

- Good use of the present continuous form.
- Good description.
- Good use of the gerund.
- A good connective to use.
- Opinion given with reasons.
- Good use of complex structure.
- Good use of complex structure.
- Good use of perfect tense (past).

¿Qué vas a hacer después de los exámenes?

Tengo muchos planes para después de mis exámenes. En primer lugar, durante el verano voy a trabajar en la tienda de mi novio y me voy a ir de vacaciones con mi familia a Portugal. En septiembre voy a volver al cole para estudiar más. Quiero ser ingeniera, así que tengo que hacer A-levels en ciencias y matemáticas – va a ser muy duro, pero estoy dispuesta a estudiar mucho.

- Good use of connective phrase.
- *Ir + a +* infinitive with future meaning.
- Good use of connective.
- Use of complex verb structure.

Vocabulario

School subjects

las **actividades extraescolares** extra-curricular activities
el **alemán** German
la **biología** biology
las **ciencias** science
las **ciencias naturales** natural sciences
la **danza** dance
los **deportes** sports
el **dibujo** art
el **diseño** design
la **educación cívica** PHSE
la **educación física** PE
el **español** Spanish
la **física** physics
el **francés** French
la **geografía** geography
la **historia** history
la **informática** ICT
el **inglés** English
el **italiano** Italian
el **latín** Latin
la **literatura** literature
las **matemáticas** maths
la **química** chemistry
la **religión** RE
el **teatro** drama
la **tecnología** technology

School timetables

las **asignaturas** subjects
el **castigo** detention
la **clase** class; lesson
los **deberes** homework
los **días** days
la **hora** time; hour
la **hora de comer** lunch time
el **horario** timetable
el **recreo** break
el **trimestre** term
las **vacaciones** holidays
el **lunes** Monday
el **martes** Tuesday
el **miércoles** Wednesday
el **jueves** Thursday
el **viernes** Friday
el **sábado** Saturday
el **domingo** Sunday

School uniform

el **abrigo** coat
la **blusa** blouse
las **botas** boots
la **bufanda** scarf
los **calcetines** socks
la **camisa** shirt
la **camiseta** T-shirt

el **chándal** tracksuit
la **chaqueta** jacket
el **cinturón** belt
la **corbata** tie
la **falda** skirt
la **gorra** cap
los **guantes** gloves
las **medias** tights
los **pantalones** trousers
los **pantalones cortos** shorts
la **sudadera** sweatshirt
el **suéter** jumper
el **traje de entrenamiento** tracksuit
los **vaqueros** jeans
el **vestido** dress
las **zapatillas de deporte** trainers
los **zapatos** shoes
amarillo/a yellow
azul blue
blanco/a white
gris grey
marrón brown
morado/a purple
naranja orange
negro/a black
rojo/a red
rosa pink
verde green

School equipment

la **agenda** diary
el **bolígrafo** biro, ballpoint pen
la **calculadora** calculator
la **carpeta** folder
el **compás** compass
la **computadora** (*LA*) computer
el **cuaderno** exercise book
el **diccionario** dictionary
el **estuche** pencil case
la **goma** rubber
la **grapadora** stapler
el **lapicero** pencil
el **lápiz** pencil
el **lápiz de color** coloured pencil
el **libro** book
el **maletín** (*Sp*) briefcase
la **mesa** table
la **mochila** backpack
el **ordenador** (*Sp*) computer
el **papel** paper
el **pegamento** glue
la **pluma** fountain pen
el **portafolio** (*LA*) briefcase
la **regla** ruler
el **rotulador** felt-tip pen; marker pen

la **silla** chair
las **tijeras** scissors

Schools and buildings

el/la **alumno/a** pupil
el **aula (f)** classroom
la **biblioteca** library
el **campo de deportes** sports field
el **comedor** dining room; canteen
el/la **director/a** headteacher
el **edificio** building
la **entrada** entrance
la **escalera** staircase, stairs
el **estudiante** student
el **gimnasio** gymnasium
el **guardarropa** cloakroom
el **laboratorio** laboratory
los **lavabos** toilets
la **oficina** office
el **pasillo** corridor
el **patio** playground
el **portero** caretaker
el/la **profesor/a**, el/la **profe** teacher
la **sala de profesores** staff room
la **secretaria** secretary
el **taller** workshop
el **teatro** theatre
el **vestíbulo** hall

School types and qualifications

aprender to learn
aprobar un examen to pass an exam
el **colegio**, el **cole** (*coll.*) school
el **colegio de primaria** primary school
el **colegio de secundaria** secondary school
el **curso** course; school year
la **escuela** primary school
estudiar to study
el **instituto** high school
la **licenciatura** degree
el **rendimiento escolar** school performance
repasar to revise
suspender un examen to fail an exam
la **universidad** university

Workplaces and activities

archivar to file
barrer el suelo to sweep the floor
coger recados to take messages
contestar el teléfono to answer the phone
escribir to write
escribir correos electrónicos to send e-mails
hablar con clientes to talk to clients
hacer el café to make the coffee

hacer las prácticas de trabajo to do work experience

ir a reuniones to go to meetings

lavar el pelo to wash hair

repartir el correo to deliver the post

trabajar en un/una... to work in/on a...

usar el ordenador to work on the computer

la **agencia de viajes** travel agency

el **banco** bank

la **empresa** company

la **fábrica** factory

el **garaje** garage

el **hotel** hotel

la **oficina** office

la **peluquería** hairdresser's

el **restaurante** restaurant

la **tienda** shop

Jobs and professions

el/la **abogado/a** lawyer

el/la **agricultor/a** farmer

el **albañil** (*no feminine form*) builder

el/la **arquitecto/a** architect

el/la **asesor/a** consultant

el/la **auxiliar de vuelo** flight attendant

el/la **azafato/a** flight attendant

el/la **bombero/a** firefighter

el/la **cajero/a** cashier

el/la **camarero/a** waiter/waitress

el/la **cantante** singer

el/la **cartero/a** postman/woman

el/la **científico/a** scientist

el/la **cirujano/a** surgeon

el/la **cocinero/a** cook, chef

el/la **conductor/a** driver

el/la **dentista** dentist

el/la **dependiente/a** shop assistant

el/la **electricista** electrician

el/la **empleado/a** employee

el/la **enfermero/a** nurse

el/la **farmacéutico/a** pharmacist, chemist

el/la **fontanero/a** plumber

el/la **ingeniero/a** engineer

el/la **marinero/a** sailor

el/la **mecánico/a** mechanic

el/la **médico/a** doctor

el/la **modelo** model

el/la **obrero/a** labourer

el/la **oficinista** office worker

el/la **peluquero/a** hairdresser

el/la **periodista** journalist

el/la **piloto** pilot

el/la **policía** policeman/woman

el/la **político/a** politician

el/la **recepcionista** receptionist

el/la **reportero/a** reporter

el/la **técnico/a** technician

el/la **torero/a** bullfighter

el/la **veterinario/a** vet

Future plans

Espero I hope to

Intento I try to

Me apetecería I'd like to

Me gustaría I'd like to

Quiero I want to

Quisiera I'd like to

Voy a I'm going to

buscar un trabajo to look for a job

cogerse un año sabático to take a year out

estudiar to study

hacer un aprendizaje to do an apprenticeship

ir a la universidad to go to university

ir de viaje to go travelling

seguir estudiando to carry on studying

ser famoso/a to be famous

trabajar como voluntario/a to work as a volunteer

Question words

¿Qué? What?

¿Quién/Quiénes? Who?

¿Cuál/Cuáles? Which?

¿Cómo? How?

¿Cuándo? When?

¿Cuánto/a/os/as? How much/many?

¿Por qué? Why?

1 **El transporte**

2 **De vacaciones**

3 **El tiempo y el medio ambiente**

☑ Talk about travelling around

☑ Compare types of transport

☑ Use interrogatives

☑ Use prepositions

1 El transporte

¿Cómo viajar?

1a 📖 Empareja las palabras con la imagen adecuada.

Ejemplo: a — el coche

a

b *Renfe*

c *Metro*

d ✈

e

f ZONA PEATONAL

g

h

i

j Estación de autobuses

k

el autobús   la bicicleta   el avión   a pie

el autocar   el coche   el metro

el taxi   la moto   el tren   el barco

b 💬 Trabaja con tu pareja. Habla de los transportes que usas.

Ejemplo: ¿Cómo viajas al colegio?
Para ir al colegio siempre voy a pie.
¿Cómo viajas cuando tienes prisa?
Cuando tengo prisa prefiero ir en taxi.

- para ir al colegio
- para ir de vacaciones
- para ir de compras
- cuando tienes dinero
- para estar seguro
- cuando tienes prisa
- para visitar la región
- para salir con amigos
- para salir con la familia
- cuando hace mal tiempo

c 🎧 Escucha lo que dicen estos jóvenes de los modos de transporte que usan. ¿Qué modos de transporte menciona cada persona?

1 Raquel

2 Sabrina

3 Miguel Ángel

4 Rafa

5 Mario

6 Enrique

2a 🎧 📖 Escucha y lee lo que dicen estos jóvenes acerca de cada método de transporte. ¿Qué piensan?

Ejemplo: *metro = más rapido —* underground is quicker

a Creo que es más rápido viajar al centro en metro.

b En mi opinión los autobuses son demasiado lentos.

c Es muy peligroso ir a pie

d Ir en autocar es muy interesante pero es caro.

e Ir en bicicleta es más sano y también es práctico.

f No me gusta viajar en avión, prefiero viajar en barco.

g Los trenes son incómodos y sucios.

h Ir en taxi es fácil pero cuesta demasiado dinero.

i Viajar en coche daña el ambiente.

b 🏛 Usando la tabla para ayudarte, escribe tus opiniones de los diferentes métodos de transporte.

Creo que	ir	en coche	es	muy	barato
En mi opinión	viajar	a pie		demasiado	caro
Prefiero				bastante	rápido
(No) me gusta					lento
					cómodo
					incómodo
					práctico
					sano
					seguro
					peligroso

c 💬 ¿Estás de acuerdo? Compara tus opiniones con las de tu pareja.

Ejemplo: A: *En mi opinión ir en avión es peligroso. También es demasiado caro. Prefiero viajar en coche.*
B: *No estoy de acuerdo. Me gusta viajar en avión. Aunque es caro, es muy rápido y práctico.*

3 🎧 ¿Quién viaja? ¿Adónde van? ¿Cómo? ¿Por qué? Copia y completa la tabla con los detalles que faltan.

	¿Quién?	¿Adónde?	¿Cómo?	¿Por qué?
Ejemplo:	padre	Londres	avión	rápido
1				

4a 📖 ✏️ Lee lo que dicen los jóvenes. Copia y rellena la tabla.

Persona	✈️	🚶	🚗	🚲	🚊	🚌	🚂	🚇	Otro
Ejemplo: Raquel	✓							✓	
Sabrina									
Miguel Ángel									
Rafa									
Mario									
Enrique									

El modo de transporte que a diario uso para ir al colegio es el metro. Vivo en el centro de la ciudad y mi colegio, San Vincente de la Vega, está a unos 15 minutos en metro. A veces voy andando con mis amigos. ¡En primavera, por ejemplo!

Raquel

A mí me gusta estar en forma y me preocupo por el ambiente, así que voy todos los días a la facultad en mi bicicleta de montaña. Tardo unos 30 minutos. Sin embargo, los fines de semana me encanta ir de compras a uno de los grandes centros comerciales y para llegar allí necesito ir en coche. Me lleva mi hermana mayor, Patricia, que tiene coche.

Sabrina

Después del cole, ¡que por cierto está al lado de mi casa!, voy a visitar a mis amigos. Como es un pueblo bastante pequeño y no hay tanto tráfico, voy patinando sobre ruedas. También voy a veces en mi pequeña moto.

Miguel Angel

Vivo en las afueras de la ciudad y tengo que coger un tren de cercanías para ir al colegio o quedar con mis amigos. Después voy unos 15 minutos a pie. ¡Es un viaje bastante largo!

Rafa

94

Interrogatives

These are the words used to ask a question.
Look at the following table.

Singular	Plural	Meaning
¿Qué?	¿Qué?	What?
¿Cuál?	¿Cuáles?	Which (one(s))?
¿Quién?	¿Quiénes?	Who?
¿Cuánto/a?	¿Cuántos/as?	How much/many?

Remember, when asking the question 'Which?' in front of a noun, use ¿Qué? rather than ¿Cuál?:

¿Cuál prefieres, el tren o el coche?
Which do you prefer, train or car?

¿Qué método de transporte prefieres, el tren o el coche?
Which method of transport do you prefer, train or car?

Write out the following sentences in Spanish:
1 How much does it cost to travel to work by taxi?
2 Who travels by bus?
3 How do you get to your friend's house?
4 How many people go to school on foot?
5 What form of transport do you prefer?

Durante la semana voy al colegio en un autobús que pasa al lado de mi casa. Los fines de semana trabajo en una granja y para ir allí tengo que coger un autocar hasta el pueblo.

Mario

Como ahora soy famoso no puedo ir andando, ¡sin que me reconozcan! Por eso, me llevan a todos los sitios en coche... ¡en una limusina! Para ir a los conciertos o en los viajes de promoción, voy mucho en avión.

Enrique

b ✏️ Contesta las preguntas.

Ejemplo: **1** *¿Cómo va Raquel al colegio?*
Raquel va al colegio andando y en metro.

2 ¿Cómo va Sabrina a la facultad?
3 ¿Qué módo de transporte usa Sabrina para ir de compras?
4 ¿Cómo va Miguel Angel a casa de sus amigos?
5 ¿Qué módo de transporte usa Rafa?
6 ¿Cómo va Mario al trabajo?

c 💬 Trabaja con tu pareja. Contesta las preguntas.

1 ¿Cómo vas al colegio/al trabajo/a casa de tus amigos?
2 ¿Qué módo de transporte usas cuando estás con amigos/con tus padres?
3 ¿Cómo viajas de una ciudad a otra?
4 ¿Cómo viajas al extranjero?

d 🏰 Haz una encuesta. Pregunta a tus compañeros cómo van a los sitios. Usa esta información para escribir frases como en el ejemplo.

Ejemplo: *Katie siempre va al colegio en autobús. Para ir de compras va en el coche de su madre. Va andando a la pista de tenis.*

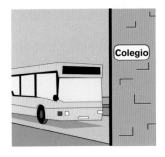  

e 📖 Empareja las frases con la imagen adecuada.

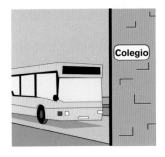  

  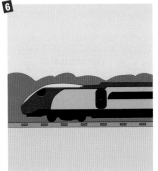

a Prefiero ir en bicicleta.
b Ir en tren es muy cómodo.
c Me encanta viajar en barco.
d El jueves voy a ir a Marbella en autocar.
e Siempre vamos andando.
f Salen de su casa a las ocho y cogen el autobús.

GRAMÁTICA

Prepositions

Most forms of transport take the preposition *en*, for example *en tren*. There is one exception: *a pie*. When using *andando*, there is no preposition: *voy andando*.

To talk about going and travelling, use the prepositions: *a* (to) or *de* (from). For example:

*Voy **a** Madrid.*
*Voy **de** mi casa.*
I am going to Madrid.
I am going from my house.

When *a* or *de* appear before the word *el*, they are shortened to *al* or *del*. This is because it is easier to pronounce. For example:

*Voy **al** colegio…(a + el)* I go to school…

*Vuelvo **del** trabajo…* (de + el) I come home from work…

Read the following sentences. Where there are errors, write out a corrected version. Translate each sentence into English.

1 Me gusta ir a el cine.
2 ¿Vas a menudo a la playa?
3 ¿Cuántas veces viajas a pie?
4 ¿Te gusta ir en coche?
5 Voy todos los días a el colegio andando.
6 Marta vuelve de el colegio a las cinco.
7 ¿A qué hora vuelves del trabajo?
8 ¿A qué hora vuelves a el trabajo?

¿Cómo vamos?

5a 🎧 📖 ✏️ Marta y Alex deciden qué transporte usar para el viaje fin de curso. Escucha y lee lo que dicen. Copia la tabla abajo y escribe los aspectos positivos y negativos de cada modo de transporte. ¿Qué deciden al final?

> ¡Así que las fechas ya están decididas! Podríamos ir en avión. Sería lo más rápido, ¡pero es más caro! Sugiero ir en barco y en autocar, ¡mucho más barato!

> Lo que pasa es que el viaje es más largo y, ¡por supuesto!, más aburrido.

> Entonces, quizás es más cómodo ir en tren y en barco. El tren es mucho más rápido y amplio.

> Claro. Ir en tren y barco es mucho mejor. Además, ir en barco me parece mucho más sano porque se puede salir a tomar el aire fresco.

Marta

> ¡Pues, ya está!

Alex

Modo de transporte	Ventajas	Desventajas
Ejemplo: avión	rápido	caro
barco		
autocar		
tren		

b 💬 Pregunta a tu pareja qué opina de cada modo de transporte.

Ejemplo:
A: ¿Qué opinas de viajar en barco?
B: En mi opinión ir en barco es muy cómodo y barato, pero se tarda más.

6 ✏️ Lee el mensaje electrónico de Luisa. Escribe tu respuesta.

> ¡Hola!
>
> Las vacaciones se acercan y, como sabes, voy a ir a Salamanca con mi familia. Vivimos bastante cerca y por eso vamos a ir en coche. Es más práctico y barato. En Salamanca hay muchos autobuses, pero prefiero ir andando porque es más sano…¡y barato! Dime, ¿adónde vas a ir de vacaciones? ¿Cómo vas a ir? ¿Y por qué?

7 💬 Haz diálogos con tu pareja.

- Quisiera un billete de ida/de ida y vuelta para…, por favor.
- ¿Cuánto cuesta (un billete sencillo)?
- Necesito un bonometro.
- ¿A qué hora sale el próximo/último tren/ autobús/metro para…?

Ejemplo:
A: *Buenos días. En que puedo servirle?*
B: *Quisiera un billete de ida para Pinto.*
A: *Aquí tiene. 3 euros.*
B: *Gracias. ¿A qué hora sale el último tren?*
A: *A las once y media.*

De viaje

8 📖 ¿Dónde están estas personas? Empareja las señales con cada declaración.

Ejemplo: *1 — b*

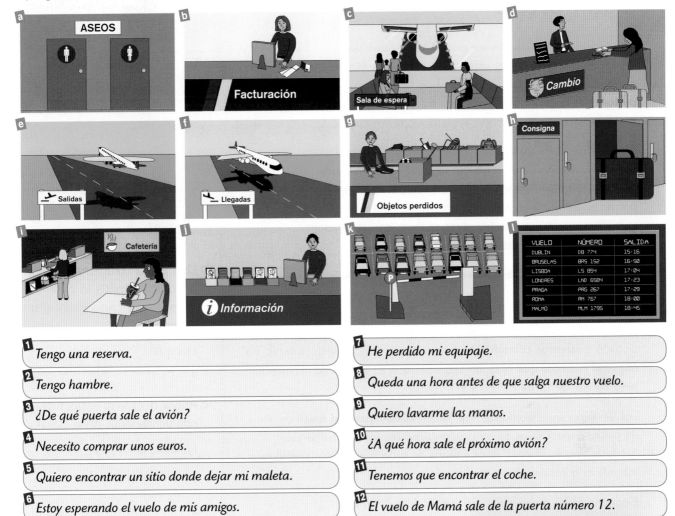

1 *Tengo una reserva.*

2 *Tengo hambre.*

3 *¿De qué puerta sale el avión?*

4 *Necesito comprar unos euros.*

5 *Quiero encontrar un sitio donde dejar mi maleta.*

6 *Estoy esperando el vuelo de mis amigos.*

7 *He perdido mi equipaje.*

8 *Queda una hora antes de que salga nuestro vuelo.*

9 *Quiero lavarme las manos.*

10 *¿A qué hora sale el próximo avión?*

11 *Tenemos que encontrar el coche.*

12 *El vuelo de Mamá sale de la puerta número 12.*

9 🎧 👤 En la agencia de viajes. Escucha a la gente hablando con el empleado. Completa la tabla de abajo.

- ¿Adónde quieren ir?
- ¿Cuándo quieren ir?
- ¿Cómo quieren viajar?
- ¿Qué más quieren saber?

	Ejemplo:	1	2	3
Destino	*Madrid*			
Transporte	*avión*			
Día/Fecha	*lunes 14 de julio*			
Hora de salir	*08:00*			
Hora de llegar	*12:30*			
Otros detalles	*sin equipaje*			

10a 🎧 📖 Escucha y lee el texto.

Un viaje en tren asombroso

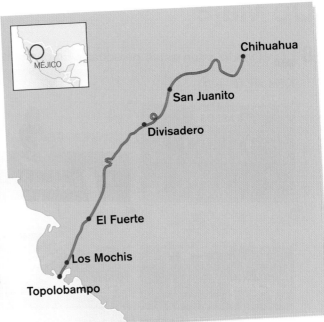

Cada año en Méjico muchísima gente hace el largo viaje de 673 kilómetros en tren entre Chihuahua y Los Mochis, **que se sitúa** en la costa pacífica. Una de las **rutas** más **pintorescas** del mundo, es un viaje a través de un paisaje impresionante.

Noventa años en construcción, el ferrocarril Chihuahua Pacífico, **conocido como** El Chepe, viaja a través de la sierra mejicana, **también llamada** El Cañón de Cobre. **Se completó** por fin en 1961 después de un esfuerzo increíble y **se considera una** de las grandes obras de ingeniería del siglo XX. Tiene en total 86 túneles y 36 puentes.

Hay **compartimentos de primera y segunda clase** y sale **a diario** en cada dirección. Cada año este ferrocarril transporta a más de medio millón de pasajeros. Para los turistas a quienes les encanta la comodidad, primera clase es **la única opción**. Los compartimentos tienen aire acondicionado y **asientos cómodos**. Hay un restaurante buenísimo. A veces, **no hay más remedio que** viajar en segunda clase. Es básico, no muy limpio, pero barato. **Se tarda** entre 14 y 17 horas.

Los pasajeros que hacen este viaje tienen **la oportunidad única** de ver un paisaje espectacular. Es un viaje precioso durante el cual se ven cataratas impresionantes, **flora y fauna** de todo tipo y color y árboles magníficos que salen de las paredes de la roca.

¡Será una de las experiencias más inolvidables de tu vida!

b Usando un diccionario para ayudarte, explica lo que significa en cado caso el texto en negrita.

Ejemplo:
que se sitúa — which is situated

c Ahora decide si estas frases son verdaderas (V) o falsas (F).

Ejemplo: 1 — (V)

1 *Este artículo habla de un viaje en tren.*
2 Las vistas no son nada buenas.
3 Es un viaje corto.
4 Se tardó mucho en construir.
5 La primera clase es mejor que la segunda.
6 Es una experiencia sin igual.
7 Se ven muchas cosas de interés.
8 Los trenes salen con frecuencia durante el día.
9 Vale la pena hacer el viaje.

2 De vacaciones

☑ **Talk about holiday plans**
☑ **Use of *ir a* + infinitive**
☑ **Talk about hotels and accommodation**
☑ **Using a dictionary**

1 🎧 Escucha lo que dicen estos jóvenes de sus próximas vacaciones. Une los dibujos y los números.

GRAMÁTICA

The immediate future

When talking about things that are about to happen, we use the immediate future tense (see also Module 3 p. 79). This is expressed in exactly the same way in both Spanish and English. We use the verb *ir* (to go) followed by *a* and the infinitive form of the main verb. For example:

Voy a ir de vacaciones.
I'm going to go on holiday.

¿Dónde vas a alojarte en vacaciones?
Where are you going to stay on your holiday?

María va a visitar las montañas.
Maria is going to visit the mountains.

Ivan y Ana van a montar a caballo.
Ivan and Ana are going to go riding.

2a 🎧 📖 Subraya todas las veces que se usa '***voy a***' o '***vamos a***'. Traduce las frases al inglés.

Ejemplo: <u>*Voy a*</u> *ir a Estados Unidos.*
    I'm going to go to the USA.

1 Este año voy a ir a Estados Unidos con mis amigos del colegio. Vamos a pasar 15 días en Nueva York y vamos a visitar todos los sitios de interés. ¡Va a ser genial!

2 En verano creo que voy a ir a Francia con mis padres. Voy a ir a la playa todos los días y al cine o a la discoteca por la tarde.

3 Voy a ir de vacaciones a Italia. Voy a pasar tres semanas con unos primos que tengo allí. ¡Me encanta! Voy a estudiar italiano y a aprender cómo preparar pasta.

4 En septiembre voy a ir a África de safari. Voy a pasar dos semanas buscando animales salvajes. Además voy a descansar y a leer.

5 En Semana Santa voy a ir con mi familia a Gran Canaria, una de las islas Canarias. Vamos a tomar el sol, visitar las islas, descansar e ir al parque acuático. ¡Guay!

b 🏔 Escribe un pequeño párrafo sobre lo que vas a hacer de vacaciones este año.

3 📖 ✏️ Lee el texto. Para cada destino, da razones en español para escogerlo para sus vacaciones.

Ejemplo: Voy a ir a Salamanca porque me interesa la cultura y quiero estudiar.

Destinos de vacaciones

1 Salamanca

Ésta es la ciudad de universidad por excelencia: la Universidad de Salamanca fue la primera en ser fundada en España y es también una de las más antiguas de Europa. Los edificios hermosos con su gran valor cultural han sido hogar para algunos de los mayores pensadores, artistas y escritores españoles.

2 Granada

Esta ciudad tiene un sabor árabe inequívoco. Sus platos típicos, sus artes y edificios son una consecuencia de la historia gloriosa de la ciudad. Este lugar tiene un encanto inolvidable. Forma parte del patrimonio universal, junto con la Alhambra y el Generalife, y ha sido un centro cultural importante a lo largo de siglos, tanto durante el período musulmán como el cristiano.

3 Madrid

La capital de España es una ciudad cosmopolita y vibrante. Como un centro de economía, finanzas, administración y servicios, esta ciudad combina la infraestructura más moderna con una herencia cultural y artística importante.

4 Mallorca

Famosa por sus playas hermosas y mar de aguas transparentes, esta isla tiene todo lo que hace falta para unas vacaciones relajantes, sobre todo para aquellos que disfrutan con los deportes acuáticos. El paisaje costero es resplandeciente con calas, playas y acantilados preciosos. Una isla hermosa y diversa con una vida cultural muy rica.

5 Barcelona

De origen romano, Barcelona tiene una larga e interesante historia. Para visitantes que disfrutan de museos, exposiciones y esculturas al aire libre esta ciudad tiene en programa durante todo el año música, teatro y baile.

6 Méjico

Se puede hacer una visita diferente a Chichén Itzá, un enclave arqueológico maya en la Península de Yucatán. Éste era el centro político y económico de la civilización maya entre 750 y 1200 A.C. Sus extraordinarios edificios ilustran el interés de los mayas por el espacio arquitectónico y la composición, así como sus conocimientos astronómicos amplios.

7 Cuba

La isla de Cuba es la más grande de las Antillas Mayores. Localizada muy cerca de la costa del sur de Florida entre el Océano Atlántico y el Mar Caribe, la isla tiene un clima subtropical que es ideal durante todo el año.

8 Argentina

Cosmopolita y vibrante, Buenos Aires es una ciudad moderna con un aire claramente europeo. La arquitectura es espectacular; tiene excelentes museos y parques en abundancia. Las calles se llenan de vida los domingos con el

mercado de antigüedades semanal. Hace falta descubrir esta ciudad, lugar de sepultura de Eva Perón. Al anochecer se puede cenar en uno de los muchos restaurantes excelentes, asistir a una obra de teatro en el famoso Teatro de Colón, o simplemente disfrutar aprendiendo un tango argentino tradicional.

4 ¿Adónde van y qué piensan hacer? Lee lo que piensan hacer estos chicos para sus vacaciones. Empareja las personas 1–8 con la letra de la imagen que corresponda.

Ejemplo: 1 — g

1 Voy a ir a Mallorca para pasar mis vacaciones descansando en la playa.

2 Las próximas vacaciones voy a ir al bosque porque me gusta mucho pasear con el perro y estar al aire libre.

3 Me gusta dormir al aire libre, así que tengo preparadas la mochila y la tienda. ¡Me voy!

4 Yo busco vacaciones con aventura y emoción y por eso voy a ir a los parques de atracciones de Florida.

5 Voy a ir de vacaciones a los ríos de Canadá porque me gustan los deportes acuáticos.

6 Como creo en la terapia que proporcionan las compras, me voy de vacaciones a la ciudad de París, donde hay cantidad de tiendas y centros comerciales.

7 En Semana Santa voy a ir con mis padres a esquiar.

8 Vamos a ir al campo para las próximas vacaciones. Preferimos estar muy lejos del ruido del tráfico y de las ciudades grandes.

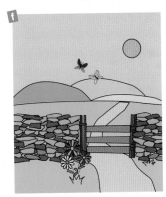
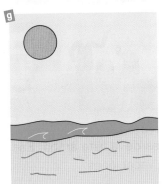

El alojamiento

5 🎧 📖 ¿Dónde se van a alojar? Empareja las imágenes con la palabra adecuada.

Ejemplo: 1 b — un camping

    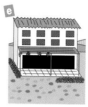 

un hotel
un albergue juvenil
un camping
un chalet
un apartamento
una casa

6a 💬 Trabaja con tu pareja. Pregunta y contesta sobre tus planes de vacaciones, como en el ejemplo.

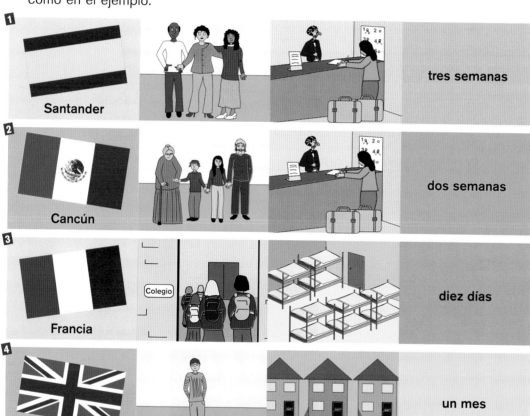

1 Santander — tres semanas
2 Cancún — dos semanas
3 Francia — Colegio — diez días
4 Londres — La familia Jones — un mes
5 Estados Unidos — diez días

Ejemplo: 1

A: ¿Adónde vas a ir de vacaciones este verano?
B: Voy a ir a Santander este verano.
A: ¿Con quién vas a ir de vacaciones?
B: Voy a ir con mis padres.
A: ¿Cuánto tiempo vas a pasar?
B: Voy a pasar tres semanas.
A: ¿Dónde vas a quedarte?
B: Voy a quedarme en un hotel.

b ✏️ Elige unas vacaciones de la lista arriba. Escribe un correo electrónico a un amigo hablándole de tus vacaciones.

Ejemplo: Este verano voy a…

7a 📖 Empareja las imágenes con la palabra adecuada.

Ejemplo: 1 — f

b 🎧 Escucha lo que dice esta gente. Empareja las imágenes del ejercicio 7a con lo que escuchas.

Ejemplo: 1 — e

c 💬 Trabaja con tu pareja. ¿Cuántas preguntas puedes hacer acerca de lo que tiene el hotel?

Ejemplo: ¿Hay una piscina?
¿A qué hora es el desayuno?
¿Dónde se puede comprar postales?
Por favor, ¿me puede cambiar dinero?

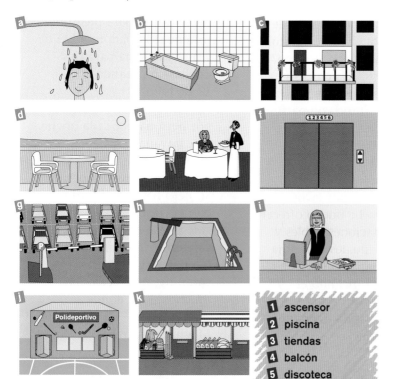

1	ascensor
2	piscina
3	tiendas
4	balcón
5	discoteca
6	ducha
7	patio para niños
8	cuarto de baño
9	restaurante
10	aparcamiento
11	polideportivo
12	recepción
13	cambio
14	vistas al mar
15	televisor

CULTURA

Paradores de Turismo de España is a chain of luxury hotels in Spain. The *Paradores* were founded by King Alfonso XIII to promote tourism, the first hotel opening in Gredos, Ávila in 1928.

A profitable state enterprise, these hotels are often situated in castles, palaces, fortresses, convents, monasteries and other historic buildings. They are very popular with tourists and are typically Spanish in character.

Parador Carmona

8 🎧 Escucha estas conversaciones y contesta las preguntas en español. Pon una ✗ en la casilla del alojamiento que mejor corresponda con las frases indicadas.

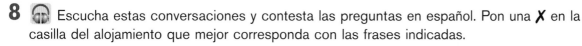

	Hotel Bella Vista	Albergue Las Olas	Camping Río Grande
Ejemplo: Es un camping.			✗
Está en la costa.			
Se puede comer allí.			
Hay que compartir con más de una persona.			
Se puede llevar mascota allí.			
Quieren pasar dos semanas allí.			
Se puede dejar el coche allí.			
Es un grupo escolar.			

9 📖 💬 Practica los tres diálogos con tu pareja.

1

A: Buenos días, hotel Bella Vista. En qué puedo servirle?

B: Nos gustaría reservar dos habitaciones con cuarto de baño para quince días a partir del quince de agosto, si es posible.

A: ¿Pensión completa o media pensión?

B: Pensión completa, por favor, y a ser posible con vistas al mar o a la piscina.

A: Todas nuestras habitaciones tienen vistas al mar. ¿Algo más?

B: Sí, una cosa más. ¿Hay aparcamiento?

A: Sí, señor.

2

A: ¿El albergue juvenil Las Olas?

B: Sí, ¿en qué puedo servirle?

A: ¿Tiene habitaciones libres para un grupo de estudiantes desde el 27 de julio hasta el 16 de agosto?

B: ¿Cuántos estudiantes son?

A: Seis chicos, seis chicas y dos profesores.

B: ¿Les importaría compartir habitación?

A: Los estudiantes pueden compartir sin problema, pero para los profesores individuales, por favor.

B: Muy bien. Le puedo ofrecer seis habitaciones dobles y dos individuales cada una con ducha. ¿Eso le vale?

A: Vale. ¿Está incluido el desayuno?

B: Sí, pero la cena es aparte.

A: Muchas gracias.

3

A: Hola, aquí el camping Río Grande.

B: Hola. Llamo para preguntar si tiene sitio para una tienda y una caravana para tres noches empezando el 12 de julio.

A: Sí, tenemos. El precio es por persona por cada noche. La caravana y la tienda cuestan más.

B: Muy bien. ¿Aceptan perros?

A: Sí, pero hay que llevarlos con la correa puesta.

B: ¿Me puede decir si hay cafetería y restaurante?

A: No hay restaurante en el camping, pero cerca hay muchos sitios donde se puede cenar.

B: Muchas gracias.

10 📖 Lee la carta abajo.

lunes el 4 de agosto

Querida Angelina,

¡Escribo para contarte mi plan de vacaciones para el verano y, por supuesto, ¡para averiguar lo que vas a hacer! Sabes que mis padres acaban de comprar un chalet en el sur de España y naturalmente allí es adonde vamos este verano. Viajamos en coche y como es un camino muy largo vamos a pasar una noche en un hotel por el camino. ¡A mi familia no nos gusta nada pasar todo el día en el coche! No voy a estudiar en absoluto para mis exámenes durante las vacaciones, solo voy a relajarme y a pasar el tiempo en la piscina o en la playa. Tendré tiempo para estudiar cuando volvamos.

¿Y tú? ¿Vas a Florida otra vez este verano? Si la respuesta es sí, ¿a qué parques vas esta vez? ¿Qué tiempo hará? Mi amigo Javier, que estuvo allí el año pasado, dice que hace muchísimo calor. ¿Vas a comprar mucho? Mi padre dice que todo es muy barato en los EE.UU. ¿Va tu hermana contigo este año o va a buscar un trabajo? Salúdala de mi parte, ¿vale?

Contéstame y cuéntamelo por favor.

Un saludo de tu amigo

Alberto

a 📖 Busca las seis frases correctas.

Ejemplo: 1

1 *Es una carta de Alberto.*
2 Pasa sus vacaciones en un hotel.
3 Su familia viaja a España.
4 El viaje durará mucho.
5 Alberto tiene que estudiar para sus exámenes.
6 Va a quedarse en la costa.
7 Va a estar muy ocupado durante las vacaciones.
8 Alberto busca información.
9 En Florida hay pocos parques temáticos.
10 Estados Unidos no es caro.
11 La hermana de Angelina trabaja en los EE. UU.

b 🏔 Imagínate que eres Angelina. Escribe una respuesta a la carta de Alberto. Asegúrate de que contestas a todas sus preguntas y luego pregúntale algo tú. Por ejemplo, pregúntale cuándo se va de vacaciones; cuánto tiempo se queda allí; dónde está su casa etc.

11a ▥ Lee esta carta.

C/ Portaceli, 11–8°D
42011 SEVILLA
Tel: 754 008 426
E-mail: famjuan@yahoo.es

10 de mayo

Estimado señor,

Me gustaría reservar dos cuartos
individuales en su hotel, cada
uno con cuarto de baño y balcón,
por una semana desde el 6 hasta
el 12 de julio. Nos gustaría pensión
completa.

Por favor, ¿puede decirme cuánto
cuesta esta reserva?

En espera de su respuesta,
Atentamente,
Juan García-Mendez

Pienso... Quisiera... Me gustaría...	...pasar quince días ...una semana	...desde el 2 de agosto. ...hasta el 20 de agosto.
Me gustaría reservar una habitación...		...con una cama para dos personas ...con dos camas ...con una ducha ...con cuarto de baño
¿Tiene sitio libre...		...para una caravana? ...para una tienda?
Quisiera...		...pensión completa ...media pensión
Me gustaría saber... ¿Puedes decirme...		
En espera de su respuesta...		

1

Hotel María Cristina,
Puerto Banus

4 estrellas ★★★★

Muy cerca del
casco viejo

Rodeado de paseos
y jardines

A cuatro manzanas
de la playa principal

Piscina grande
y restaurante

2

Delfin el-Verde

4 estrellas ★★★★

Es imposible no volver a
casa bronceado dado su
playa, sol interminable,
arena y deportes.
Querrás volver aquí
año tras año.

Abierto desde el
31 de marzo hasta
el 14 de septiembre.

b ▥ 💬 Practica una conversación en la
oficina de turismo con tu pareja.

¿Dónde está
Correos?
¿Dónde hay
un banco/
una oficina de
Correos/un
cine por aquí?

Quisiera un
mapa de
la ciudad/
información
sobre.../un
horario.

¿Qué se
puede hacer
por aquí?

Buenos días.
¿En qué puedo
servirle/
ayudarle?

Aquí tiene un
mapa/un folleto/
un horario.

Aquí se puede
visitar los
monumentos y
museos, hacer
compras, hacer
deportes acuáticos
y se celebra(n)
la(s) fiesta(s) de...

12 ¿Qué tal tu geografía? Encuentra estos países en un atlas y busca los nombres en español. Después, añade las nacionalidades apropiadas en la tabla siguiente.

Europa	
País	Nacionalidad
España	español/la
Inglaterra	inglés/esa
Francia	francés/esa

América Latina	
País	Nacionalidad
Méjico	mejicano/a

LENGUA CLAVE

When you look up a word in a bilingual dictionary, it is followed by a number of related words. The part of speech of each word is indicated as follows:

- (v.) — verb
- (n.m.) — masculine noun
- (n.f.) — feminine noun
- (adj.) — adjective

For example:
viajar (v.) — to travel
viaje (n.m.) — journey
viajero (n.m.) — traveller/passenger

Look up the following verbs related to travel and transport. Can you find the Spanish for the English nouns listed?

- *parar* (to stop) — bus stop
- *sentarse* (to sit) — seat
- *entrar* (to enter) — entrance
- *salir* (to go out) — exit
- *volar* (to fly) — flight
- *conducir* (to drive) — driver
- *visitar* (to visit) — visitor
- *llegar* (to arrive) — arrival

Can you find any more related words?

3 El tiempo

☑ **Talk about the weather**

☑ **Compare climates**

☑ **Use different tenses and verbs to describe the weather**

☑ **Learn about fiestas**

1 📖 Une los dibujos y las frases.

Ejemplo: 1 — d

1 hace calor
2 hace mal tiempo
3 llueve
4 hace frío
5 hay hielo
6 hace viento
7 hace sol
8 hace buen tiempo
9 está nublado
10 hay niebla
11 hay tormenta
12 nieva

2a 🎧 Escucha el pronóstico del tiempo y empareja el tiempo con la ciudad correcta.

Alicante

Barcelona

La Coruña

Las Palmas

Madrid

Málaga

Palma de Mallorca

Sevilla

Valencia

Zaragoza

b 💬 Trabaja con tu pareja. Usa la información en 2a para hablar del tiempo en diferentes ciudades de España.

Ejemplo: ¿Qué tiempo hace en Madrid?
En Madrid hace calor y hace sol.

3a 📖 Mira el mapa de Chile. Usa la información para decidir cuáles de las frases siguientes son verdaderas (V) y cuáles son falsas (F).

1 Hoy hace sol en Antofagasta.
2 Hoy hace calor en Santiago.
3 Hoy está nublado en Temuco
4 Hoy hay nieve en Punta Arenas.
5 Hoy llueve en Concepción.

b 💬 Mira el mapa otra vez. Con tu pareja, contesta las preguntas utilizando las expresiones en la página 109 (Grámatica).

Ejemplo:
A: ¿Qué tiempo hace hoy en Concepción?
B: Hoy en Concepción hace calor, pero está lloviendo.

1 ¿Qué tiempo hace hoy en Santiago?
2 ¿Qué tiempo hace hoy en Antofagasta?
3 ¿Qué tiempo hace hoy en Temuco?
4 ¿Qué tiempo hace hoy aquí?

4 📖 Empareja la estación del año con la imagen adecuada.

1 verano
2 invierno
3 primavera
4 otoño

5 📖 🏛 Trabaja con tu pareja. Copia y rellena la tabla siguiente con palabras y frases que asocies con diferentes estaciones.

Verano ☀		Invierno ❄	
Tiempo	**Actividades**	**Tiempo**	**Actividades**
hace sol	*ir a la playa*	*llueve*	*ir al cine*

6 🎧 🏛 Escucha la descripción del clima de Chile. Copia los puntos cardinales de la brújula abajo y haz apuntes sobre el tiempo.

7 📖 🏛 Completa las frases siguientes con el nombre correcto de las estaciones según el hemisferio.

Ejemplo: En junio, julio y agosto en Chile es **invierno** y en España es **verano**.

1 En diciembre, enero y febrero en Chile es _____ y en España es _____ .
2 En septiembre, octubre y noviembre en Chile es _____ y en España es _____ .
3 En marzo, abril y mayo en Chile es _____ Y en España es _____ .

8 🎧 📖 💬 Escucha otra vez la información sobre el clima de Chile, pero esta vez léela también y hazle preguntas a tu pareja sobre el clima.

Ejemplo: A: ¿Qué tiempo hace en el norte de Chile en verano?

B: En el norte de Chile en verano hace calor.

La República de Chile es uno de los muchos países hispanohablantes. Como se ve en el mapa, se encuentra en América del Sur, a lo largo de la costa, entre las montañas de los Andes y el océano Pacífico. Comparte su frontera con Argentina al este, Bolivia al noreste y Perú hacia el norte.

Dado que el país tiene cuatro mil kilómetros de largo, no es ninguna sorpresa que el clima de Chile sea tan variado como sus tierras.

El verano en Chile es de diciembre a marzo. En el centro del país durante esta estación el clima es cálido y seco, con pocas lluvias, y la temperatura llega a unos 30 grados centígrados. En invierno, sin embargo, la región central recibe muchas precipitaciones, mientras que sus zonas más expuestas experimentan vientos violentos.

En las zonas del sur, donde hay muchos lagos, en verano las temperaturas no llegan a más de 14 grados. Aquí el clima es más lluvioso y más fresco. En invierno llueve más que en el centro. En el extremo sur incluso se registran vendavales. Las lluvias son abundantes excepto en Patagonia, donde tienen un clima muy seco.

En el este del país está la cordillera de los Andes, que sirve de frontera entre Chile y Argentina. Aquí el clima es típico de las regiones montañosas. En las elevaciones altas hay un clima de hielo.

La zona del norte de Chile se caracteriza por veranos cálidos e inviernos suaves. En esta región está el desierto más seco del mundo, el Atacama: aquí las lluvias son encasas y las temperaturas muy altas.

vendaval = gale

GRAMÁTICA

Different tenses and verbs to describe the weather

To talk about the weather in Spanish, we usually use the third person of *hacer*, *estar* or *haber*.

¿Qué tiempo hace en Inglaterra?	What's the weather like in England?
Hace frío.	It's cold.
Hace calor.	It's hot.
Hace sol.	It's sunny.

To say it's very hot, cold or sunny, just add *mucho*:

Hace mucho calor.	It's very hot.
Hace mucho frío.	It's very cold.
Hace mucho sol.	It's very sunny.

However, when talking about any form of precipitation (rain, snow etc.), use *estar*:

Está lloviendo.	It's raining.
Esta nevando.	It's snowing.
Está nublado.	It's cloudy.

Mucho can be used after the verb, except with *está nublado*, which requires *muy* (*está muy nublado*)

It is also possible to use *hay* plus a noun:

Hay sol.	It's sunny.
Hay niebla.	It's foggy.
Hay lluvia.	It's raining.

If you want to talk about the weather in the past, simply use the past tense of *hacer*, *estar* or *haber*:

Hizo sol.	It was sunny.
Estuvo lloviendo.	It was raining.
Hubo tormenta.	There was a storm.

An easy way to talk about the weather in the future is to use the third person of the present tense of *ir* with the infinitive of the relevant verb:

Va a hacer sol.	It's going to be sunny.
Va a hacer calor.	It's going to be hot.
Va a haber tormenta.	There will be a storm.

Finally, there are two verbs relating to the weather, namely *llover* and *nevar*, that can be used on their own in the relevant tense:

Llovió.	It rained.
Llueve.	It's raining.
Va a llover.	It's going to rain.
Nevó.	It snowed.
Nieva.	It's snowing.
Va a nevar.	It's going to snow.

Care must be taken with these verbs as they are radical changing.

9 Haz investigaciones por Internet para descubrir el clima de otro país hispanohablante, y después úsalo como modelo para escribir y dar tu propia presentación sobre ese país. ¡Podrías hacer un PowerPoint para acompañarlo!

10 Empareja el español con la frase adecuada en inglés.

1 En mi pueblo hace mucho frío en invierno.
2 Ayer hizo mucho calor en la playa.
3 Mañana va a hacer mucho viento.
4 En vacaciones hizo mucho sol.
5 En otoño llovió todos los días.
6 Hoy está nublado.
7 En el centro del país normalmente hace mucho calor.
8 En Navidades nevó todos los días.

a Tomorrow it's going to be very windy.
b In my town it's very cold in winter.
c At Christmas it snowed every day.
d Yesterday it was very hot on the beach.
e On holiday it was very hot.
f In autumn it rained every day.
g It's cloudy today.
h In the centre of the country it's usually very hot.

11a Escucha y lee la información de cómo afecta al Polo Norte el cambio de clima. Toma apuntes y decide cuál de las frases siguientes es la más apropiada.

1 El clima mundial es más o menos consistente y constante y no debemos estar preocupados.
2 No tienen importancia para la raza humana los cambios que están ocurriendo en el clima global.
3 Ha habido unos cambios en el clima mundial que ya tienen consecuencias significativas.

Estamos destruyendo nuestro mundo

Parece ser que durante los últimos **cien años** la temperatura **del mundo ha aumentado** medio grado. No parece mucho, pero incluso medio grado puede tener un efecto **profundo** en nuestro planeta.

La principal causa de este calentamiento global es la actividad humana, que genera gases contaminantes, sobre todo en los países industrializados. Estos gases retienen el calor del sol en la atmósfera, lo que produce el llamado "efecto invernadero".

Según muchos estudios, el nivel del mar ha subido entre seis y ocho pulgadas (quince a veinte centímetros).

Se piensa que estas temperaturas **elevadas** están causando la descongelación de las capas polares, y que son una **consecuencia** del calentamiento global.

Esa subida de temperaturas aumenta **el volumen** de agua en el océano, lo cual hace que algunas partes del mundo hoy en día **sufran** inundaciones catastróficas — como en partes de Gran Bretaña, India y Bangladesh. También **quiere decir** que aumenta la cantidad de icebergs.

Otras consecuencias graves del calentamiento global son los huracanes y las tormentas, que son cada vez más frecuentes en ciertas regiones. También aumentará el número de muertes por enfermedades como la malaria y el cólera, que afectarán a más población porque las zonas tropicales van a extenderse.

Lo que **está claro** es que está cambiando el clima global y tendremos que prepararnos para las consecuencias.

b 📖 🖼 Ahora, con la ayuda de un diccionario, busca las palabras del texto en negrita que correspondan con las palabras o frases siguientes.

Ejemplo: **1** *un siglo — cien años*

1 un siglo	**6** resultado
2 se ha hecho más grande	**7** es obvio
3 altas	**8** significa
4 de la Tierra	**9** padezcan de
5 la cantidad	**10** creen que

12 📖 Mira las imágenes. ¿Puedes emparejar cada una con estas actividades? Usa un diccionario para ayudarte.

Ejemplo: **a** *— una corrida de toros*

cantar

una procesión

una hoguera

beber

una fiesta

un belén

el baile flamenco

una corrida de toros

una verbena

la misa

una batalla

una imagen

un disfraz

montar a caballo

fuegos artificiales

comer

España, ¡el hogar de las fiestas!

En cada uno de sus múltiples pueblos y ciudades se puede ver algún tipo de fiesta casi todas las semanas del año. Estas fiestas hacen que la gente salga a la calle para compartir las celebraciones. Puede ser esto el motivo de las buenas relaciones y camaradería entre los vecinos en la península.

Las fiestas más famosas en el extranjero son los encierros de Pamplona, las Fallas de Valencia con sus impresionantes fuegos artificiales, las batallas de moros y cristianos representadas en Alcoi, o quizás las fiestas de Semana Santa por toda Andalucía, sin olvidarse de la enorme Feria de Abril de Sevilla.

En Andalucía hay corridas de toros, flamenco, conciertos, música y fiestas de vino, mientras que en otros sitios se puede encontrar todo tipo de celebraciones extrañas, como la fiesta del caracol en Lleida, la del marisco en Logroño y la de la paella de Chueca.

Cara, la revista del momento, les ofrece aquí toda la información imprescindible sobre dos de las fiestas inolvidables de España. ¡No te las pierdas!

San Isidro – Madrid

San Isidro es el patrón de la capital de España, Madrid. El 15 de mayo los madrileños van andando hacia el Prado de San Isidro donde es costumbre tomar agua bendita que sale de una fuente que hay en el patio. Es tradicional vestirse de chulapo o chulapa (el traje típico de la ciudad de Madrid).

A pesar de su significado religioso, San Isidro es una buena excusa para celebrarlo con comida, copas, música y baile hasta la madrugada. Es típico, por ejemplo, comer barquillos y rosquillas. Esta fiesta dura varios días repletos de actividades culturales — concursos de chotis, conciertos de música y ferias de artesanía.

Las Navidades españolas

En España, las vacaciones de Navidad están llenas de festividades tradicionales, pero hay una que es única. Llamada 'Hogueras', esta tradición es anterior a la Navidad cristiana. Es la fiesta del invierno, el día más corto del año. En ella, la gente salta por encima del fuego como símbolo de protección contra las enfermedades. Se celebra principalmente en Granada y Jaén.

Las tradiciones más comunes incluyen la construcción de enormes belenes — representando el Nacimiento, árboles de navidad, mercadillos por todo el país, donde se venden frutas, flores, dulces de navidad (mazapanes, turrones y polvorones), velas, decoraciones y artesanías — y por supuesto hoy en día regalos para todos. A menudo, con la aparición de la estrella navideña en el cielo, se encienden lámparas de aceite. Con el avance de la noche disminuyen las muchedumbres y se puede ver a la gente que se retira hacia sus hogares.

La alegría familiar se interrumpe con el canto de las campanas que llaman a todos a la iglesia para celebrar la Misa del Gallo. La más bella de estas celebraciones se ve en el monasterio de Montserrat, que se sitúa en lo alto de una montaña cerca de Barcelona. Se distingue por el coro de niños que cantan con una voz dulce y única.

No se come la cena hasta después de medianoche. Es una celebración familiar y uno de los platos típicos es el pavo trufado. Después de la cena se cantan los villancicos y a continuación los jóvenes salen de juerga. Las celebraciones siguen hasta la madrugada que como dice en la canción: 'Esta noche es Nochebuena, Y no es noche de dormir'.

El Día de Navidad se va otra vez a la iglesia antes de los aperitivos y la comida.

En España Santa Claus y los regalos en Navidad no es una costumbre tradicional. Los regalos los traen el día 6 de enero los Reyes Magos. La víspera del día 6 los niños dejan sus zapatos limpios fuera para que los encuentren los Reyes. Si el niño ha sido bueno durante el año, le dejan regalos. Si ha sido malo solo recibe carbón de reyes (un dulce hecho de azúcar de color negro que parece carbón). El día 6 es fiesta nacional, y lo tradicional es comer el roscón de reyes (un bollo dulce en forma de anillo grande que contiene frutos secos y a menudo relleno de nata). Quien encuentre al comer su trozo la sorpresa escondida en la masa, se supone que tendrá suerte durante el resto del año.

a 🎨 Empareja estos verbos con su significado en inglés. Usa un diccionario para ayudarte.

1 comer
2 beber
3 tomar copas
4 bailar
5 cantar
6 celebrar
7 originarse
8 se ve
9 se caracteriza por

GRAMÁTICA

Se puede + infinitive

This means 'one/you can do something'. For example:

En mi pueblo se puede pasear a orillas del mar.
In my village you can walk by the sea.

14 💬 Trabaja con tu pareja. Contesta las preguntas siguientes usando las pistas en la casilla.

Ejemplo:
¿Qué se puede hacer en la fiesta de San Isidro? En la fiesta de San Isidro se puede bailar hasta la madrugada.

> **San Valentín**
> **El día de los Inocentes**
> **Semana Santa**
> **La Víspera de Todos los Santos**
> **Navidad**

1 ¿Qué se puede hacer en _____?
2 ¿Qué fiestas celebras?
3 ¿Qué se puede hacer?
4 ¿Qué se puede ver?

Paper 1: listening

This sample listening task has two parts:

- a multiple-choice question, for 1 mark, with three images to choose from
- five statements, each with a gap to fill; the five words that fill the gaps are chosen from 10 words in a box

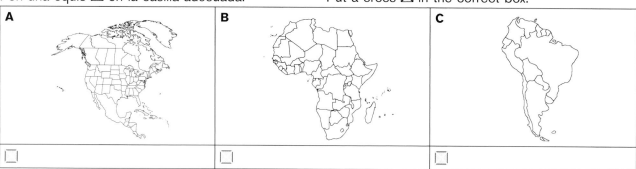

Unas vacaciones especiales

Lola habla de sus vacaciones familiares.

Lola talks about her family holiday.

(a) ¿Adónde va a ir Lola de vacaciones?
  Where is Lola going on holiday?   (1)

Listen carefully for any countries mentioned.
Which continent are they in?

Pon una equis ⊠ en la casilla adecuada.

Put a cross ⊠ in the correct box.

A	B	C
☐	☐	☐

(b) ¿Qué va a hacer su familia?

What is her family going to do?

Completa las frases con las palabras correctas. Complete the sentences with the correct words. (5)

regalo   primavera   premio canción   comida invierno   lengua nación mar puerto

(i) Harán el viaje porque los padres
   recibieron un ....

Only two of the words in the box refer to something that can be given: *regalo* and *premio*. Which do you think it is? Why?

(ii) Van a ir en ....

In which season of the year is the holiday? Listen out for the month.

(iii) Pasarán unos días en el ....

You are looking for a masculine noun here. Only two of those in the box could fill the gap. Which is it, according to the context?

(iv) Lola quiere descubrir cómo
   es la ....

Lola wants to find out about something; only two words are possible. Be careful not to confuse this answer with that for part (v).

(v) Lola necesita aprender otra ....

At the end of the extract Lola says she must learn something? What is it? *Una canción or una lengua?*

(Total for Question = 5 marks)

Hints to answer the question

For part (b):

- Before you listen to the extract it is essential to take time to read carefully the five statements and the 10 words in the box.
- The statements, which are in the order of the text, summarise aspects of the extract expressed in different words.
- Understanding the context is the key to success in this type of question.
- When choosing the words to fill the gaps be aware that they are often chosen in 'pairs' (e.g. *primavera* and *invierno* in the box above), only one of which is correct according to the context.

Paper 2: reading

In paper 2 reading tasks, you may be asked to match statements with quotes from speakers, as in the sample task below.

El tiempo

Lee estas frases.   Read these comments.

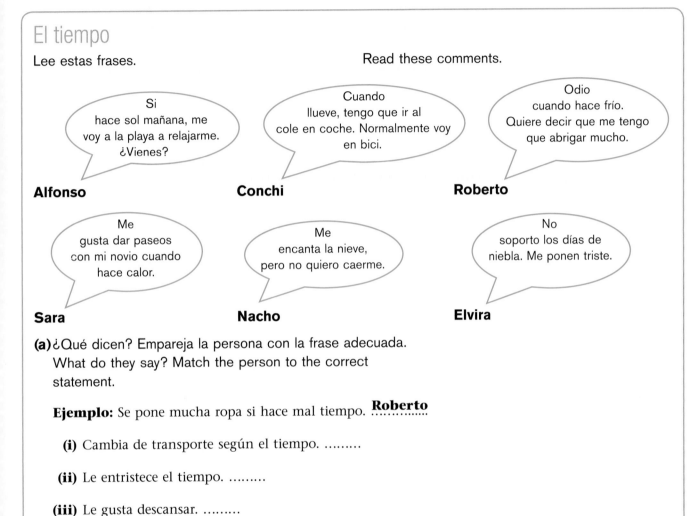

Alfonso — Si hace sol mañana, me voy a la playa a relajarme. ¿Vienes?

Conchi — Cuando llueve, tengo que ir al cole en coche. Normalmente voy en bici.

Roberto — Odio cuando hace frío. Quiere decir que me tengo que abrigar mucho.

Sara — Me gusta dar paseos con mi novio cuando hace calor.

Nacho — Me encanta la nieve, pero no quiero caerme.

Elvira — No soporto los días de niebla. Me ponen triste.

(a) ¿Qué dicen? Empareja la persona con la frase adecuada. What do they say? Match the person to the correct statement.

Ejemplo: Se pone mucha ropa si hace mal tiempo. **Roberto** ....

  (i) Cambia de transporte según el tiempo. ....

 (ii) Le entristece el tiempo. ....

(iii) Le gusta descansar. ....

 (iv) Tiene miedo de caerse. ....

  (v) Le gusta estar al aire libre. ....

(Total for Question = 5 marks)

Hints to answer the question

- Think carefully about what each of the statements (i)–(v) mean. Ask yourself how you might say the same thing using different language. Then the task is just a matching exercise.
- Remember your exam technique: once you have solved a few, the others become easier by a process of elimination.
- Look for key verbs like *salir* (to go out) or *cambiar* (to change). They may help you to make connections.
- Remember that there is likely to be some vocabulary you don't recognise, so look for cognates to help you, such as *triste* in Elvira's statement and *le en**triste**ce* in part (ii).

Paper 2: writing

The short writing task 3(b) follows on from the theme of the preceding reading task 3(a). Try this short writing task on the same theme as the reading question above. Remember the tips given earlier when tackling this type of question (pages 28 and 58), especially the link with the previous reading question.

(b) ¿Y tú? ¿Qué haces según el tiempo que hace? ¿Cómo viajas?

Escribe unas 50 palabras en español.

Aquí tienes algunas ideas.

And you? How do you react to the weather? How do you travel?

Write about 50 words **in Spanish.**

Here are some ideas.

tiempo/weather **lugares/places** **actividades/activities** (10)
transporte/transport **ropa/clothes**

Look at the following sample answer. It is of a good standard, but there are a few slips. Note that the student has addressed all the required points in approximately 50 words.

Paper 3: speaking (section A)

The first part of the speaking test (section A) is a presentation and discussion based on a picture and you can take in a picture of your choice. This part of the exam lasts a maximum of 4 minutes. You have a maximum of 1 minute to make your presentation.

After your presentation, the interviewer intervenes with a series of questions based on the picture. The conversation must relate to the picture but may also include some questions prompted by your chosen image. The questions will not duplicate material already covered in your initial presentation.

Listen to this very good presentation about the photo at the top of page 117 and note how and when the interviewer steps in to ask relevant questions. The transcript is presented below, along with comments on some of the inaccuracies you should try to avoid. Note the excellent use of verbs in this sample.

Sample student answer

Accurate use of complex structure.

Careful with the preterite tense of *ser.* What should it be?

Check verbs. This should be *sentarse*. Do you know what *sentirse* means?

Clear demonstration of ability to move from one verb tense to another with ease (from present *está* to past (*pasó*).

Effective use of past tense.

This should be estupendas.

El año pasado pasé unas vacaciones estupendos en el Caribe. Pero antes de poder llegar allí, tuvimos que pasar veinticuatro horas en el aeropuerto porque hubo huelga de pilotos. Fui incomodísimo porque no había ningún sitio donde sentirse y tuve que dormir en el suelo. Mi madre está muy mal de la espalda, así que pasó la noche con mi padre en un hotel cerca del aeropuerto y mis hermanos y yo nos quedamos allí en el suelo. Nos trataron bien porque nos dieron comida y bebida y más tarde pagaron una compensación mis padres. Pero fue un gran desilusión y una mal comienzo para unas vacaciones de ensueño. Fui a Jamaica con mi familia y con amigos nuestros. Después de ese problema, todo fue bien. Una vez allí, nos alojamos en un hotel de lujo en la playa con media pensión.

¿Y qué tiempo hace en Jamaica?

¡Pues siempre hace sol! A pesar de ser octubre, hizo un calor agradable, lo que quería decir que podía bañarme cada día en el mar.

¿Y qué más pueden hacer los turistas allí?

Se pueden hacer, por ejemplo, muchos deportes. Cada tarde jugábamos todos al voleibol en la playa. Me puse morena y muy en forma.

¿Y dónde comiste cuando no lo hiciste en el hotel?

Había muchos sitios diferentes donde cenar, pero lo que más me gustó fue un restaurante en el puerto donde se come pescado fresco que se compra a los barcos pesqueros. Se llama Sami's.

¿Crees que volverás?

Sí. Nos reímos mucho y fueron mis mejores vacaciones. Tengo muchas ganas de volver allí otra vez algún día.

Effective use of past tense.

Don't forget the personal *a*. This should read: *pagaron una compensación a mis padres*

Be careful with the gender of nouns — the articles for these are the wrong way round.

Good use of connectives.

Good use of imperfect tense.

This student has missed the opportunity to show off a future tense. The teacher sets this up with the question about the future.

Now look at the photo on the right. What could you say about it? Prepare a short presentation. List the questions you might be asked and prepare some answers. Work with a partner to prepare and then role-play the exam.

Exam tip

Remember to use a variety of tenses and structures, to give opinions and to ensure you give details about what is in the picture.

Vocabulario

Transport

el **autobús** bus
el **autocar** coach
el **avión** plane
el **barco** boat
la **bicicleta** bicycle
el **coche** car
el **metro** underground/tube
la **moto** motorbike
a **pie** on foot
el **taxi** taxi
el **tren** train

Adjectives

barato/a cheap
caro/a expensive
cómodo/a comfortable
fácil easy
incómodo/a uncomfortable
lento/a slow
limpio/a clean
peligroso/a dangerous
práctico/a practical
próximo/a next
rápido/a fast
sucio/a dirty
último/a last

Travelling

el **andén** platform
los **aseos** toilets
el **billete** ticket
la **cafetería** café
el **cambio** bureau de change
(el billete) de ida y vuelta return (ticket)
el **equipaje** luggage
la **maleta** suitcase
objetos perdidos lost property
la **puerta de embarque** departure gate
el **puerto** port, harbour
la **reserva** reservation
la **sala de espera** waiting room
la **salida** exit
(el billete) sencillo single (ticket)
el **viaje** journey, trip
el **vuelo** flight

Countries

Alemania Germany
Argentina Argentina
Austria Austria
Bélgica Belgium
Brasil Brazil
Canadá Canada
Chile Chile
Chipre Cyprus
Colombia Colombia
Dinamarca Denmark
España Spain
los **Estados Unidos** United States
Francia France
Gales Wales
Grecia Greece
Hungría Hungary
Inglaterra England
Irlanda Ireland
Islandia Iceland
Italia Italy
Luxemburgo Luxembourg
Marruecos Morocco
Méjico Mexico
Nueva Zelanda New Zealand
(los) Países Bajos the Netherlands
Perú Peru
Polonia Poland
(el) Reino Unido United Kingdom
Sudáfrica South Africa
Suecia Sweden
Suiza Switzerland
Venezuela Venezuela

Places to stay

el **albergue juvenil** youth hostel
el **apartamento** apartment
el **camping** campsite
el **campo** countryside
la **casa** house
el **chalet** bungalow, house, cottage
la **costa** coast
el **hotel** hotel
las **montañas** mountains
el **parador** (Sp) state-run hotel
el **piso** flat

Accommodation

el **aparcamiento** car park
el **ascensor** lift
el **balcón** balcony
la **cama** bed
la **caravana** caravan
la **discoteca** disco
la **ducha** shower
(la) **media pensión** half board
(la) **pensión completa** full board
la **piscina** swimming pool
la **recepción** reception
el **sitio** place; pitch; space
la **terraza** terrace; balcony
la **tienda** shop
vistas al mar sea views

Weather

el **clima** climate
Está lloviendo. It's raining.
Está nevando. It's snowing.
Está nublado. It's cloudy.
Hace buen tiempo. The weather is good.
Hace calor. It's hot.
Hace frío. It's cold.
Hace mal tiempo. The weather is bad.
Hace sol. It's sunny.
Hace viento. It's windy.
Hay hielo. It's icy.
Hay niebla. It's foggy.
Hay relámpagos. There's lightning.
Hay tormenta. There's a storm.
Llueve. It is raining.
Nieva. It is snowing.
el **pronóstico** weather forecast
el **tiempo** weather

Seasons and months

las **estaciones** seasons
la **primavera** spring
el **verano** summer
el **otoño** autumn
el **invierno** winter
el **mes** month
enero January
febrero February
marzo March
abril April
mayo May
junio June
julio July
agosto August
septiembre September
octubre October
noviembre November
diciembre December

Festivals and celebrations

el **Año Nuevo** New Year
bailar to dance
la **batalla** battle
beber to drink
el **belén** crib
la **boda** wedding
brindar to drink a toast
cantar to sing
celebrar to celebrate
el **champán** champagne
comer to eat
la **corrida de toros** bullfight
el **cumpleaños** birthday
el **Día de la Madre** Mother's Day

el **disfraz**   disguise, costume
los **dulces**   sweets
la **feria**   festival, fair
la **fiesta**   party, (public) holiday
el **flamenco**   type of dance
los **fuegos artificiales**   fireworks
la **hoguera**   bonfire
la **iglesia**   church
la **imagen**   image; picture; photo
la **misa**   mass
montar a caballo   to ride a horse
la **Navidad**   Christmas
la **Nochebuena**   Christmas Eve
la **Pascua**   Easter
el **pavo**   turkey
la **procesión**   procession
el **regalo**   present
religioso/a   religious
los **Reyes Magos**   Three Kings, Magi
San Valentín   Valentine's day

la **Semana Santa**   Holy Week
la **tarjeta**   card
la **tradición**   tradition
el **turrón**   nougat (Sp)
la **verbena**   festival
el **villancico**   carol

Holiday activities

bañarse en el mar   to swim in the sea
comprar recuerdos   to buy souvenirs
descansar   to relax
hacer surf   to go surfing
ir de compras   to go shopping
dar un paseo   to go for a walk
montar en bici   to go for a bike ride
practicar deporte   to do sports
sacar fotos   to take photos
salir a cenar   to go out to eat
tomar el sol   to sunbathe
visitar lugares de interés   to visit places
         of interest

Places of interest

la **agencia de viajes**   travel agency
el **banco**   bank
el **bar**   bar
la **bodega**   wine cellar; winery
el **castillo**   castle
la **catedral**   cathedral
Correos   post office
el **jardín**   garden
el **mercado**   market
el **museo**   museum
el **museo de arte**   art gallery
la **oficina de turismo**   tourist office
el **palacio**   palace
el **parque de atracciones**   amusement park
la **playa**   beach
la **plaza**   square
el **río**   river
el **teatro**   theatre
el **zoo**   zoo

Así es mi vida

1 **Una vida sana**

2 **De compras**

3 **¡A comer fuera!**

4 **¡Vivir a tope!**

1 Una vida sana

1a 📖 ✏️ ¿Qué sabes ya? Descifra las palabras y emparéjalas con la imagen adecuada.

Ejemplo: **a** — *la cabeza*

al bazeca
al zíran
sol ídsoo
al cabo
le razob
al ripnea
le ipe
al noam
le locule
le bromho
al drollia
al palesad
le joo
le masetógo

b 🎧 En el gimnasio. Apunta las partes del cuerpo en el orden en que las oyes. Usa el vocabulario del ejercicio arriba.

c ✏️ 💬 Inventa tu propia rutina de ejercicio. Pruébalo con tu pareja.

GRAMÁTICA

The imperative

To give someone an instruction or to tell him or her what to do we use the imperative. There are two forms for the informal imperative, singular (*tú*) and plural (*vosotros*).

Look at the box below

	-ar	-er	-ir
tú	*habla*	*come*	*escribe*
vosotros	*hablad*	*comed*	*escribid*

A few imperatives are irregular in the *tú* form:

decir	*di* (say)
salir	*sal* (go out)
hacer	*haz* (do/make)
ser	*sé* (be)
ir	*ve* (go)
tener	*ten* (have)
poner	*pon* (put)
venir	*ven* (come)

Write these instructions in English.

1 Respira hondo.
2 Levantad las manos.
3 Estira las piernas.
4 Haz unos ejercicios de calentamiento.
5 Doblad las piernas.
6 Abre los ojos.
7 Ten cuidado cuando haces ejercicios.
8 Ven conmigo al gimnasio.
9 Levanta las manos.
10 Agáchate hacia el suelo.

2 📖 Lee este artículo y apunta verdadera (V) o falsa (F) para cada una de las frases abajo.

Ejemplo: **1** *Hace falta hacer ejercicio para mantenerse en forma.* — V

¿Qué tipo de ejercicio debería ser parte de mi rutina diaria?

Mantenerse sano requiere una rutina adecuada de actividad física. El ejercicio aeróbico es un buen ejemplo. Aumenta el pulso, trabaja los músculos, y altera la respiración. Para la mayoría de la gente es mejor intentar hacer 30 minutos diarios por lo menos 4 veces a la semana. Si llevas bastante tiempo sin hacer ejercicio, puedes empezar con 5 o 10 minutos al día y aumentarlo poco a poco. Por ejemplo, se puede comenzar con un paseo de 10 minutos después de cada comida. Otro beneficio del ejercicio es que ayuda a controlar el peso. Unos ejemplos de ejercicio aeróbico son:

- dar un paseo rápido cada día dentro, en una máquina de correr, o al aire libre
- bailar
- hacer una clase de aerobic
- nadar
- patinar o hacer patinaje sobre ruedas
- jugar al tenis
- montar en bici

Además, hay muchas posibilidades cada día para ser más activo. Si te mueves mucho gastarás muchas calorías! Cuanto más te mueves, más calorías gastas. Lo siguiente puede ayudarte a aumentar tu actividad:

- Cuando tengas la oportunidad, anda en vez de coger el autobús o pedir que te lleven tus padres en coche.
- Sube por las escaleras en vez de usar el ascensor.
- Trabaja en el jardín o haz algo de limpieza en casa cada día.
- Baja del autobús una parada antes del colegio y anda desde allí.

1 *Hace falta hacer ejercicio para mantenerse en forma.*
2 El ejercicio aeróbico es bueno para el corazón.
3 Hay que hacer 30 minutos de ejercicio cada día.
4 Hay que hacer ejercicio inmediatamente después de comer.
5 No perderás peso si no haces ejercicio.
6 El ejercicio aumenta la energía.
7 El tenis es un ejercicio aeróbico.
8 Hacer tareas de casa es buen ejercicio.

3 🎧 How do you lead a healthy life? Listen to the recording and answer the questions in English.

1 What does Señora Fernández mean by the 'magic number 5'?
2 How much sleep does she recommend?
3 What does she say is the best sleeping pattern?
4 What two things should we avoid to ensure a good night's sleep?
5 What four things does she view as the common-sense approach to achieving a healthy lifestyle?

GRAMÁTICA

Giving instructions and advice

For instructions and advice in Spanish in a **formal** context the *usted* form of the imperative is used.

- *-ar* verbs end in *-e*
  ¡Escuche! Listen!
- *-er* and *-ir* verbs end in *-a*
  Coma fruta cada día.
  Eat fruit every day.

  ¡Escriba la carta ahora!
  Write the letter now!

Many irregular verbs form the *usted* imperative from the irregular first person singular of the present tense:

Haga mucho ejercicio.
Do a lot of exercise.

For more information see pp. 162–63 of the grammar summary. Look at the following examples:

¡Coma cinco raciones de fruta y verdura al día!
Eat five portions of fruit and vegetables every day!

¡Tome por lo menos cinco vasos de agua diarios también!
Have at least five glasses of water a day as well!

¡Siga una dieta equilibrada!
Make sure you have a balanced diet!

Traduce estas frases utilizando el imperativo formal:
1 Eat salad and lean meat.
2 Drink water with every meal.
3 Follow a varied diet.
4 Don't eat too much fat, salt or sugar.
5 Do aerobic exercise.

4a 💬 Haz una entrevista con tu pareja. Utiliza el cuadro de abajo para ayudarte.

Ejemplo: **A:** *¿Qué haces para estar en forma?*
B: *Duermo ocho horas cada noche y bebo mucha agua.*
A: *¿Qué actividades me aconsejas para estar en forma?*
B: *Haz deportes y evita el estrés.*
A: *¿Qué hay que hacer para llevar una vida sana?*
B: *Hace falta relajarse durante el día y no se debe fumar o tomar alcohol.*

¿Qué haces para estar en forma?	Duermo/Como/Bebo/Evito/Hago...
¿Qué actividades me aconsejas para estar en forma?	Duerme/Come/Bebe/Evita/Haz...
¿Qué hay que hacer para llevar una vida sana?	Hay que relajarse/dormir... Hace falta comer/acostarse... No se debe fumar/tomar drogas/estresarse.

b ✏️ Escribe un párrafo contestando a las preguntas.

5 📖 ¿Qué te pasa? Empareja las imágenes con las frases.

Ejemplo: **1 — d**

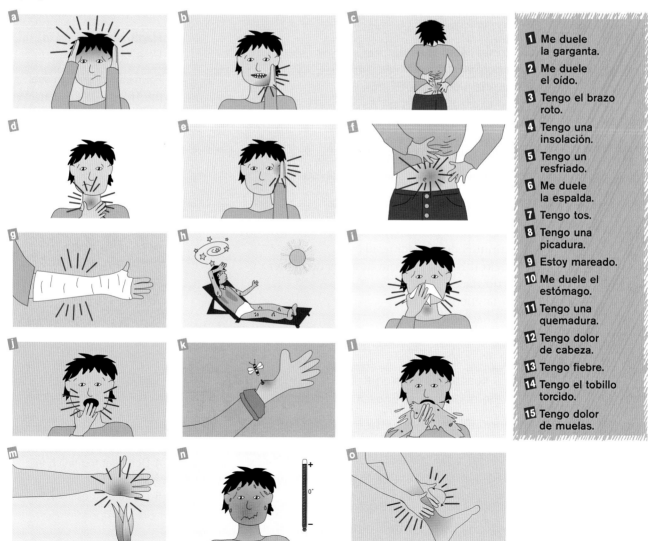

1. Me duele la garganta.
2. Me duele el oído.
3. Tengo el brazo roto.
4. Tengo una insolación.
5. Tengo un resfriado.
6. Me duele la espalda.
7. Tengo tos.
8. Tengo una picadura.
9. Estoy mareado.
10. Me duele el estómago.
11. Tengo una quemadura.
12. Tengo dolor de cabeza.
13. Tengo fiebre.
14. Tengo el tobillo torcido.
15. Tengo dolor de muelas.

6a 🎧 👤 En la farmacia. Escucha el diálogo. Luego copia y completa la tabla con los detalles que faltan.

	Problema	Remedio	Precio
Ejemplo:	*dolor de cabeza*	*aspirinas*	*6 euros*
1			

b 💬 Trabaja con tu pareja. Adapta el diálogo de abajo para practicar comprando medicamentos en una farmacia.

Ejemplo: **A:** *Buenos días.*
B: *Buenos días. ¿Qué le pasa?*
A: *No me siento bien. Me duelen la garganta y la cabeza.*
B: *Le recomiendo estos comprimidos y estas pastillas. ¿Qué tamaño quiere?*
A: *Grande por favor. ¿Cuánto le debo?*
B: *Son ... euros.*
A: *Aquí tiene. Gracias. Adiós.*

7 📖 Lee el artículo siguiente. Pon títulos para los contenidos como en el ejemplo.

Guía para exploradores

Botiquines

Un botiquín bien provisto de cosas para primeros auxilios es imprescindible. Elige una caja resistente y suficientemente grande para tener el contenido visible y accesible sin tener que sacar todo a la hora de usarlo. Guarda una lista del contenido y mantenlo en un sitio apropiado.

Sugerencias para el contenido del botiquín:

- jabón
- vendas
- tiritas
- termómetro
- tijeras
- pinzas
- crema de sol
- linterna
- algodón hidrófilo
- agua esterilizada
- imperdibles
- crema antiséptica

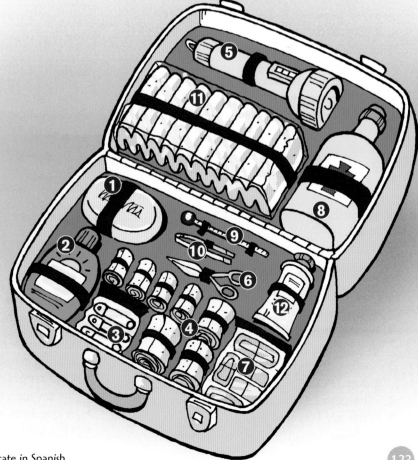

Impersonal verbs

To talk about ailments and symptoms in Spanish, the verb *doler* is very important.

Me duele(n) + body part
Te duele(n)
Le duele(n)
Nos duele(n)
Os duele(n)
Les duele(n)

Look at the examples below:

Me duele la cabeza.	My head hurts.
Me duelen los dedos.	My fingers hurt.
Me duele la garganta.	My throat hurts.
Me duelen las piernas.	My legs hurt.

Doler as an impersonal verb is similar to the verb *gustar*. See page 34.

Alternatively, *tengo dolor de* + body part can be used:

Tengo dolor de cabeza.
Tengo dolor de dedos.
Tengo dolor de garganta.
Tengo dolor de piernas.

Note that the article is not necessary here.

8 🎧 📖 Read and listen to this article and then answer the questions in English.

La comida sana

¿Sabías que la mayoría de las personas deberíamos comer más?

Una dieta bien equilibrada puede ayudar a mantener un peso corporal sano, mejorar el bienestar general y reducir el riesgo de enfermedades serias. Sigue estas simples reglas para asegurarte de la mejor rutina alimenticia posible.

Primero y lo más importante es elegir una variedad de estos cuatro grupos de alimentos cada día:
1 pan, otros cereales y patatas
2 fruta y verduras
3 leche y productos lácteos
4 carne y pescado
5 aceite, mantequilla, azúcar

Las comidas del quinto grupo que contienen grasa y azúcar pueden formar parte de tu régimen, pero solo si no sustituyen alimentos de los otros grupos. Tampoco es bueno comerlas en cantidades grandes o muy a menudo. Aprovechar de una amplia variedad de alimentos en tu dieta es importante para la salud. Por último, sigue los siguientes consejos adicionales:
- Disfruta de lo que comes.
- Come una dieta variada.
- Bebe mucha agua.
- Come lo suficiente para mantener un peso sano.
- Come muchos alimentos ricos en carbohidratos y fibra.
- Come mucha fruta y verdura.
- No comas demasiados alimentos con mucha grasa.
- No comas demasiados alimentos abundantes en azúcar.
- Si bebes alcohol, sé moderado.

1 Give two advantages of maintaining a healthy diet.
2 Which group of foods is least favourable to your health?
3 Name one item noted in each of the food groups 1–5.
4 What should you **not** do with fatty foods?
5 What are you told about drinking?

9 📖 ✏️ Copia y completa esta tabla añadiendo las palabras adecuadas del recuadro. ¿Cuántas palabras puedes añadir a la lista? Usa un diccionario para ayudarte.

Bread, cereals and starch	Vitamins and fibre	Dairy products	Meat/fish and alternatives	Sugar and fats
pan	naranjas	leche	pollo	mantequilla

zanahorias   queso   pasta   aceite   yogur
mermelada   atún   huevos   nata   arroz
manzanas   jamón   patatas   zumo de frutas

10 💬 Trabaja con tu pareja. Habla de las comidas que tomaste ayer. Decide si eran sanas o no.

Ejemplo: **A:** *Ayer comí pizza con patatas y bebí agua.*
B: *Eso no es sano. Debes tomar ensalada.*

11a 🎧 📖 Escucha a Ana y Carlos. ¿Qué comen y beben? Copia la tabla y complétala con la información correcta, utilizando las palabras del recuadro.

	Desayuno	Almuerzo	Merienda	Cena
Ana	cereales	ensalada		
Carlos	leche		yogur	carne

zumo de frutas   mantequilla   chocolate   pan   galletas
ensalada   cereales   café
mermelada   fruta   tostada
arroz   atún   carne   tortilla   leche
helado   sopa   pizza   yogur   pollo
carne   tarta   manzana   pescado   agua mineral

b 💬 Trabaja en pareja. Pregunta y contesta las siguientes preguntas.

- ¿Qué desayunas normalmente?
- ¿Dónde comes?
- ¿Qué comes?
- ¿Sueles merendar durante el día?
- ¿A qué hora cenas?
- ¿Qué sueles comer y beber para la cena?

12a 🎧 📖 Escucha y lee lo que dicen estas personas.
Luego copia y completa la tabla.

Normalmente no tengo tiempo para desayunar, pero sí tomo un vaso de agua y un vaso de zumo. Sé que no es sano y como consecuencia cuando llego al colegio estoy muerta de hambre. Durante el recreo suelo comer un plátano o una manzana. Luego por las tardes mi madre insiste que nos sentemos todos juntos a cenar en familia. Tomamos la cena a eso de las ocho y normalmente es algo como pasta con ensalada. No hago mucho deporte o ejercicio, pero voy al cole cada día en bici. No peso demasiado y eso probablemente es porque, como dicen en los estudios, no como suficiente. Mi madre siempre me da la lata con ello, pero por lo menos no fumo ni bebo alcohol.

Elena

Soy muy particular con respecto a la comida, según mis padres. No me gustan las verduras y solo tomo los refrescos con gas. Supongo que eso no es muy sano, pero no me importa. Sin embargo me gusta desayunar bien y cada día me tomo fruta con yogur. Me encantan el chocolate y los caramelos y como mucho de ello durante el día. Eso me da energía. La comida que más me gusta es la comida rápida. Hamburguesas y patatas es lo que compro para mi comida. Por las tardes tomamos pollo con patatas o algo así. ¿Deporte? ¡Nunca lo hago! Prefiero ver en vez de practicar.

Conchi

Generalmente me levanto a las 7 de la mañana, me ducho deprisa y después me siento a tomar un desayuno fuerte de cereales, leche y fruta. Durante el recreo tomo más fruta y a la hora de comer algo como ensalada con jamón o pollo. Después del cole hago natación y dos veces a la semana voy al gimnasio local. Por las tardes comemos arroz o patatas con pescado o carne. Me gusta acostarme bastante temprano durante la semana, pero no los fines de semana. ¿Fumar? ¡Ni hablar! ¡Es una locura!

Ramón

	Desayuno	Mediodía	Tarde	Otra información
Elena				
Ramón				
Conchi				

b ✏️ Escribe un párrafo sobre lo que comes y bebes y lo que haces para mantener la salud.

Ejemplo: *Suelo desayunar cereales con leche cada mañana.*
Intento no beber café o té porque no son buenos para la salud…

13 📖 Descifra estas palabras y emparéjalas con la imagen adecuada. Usa un diccionario para ayudarte.

Ejemplo: **a** — *mantel*

talpolil   cochulil   naltem

llivtersea   zaat   lapot

osva

rachacu   raraj   netoder

y las neitimpa

topal donoh

14 📖 Lee este artículo. Pon una X en las casillas con las cuatro frases correctas en la tabla abajo.

Querido Doctor David,

¿Me pregunto si es grosero comer con los codos en la mesa? Tengo dos hijos, de 9 y 10 años, que me miran con cara de alucine cuando les digo que eso no se hace. Le agradecería cualquier consejo sobre las buenas maneras en la mesa que pudiera ofrecerme. Quiero que mis hijos crezcan bien educados.

¡Espero que pueda ayudarme!
Una madre preocupada
Málaga

Querida preocupada,

En comidas informales es aceptable tener los codos encima de la mesa. Pero solo si no estás comiendo. Mientras comes, hay que evitarlo.

Sería aconsejable decirles a tus hijos que las normas de la mesa no solo tratan de comer educadamente, sino que también son consideración hacia los demás. Diles que aunque tú sabes que son majos y bien educados, los demás también les juzgarán.

Ser bien educado en la mesa da una buena impresión a los demás. Tus hijos no querrán ser maleducados. ¿Verdad?

No importa si estás en casa o en un restaurante, aquí hay diez normas básicas para tus hijos:

1 Come con cuchillo y tenedor a no ser que sea comida en plan estilo *buffet*. ¡Solo los bebés comen con sus dedos!

2 No te llenes la boca demasiado – queda horrible y no es sano.

3 Mastica siempre con la boca cerrada. Nadie quiere verte la comida. Eso quiere decir que no se debe hablar con comida en la boca.

4 No digas cosas despectivas sobre la comida que te sirvan. Eso ofende mucho.

5 Siempre di 'gracias' cuando alguien te sirve. Es cortesía básica y demuestra que aprecias al chef o al anfitrión.

6 No empieces hasta que todos tengan la comida servida en sus platos.

7 Come despacio. Alguien habrá pasado bastante tiempo preparando la comida, así que es apropiado disfrutarlo como es debido. Eso quiere decir que debes esperar por lo menos 5 segundos después de tragar antes de meter más comida en la boca.

8 No te asomes para coger algo por delante de otra persona – pide que te lo pasen.

9 Siempre usa una servilleta para limpiarte la boca o las manos. Mantén la servilleta en tus rodillas cuando no lo estás usando.

10 Siempre recuerda dar las gracias al cocinero y decirle lo delicioso que es la comida – ¡incluso si no te gustó!

Ejemplo:	*Normalmente hay que usar cuchillo y tenedor.*	**X**
1	No se debe mantener la boca cerrada.	
2	¡Habla y canta con la boca llena!	
3	Solo di cosas positivas sobre la comida servida.	
4	A veces hay que dar las gracias.	
5	Es de buena educación esperar a los demás.	
6	No hay que darse prisa comiendo.	
7	Las servilletas no sirven para nada.	
8	Hay que echar piropos al cocinero.	
9	Hay que pelear para conseguir la comida.	

2 De compras

- ☑ **Talk about shops and places of business**
- ☑ **Learn quantities, sizes and shapes**
- ☑ **Discuss eating out**
- ☑ **Use ordinal numbers**

1a 🎧 ¿Cómo es donde vives? Pon las imágenes en el orden en que oyes los lugares.

Ejemplo: **1 — c**

b 📖 Empareja las palabras con las imágenes.

Ejemplo: **a** *— la carnicería*

el quiosco de periódicos
la farmacia
Correos
la carnicería
el estanco
los grandes almacenes
la panadería
el supermercado
el mercado
la frutería
la librería
la pescadería
la tienda de ropa
el banco
la floristería

2a 🎧 📖 Escucha y lee el texto. Escribe el nombre de la persona que corresponda con las frases abajo.

Ejemplo: *Vive en una ciudad turística. — Alina*

> No me gusta mucho ir de compras, aunque sí compro música y revistas — cosas que me encantan — normalmente por Internet. Cerca de donde vivo no hay muchas tiendas interesantes, pero hay una ciudad grande a unos kilómetros. Aunque para mí es bastante difícil llegar.
>
> **Jesulín**

> A mí me encanta ir de compras, pero hay pocas tiendas en mi barrio. Para comprar comida normalmente vamos al centro comercial donde hay un supermercado bueno. Está bastante lejos, pero tiene un aparcamiento grande, así que es bastante práctico.
>
> **Vicky**

> Vivo en una zona turística así que te puedes imaginar que hay todo tipo de tiendas. Puedes comprar regalos y recuerdos para cualquiera. A veces voy a la ciudad de compras con mis amigos porque nos gustan los grandes almacenes y no hay muchos en nuestro pueblo. La verdad es que hay mayor surtido en la ciudad.
>
> **Alina**

> No suelo ir a la ciudad para comprar porque el supermercado del barrio tiene todo lo que necesito. En el centro no hay tantas tiendas y son bastante caras. En el supermercado de aquí las cosas tienen precios más razonables y a veces encuentras gangas.
>
> **Bernardo**

> Me encanta ir al mercado de mi barrio para comprar. Se puede comprar fruta y verduras frescas y hay mucha variedad. También venden ropa, libros y CDs. Tiene un ambiente animado gracias a toda la gente que compra allí.
>
> **Marina**

1 Dice que las compras son más baratas en su barrio.
2 No compra comida en su barrio.
3 Le entusiasma el ambiente de donde compra.
4 De vez en cuando va de compras a la ciudad — pero no sola.
5 Compra por Internet.
6 Le gusta leer.

b 💬 Trabaja con tu pareja. Pregunta y contesta las preguntas siguientes.

- ¿Te gusta ir de compras?
- ¿Qué tiendas hay en tu barrio?
- ¿Adónde vas normalmente para comprar?
- ¿Por qué?

3a 📖 Read this e-mail. Write down in English what Sergio says about shopping.

Ejemplo: bakery — opens early

¡Hola!

Me has pedido información sobre las tiendas de mi barrio. Sé que es muy diferente en Inglaterra y que no tenéis muchas tiendas pequeñas. Pero aquí en España todavía hay muchos locales pequeños – sobre todo en los barrios de las afueras y en los pueblos.

La gente no suele ir lejos para comprar, a pesar del sistema de transporte público maravilloso. Por ejemplo, tenemos una panadería donde compramos pan. Nos conviene porque abre temprano cada mañana, así que tenemos pan recién hecho cada día para desayunar.

La mayoría de la gente hace la compra en los supermercados porque es práctico y ahorra mucho tiempo, lo que supongo es una verdadera ventaja. Tenemos mercadillo los miércoles y sábados donde compramos fruta y verduras frescas. También hay hipermercados que normalmente se ubican en las afueras de las ciudades.

En todos los barrios suele haber una farmacia y a veces también una librería. Por todas partes hay quioscos donde se compran bonos de lotería o quinielas.

Para tiendas buenas especializadas – como las de ropa o música – hay que ir a las ciudades. En pueblos turísticos normalmente hay también tiendas de recuerdos. Las tiendas suelen estar abiertas más horas que en tu país, aunque las tiendas pequeñas cierran a la hora de comer y de echar la siesta.

Si compras en el barrio normalmente resulta barato. Sin embargo, en las ciudades las cosas suelen ser más caras.

Bueno, espero que esto te ayude con tus estudios – y que estés bien.

Por favor, escríbeme pronto con noticias tuyas.

Un abrazo,
Sergio

¡ojo!

Intenta acordarte de estas frases útiles que tienen que ver con las compras.

echar un vistazo	to have a look
buscar una ganga	to look for a bargain
tres por el precio de uno	three for the price of one
de oferta	on offer
las rebajas	the sales
la caja	the checkout/pay point
los probadores	the changing rooms

b 👥 Escribe una respuesta a Sergio. Háblale de las tiendas que hay donde vives y de tus hábitos a la hora de hacer la compra.

En mi barrio hay...

¿Dónde se compra?

4a 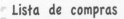 ¿Dónde se encuentra cada cosa en la lista de compras?

Ejemplo: **1** — *e*

Lista de compras

1 manzanas
2 leche
3 gambas
4 pasta de dientes
5 aceite
6 patatas fritas
7 mermelada
8 periódico
9 panecillos
10 limonada

Sección de congelados

Panadería

Pescadería

Quiosco

Frutería

Bebidas

Lácteos y huevos

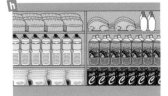

Sección de alimentación

Droguería

Ultramarinos

b ¿En qué tienda/puesto están? ¿Qué quieren comprar? ¿Cuánto gastan? Copia y completa la tabla.

	Puesto	Artículo	Precio
Ejemplo:	*frutería*	*naranjas*	*5,60€*
1			

5 Completa la lista siguiente añadiendo una cantidad apropiada.

Ejemplo: una lata de sardinas

Lista de compras

sardinas   pasteles
tomates   azúcar
jamón   aceitunas
queso   zanahorias
vino   café
leche   pan

6 Trabaja con tu pareja. Practica comprando comida y bebida.

¿Qué desea?   ¿Algo más?   ¿Tiene…?   ¿Cuánto es?

Quisiera…   Déme…   Eso es todo.

LENGUA CLAVE

un kilo	a kilo
medio kilo	half a kilo
un cuarto kilo	quarter of a kilo
cien gramos	100 grams
quinientos gramos	500 grams
un litro	a litre
medio litro	half a litre
un vaso	a glass
una botella	a bottle
una lata	a tin
un paquete	a packet
un pedazo	a slice
un trozo	a piece
una bolsa	a bag
una caja	a box
una docena	a dozen
un cartón	a carton
un tubo	a tube
una barra	a loaf

7 📖 En los grandes almacenes. Mira el directorio de abajo. ¿En qué planta se compra cada artículo?

Ejemplo: **a — 1a**

Directorio

6ª	Cafetería, Agencia de viajes
5ª	Electrónica, sonido, informática
4ª	Deportes
3ª	Moda Él y Ella
2ª	Regalos de boda y juguetes
1ª	Papelería
PB	Complementos moda: cinturones, bolsos, zapatos
Sot	Supermercado

6a	Sexta planta
5a	Quinta planta
4a	Cuarta planta
3a	Tercera planta
2a	Segunda planta
1a	Primera planta
PB	Planta baja
Sot	Sótano

8 💬 Trabaja con tu pareja. Usa el directorio de arriba. ¿Adónde hay que ir para ver las cosas en las imágenes?

Necesito unos zapatos   *Hay que ir a la planta baja.*

130

Ordinal numbers

An ordinal number is an adjective that describes the numerical position of an object, for example first, second, third etc.

Below are the ordinal numbers, first to tenth:

primero	first	*sexto*	sixth
segundo	second	*séptimo*	seventh
tercero	third	*octavo*	eighth
cuarto	fourth	*noveno*	ninth
quinto	fifth	*décimo*	tenth

Like many other adjectives, the ordinal numbers have both a masculine and a feminine form, singular and plural. In other words, ordinal numbers have four forms, just like other adjectives that end in *-o*.

For example:
primero(s), primera(s)
segundo(s), segunda(s)
tercero(s), tercera(s)

When used before a noun, *primero* and *tercero* drop the *-o* in the masculine singular form:
el primer día, el tercer año.

Ordinal numbers usually precede the noun. However, if the noun they refer to is royalty, a pope or a street, they come after the noun:

Isabel II (segunda)	'*segunda*' comes after 'Isabel' (royalty)
Alejandro VI (sexto)	'*sexto*' comes after 'Alejandro' (pope)
la calle octava	'*octava*' comes after 'calle' (street)

Ordinal numbers are not normally used after 10:
el siglo veintiuno   the twenty-first century

1st, 2nd, 3rd, 4th and so on are normally indicated in Spanish as *1°, 2°, 3°, 4°*.

Escoge la forma correcta del número en cada frase.

1 Vivo en el tercer/tercero piso.
2 Hay que ir al primer/a la primera planta.
3 Julio es el quinto/la quinta hijo de mi vecina.
4 Hoy es el primer/el primero/la primer de julio.

9 📖 Read the text and answer the questions that follow in English.

De compras en España

A pesar de la gran cantidad de supermercados e hipermercados que hay ahora en España — como en la mayor parte del mundo — todavía existen algunas tiendas que pertenecen a empresas familiares. Como en otros países, los centros comerciales, que ahora son tan populares, tienden a estar en los alrededores de las ciudades.

Horarios

Esto varía mucho entre regiones, ciudades, pueblos y también depende del tipo de tienda. Las tiendas pequeñas abren cada vez más horas para competir con sus rivales más grandes.

Las que siguen horarios tradicionales abren entre 08.30 y 09.30 (o más temprano si son tiendas de comida) y cierran de las 14.00 hasta las 17.00, y abren por la tarde hasta las 21.00. Este horario se debe a las temperatures altas que hay durante los meses de verano y justifican la popular siesta española — tan conocida en todo el mundo. Antes, en un país católico las tiendas no abrían los domingos. Ahora, sin embargo, se puede hacer compras todo el fin de semana sin problema. ¡Los tiempos han cambiado mucho!

Es menos común ahora, pero algunas tiendas pequeñas cierran un día entre semana y el domingo.

Muchos grandes almacenes y centros comerciales tienen horarios alargados — de 09.30 o 10.00 hasta las 20.00 o las 22.00 de lunes a sábado.

¿Qué comprar?

Se puede comprar de todo en España, pero los productos más populares entre turistas son artículos de cerámica y artesanía de cada región, vinos y dulces típicos. Calzado y ropa de cuero se venden mucho también, aunque los españoles se han dado cuenta del valor artístico de sus productos y hoy en día no suelen ser tan baratos como en el pasado. Además, ahora hay muchos diseñadores españoles famosos por todo el mundo — ¡Agata Ruíz de la Prada y Alfonso Domínguez son solo dos ejemplos!

Mercados

El mercado sigue siendo una institución en España. Todavía hay un mercado cubierto en cada barrio, donde se encuentran puestos de todo tipo de comida y bebida. Suelen seguir el mismo horario que las demás tiendas de los barrios.

En ciertos lugares hay mercados tradicionales cada semana o varias veces al mes donde se pueden ver calles enteras de puestos variados. Un buen ejemplo de esto es el Rastro de Madrid, famoso también por la cantidad de puestos dedicados a artículos de segunda mano. Son tan populares como aquí nuestros 'car boot sales'. Siempre se puede encontrar una ganga, pero como en todos los sitios ¡hay que tener cuidado con los posibles engaños y la seguridad personal! Como se suele decir, ¡no es oro todo lo que reluce!

1 What are you told about the building of new supermarkets and shopping centres in Spain?

2 What are you told about traditional shop opening and closing times in Spain?

3 Why do shops close during the middle of the day?

4 What are the most popular ítems on sale to tourists in markets?

5 What is the Rastro in Madrid famous for?

10 🎧 ¿A qué hora? Escucha los mensajes y emparéjalos con la hora adecuada.

Ejemplo: *1 — a*

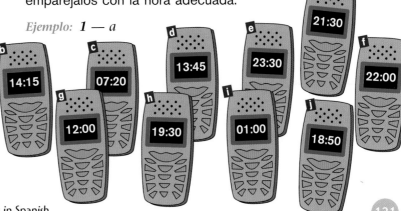

3 ¡A comer fuera!

1a 📖 Empareja las imágenes con las palabras adecuadas del menú. Usa un diccionario si hace falta.

Ejemplo: **b** — *fruta del tiempo*

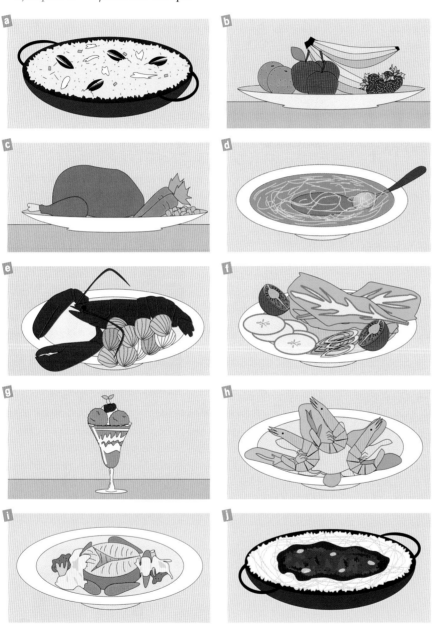

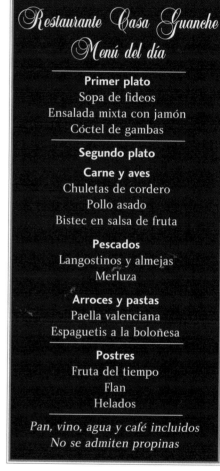

Restaurante Casa Guanche
Menú del día

Primer plato
Sopa de fideos
Ensalada mixta con jamón
Cóctel de gambas

Segundo plato

Carne y aves
Chuletas de cordero
Pollo asado
Bistec en salsa de fruta

Pescados
Langostinos y almejas
Merluza

Arroces y pastas
Paella valenciana
Espaguetis a la boloñesa

Postres
Fruta del tiempo
Flan
Helados

Pan, vino, agua y café incluidos
No se admiten propinas

b 🎧 ¿Qué pide cada persona? Copia y completa la tabla con los detalles que faltan.

	Primer plato	Segundo plato	Postre
Ejemplo:	*sopa*	*chuletas*	*helado*
1			

2 🎧 Pon las imágenes en el orden correcto según el diálogo.

3a 🎧 📖 Escucha el diálogo.
Pon las frases en el orden correcto.

1. *Para empezar, para mí, paté, y para mi amigo melón.*
2. *De acuerdo.*
3. *¿Y qué quieren para beber?*
4. *Un helado de piña para mí y para mi amigo un helado de vainilla.*
5. *Gracias. Tráiganos el menú, por favor.*
6. *Muy bien. ¿Y de segundo plato?*
7. *Entonces, dos helados de vainilla.*
8. *Pollo con patatas para dos, por favor.*
9. *Una botella de vino tinto y una botella de agua mineral con gas.*
10. *¿Y de postre?*
11. *Buenas tardes. ¿Tiene una mesa para dos personas?*
12. *Aquí tiene. ¿Qué van a tomar?*
13. *Sí. Hay esta mesa aquí, en la terraza.*
14. *Lo siento, señor, pero de piña no hay.*

GRAMÁTICA

Disjunctive pronouns

Look at the following example phrase from the dialogue in Exercise 3a:

Para *mí* paté.   Pâté for *me*.

Here, *mí* is a disjunctive pronoun. It is used because the word *mí* (me) follows the preposition *para* (for). Disjunctive pronouns are used after prepositions and are listed in the table below.

	Singular	Plural
First person	*mí* (me)	*nosotros/as* (us)
Second person	*ti* (you) *usted*	*vosotros/as* (you)
Third person	*él* (him) *ella* (her)	*ellos* (them) *ellas*

Escribe estas frases en español.

1 A coffee for me and a tea for her.
2 I'd like chicken for them, Pablo and Juan.
3 Water for him and wine for us.
4 An ice cream for her and fruit for him.
5 Ana and María? A glass of water for them.

b 💬 Trabaja con tu pareja. Practica el diálogo.
Inventa tus propias conversaciones.

4 📖 Busca la palabra intrusa. Usa un diccionario para ayudarte.

Ejemplo: desayuno almuerzo cena **comedor** merienda

1 zumo	naranja	pomelo	melocotón
2 sopa	consomé	tortilla	gazpacho
3 merluza	gambas	bacalao	cerdo
4 carne	pescado	aves	legumbres
5 arroz	postre	pasta	patatas
6 queso	mantequilla	huevos	leche

5 Read the article and answer the questions that follow in English.

Las regiones culinarias de España

España está rodeada de mar; tiene tres lados de costas. En el norte tiene el mar Cantábrico; al oeste está el océano Atlántico y hacia el este hay el mar Mediterráneo. Justo al otro lado del estrecho de Gibraltar están Marruecos y Argelia. Con tantas millas de costa se puede entender por qué los españoles comen tanto marisco y pescado. En el pasado, las barreras naturales — sobre todo las cadenas monañosas — hicieron difícil la comunicación entre las regiones. Así, aunque ciertos ingredientes, como el aceite de oliva y el ajo, son comunes, se desarrollaron diferencias importantes entre las regiones. Los alimentos de cada región son, en general, sencillos y típicos de la zona. Los españoles tienen una dieta bien muy variada y sana.

España se caracteriza por la diversidad culinaria de sus regiones.

¡Hola! Me llamo Arturo y soy de Bilbao en el norte de España. Mi región es famosa por el pescado, sobre todo el bacalao. También comemos mucho marisco, cordero y verduras.

Soy María de la zona montañosa de los Pirineos. Somos muy conocidos en España por nuestros pimientos, tomates y cebollas.

Soy Marcelo de Guadalajara en el centro de España. Aquí comemos mucha carne: cerdo, cordero y ternera. Son conocidos nuestros quesos, como el delicioso queso Manchego, uno de los mejores quesos del mundo.

Soy Ángel. Mi región es Andalucía en el sur de España. Cultivamos mucha fruta aquí. Esta zona es famosa por sus aceitunas y exportamos el aceite de oliva a países de todo el mundo. Quizás nuestro plato más famoso es el gazpacho, una sopa fría hecha de tomates y pepino. ¡Qué rico!

Me llamo Juan y soy de Barcelona en Cataluña. Lo más típico de allí son nuestros guisos de carne o pescado. También son conocidos los embutidos.

Hola! Soy Alicia y soy de Valencia en el este. Esta región es famosa por el arroz y sus platos típicos como la paella. ¡Deberías probarla!

1 Why do the Spanish eat a lot of fish?
2 Which region is famous for its cheese?
3 What are the main ingredients of *gazpacho*?
4 Where in Spain is rice the staple diet?
5 What meat can you find in particular in central Spain?

6a Completa lo siguiente eligiendo las palabras adecuadas de la lista de abajo.

¡Hola! ____ Ana. Soy de Lancashire en el ____ de Inglaterra. Mi región es famosa por sus productos lácteos, como el ____ . También comemos mucho ____ aquí porque estamos cerca de la costa atlántica. Nuestro plato más famoso es el Lancashire Hotpot. Es un ____ hecho de ____ y ____ .

> guiso soy pescado norte
> queso patatas cordero

b Prepara una breve presentación sobre los platos típicos de tu región. Usa el ejemplo arriba para ayudarte.

7 📖 Lee la receta. Empareja las instrucciones con la imagen adecuada.

Ejemplo: a — Añade los tomates, guisantes, gambas y azafrán.

Paella Valenciana

Ingredientes
4 tazas de arroz de paella
8 tazas de caldo de pescado
8 langostinos
8 mejillones
200 gramos de gambas (50 gramos sin pelar)
200 gramos de guisantes (frescos o congelados)
2 tomates, pelados y trozeados
2 dientes de ajo picados
unos hilos de azafrán machacados
cuartos de limón
aceite de oliva para freír

Método
1 Fríe el ajo en la paellera.
2 Añade los tomates, guisantes, gambas y azafrán.
3 Cocínalo durante unos minutos.
4 Añade el arroz y el caldo.
5 Cuece durante aproximadamente veinte minutos.
6 Cuece el marisco durante unos minutos.
7 Decora con gambas y mejillones.
8 Decora la paella con cuartos de limón.
9 Sirve directamente de la paellera.

8a 📖 Lee las instrucciones para preparar la tortilla. Usando un diccionario para ayudarte, explica lo que significa cada palabra o frase en negrita en el texto.

Ejemplo: **1** *pela — peel*

Tortilla española

Ingredientes
4 huevos
$\frac{1}{2}$ kilo de patatas
una cebolla
un pimiento
aceite
sal y pimiento

Método
1 **Pela** las cebollas y las patatas.
2 **Pica** las cebollas en trozos no muy pequeños y ponlas a freír en una sartén con abundante aceite.
3 Mientras tanto pica las patatas en dados, sazónalas y añádelas a la sartén. **Corta** el pimiento y **fríe** todo a fuego medio, removiendo de vez en cuando, hasta que se dore todo un poco. Retíralo y escúrrelo.
4 **Prepara** un recipiente y **bate** los 4 huevos. **Añade** las patatas, cebollas y pimiento.
5 **Pon** un poco de aceite en una sartén y vierte la mezcla. **Cuaja** el huevo, primero a fuego vivo y después un poco más suave. **Da la vuelta** a la tortilla para que se dore por ambos lados y **sírvela** caliente con una ensalada.

¡OJO!

The *tú* imperative form is generally used to give recipe instructions.

-ar	-er	-ir
corta	cuece	sirve

Corta la carne.
Cut the meat.

Cuece el marisco durante 20 minutos.
Cook the shellfish for 20 minutes.

Sirve caliente.
Serve hot.

b Escribe una receta.

La comida rápida. ¿Cuáles conoces?

A pesar de la enorme expansión en los siglos XX y XXI de la industria que proporciona la comida rápida, todavía quedan muchas tradiciones interesantes con respecto a la comida y la merienda callejera. ¿Cuántos de estos conoces?

Tapas españolas

'Tapas' es como se denomina una gran variedad de platos que 'se pican' (se toman) normalmente en bares y cafeterías. Tradicionalmente se sirven acompañando a vinos y cañas para **reducir los efectos** del alcohol cuando se bebe con el estómago vacío. Las tapas pueden ser servidas frías, como aceitunas, jamón curado o queso, o calientes, **como por ejemplo** la tortilla, el pollo, el pescado o patatas.

Como pueden ser apreciadas por **cualquiera** que las pruebe, hoy en día hay bares y restaurantes por todo el mundo donde se sirven las tapas. En muchos de esos lugares, **a pesar de** las tradiciones, se piden varias tapas diferentes para completar una comida o una cena entera. Algunos creen que las tapas tienen su origen en tiempos de Alfonso X. Como el Rey solo podía tomar porciones pequeñas de comida, solía preferir picar **cantidades muy escasas** con un buen vaso de vino.

Churros

Churros, **a menudo descritos como** 'el donut español', son cintas de masa fritas en aceite hirviendo. A menudo se venden de puestos que se encuentran por las calles. En España **son muy populares** como desayuno y por eso se sirven en bares y cafeterías.

Salchipapas

A todo el mundo le encantan los perros calientes, pero en Ecuador y Perú son muy especiales. ¡Una salchipapa es la comida rápida de Latinoamérica! Se preparan en el momento y se venden en la calle. **Proporcionan** una merienda deliciosa **compuesta de** lonchas de salchicha frita y servida con patatas fritas, huevo frito y salsa picante o mayonesa. ¡**Exquisito**!

Méjico

Méjico D. F. es una de las ciudades del mundo donde más puestos de comida rápida se encuentran. Hay uno **en cada esquina** y venden todo tipo de comida y plato rápido. Seguro que conoces los *tacos*, pero ¿**has oído hablar de** las tortas? Una torta es como un bocadillo mejicano **hecho con** ricos panecillos rellenos de todo tipo de ingrediente: aguacate, carne picada, pollo, pescado o judías. ¡Es un manjar que **no se debe perder**!

Colombia

Una comida rápida que se encuentra por zonas de Colombia, como Medellín, es la deliciosa torta *choclo* con queso. Básicamente es una torta de maíz frita rellena de queso. ¡Son deliciosas y **muy baratas**!

Por todas partes de América del Sur se encuentran puestos que venden zumos o 'jugos'. Como allí tienen tantas frutas exóticas, hay un gran surtido de sabores: maracuyá (de color amarilla), granadilla (de color naranja), papyuala, lulo (de color naranja), e higo. También **es muy popular** el zumo de papaya.

¡Hasta se venden postres! En Bogotá, por ejemplo, muy típicos son **raciones de** tarta de queso o vasitos de arroz con leche.

Chile – empanadas

Lo que más se ve por las calles en Chile son puestos de empanadas. Hechas de hojaldre, rellenas de muchos ingredientes diferentes, y fritas, son deliciosas y **fáciles de servir**. Se meten todo tipo de carne, queso, salsas, pescado — ¡lo que haya! Tienen nombres especiales también! El pino, por ejemplo, contiene carne picada, cebolla, pasas, aceitunas y trozos de huevo duro. Otra se llama *la mariscona*, y tiene marisco frito con un poco de espinacas.

a 📝 Copia las palabras y frases en negrita del texto. Encuentra los equivalentes en inglés en la lista abajo.

Ejemplo: **1** *sentirse los efectos* — feel the effects

> anyone
> very cheap   on every corner   portions of
> not to be missed   in spite of   reduce the effects
> very small amounts   easy to serve   made with
> like, for example   is very popular
> delicious   they provide
> have you heard of...?   often described as
> they are very popular   consisting of

b 📖 Lee las frases siguientes y decide si son verdaderas (V) o falsas (F).

Ejemplo: **1** *— V*

1 *Las tapas son típicamente españolas.*
2 Las tapas son postres.
3 Las tapas son normalmente raciones pequeñas.
4 Los churros se toman normalmente por las mañanas.
5 Las salchipapas se sirven en restaurantes muy elegantes.
6 No hay comida rápida en Méjico.
7 La torta *choclo* se prepara usando aceite.
8 A los sudamericanos no les gusta la fruta.
9 En Sudamérica no suelen tomar postres.
10 Una empanada contiene muchos ingredientes.

10 📖 📝 Ahora busca comida típica callejera del mundo hispanohablante. Usa Internet y prepara una pequeña presentación sobre la información que has encontrado. Escribe una lista de páginas web útiles para tus compañeros.

Ejemplo:

En Guatemala se come mucho los rellenitos de plátano. Estos plátanos están fritos. Se preparan en casa para el desayuno o se compran en un puesto de la calle. Son muy fáciles de preparar y son deliciosos.

4 ¡Vivir a tope!

☑ Talk about youth issues
☑ Give opinions
☑ Use the subjunctive mood

1 📖 Lee el texto.

¿Eres un joven a quien le importa el mundo a su alrededor? ¿Tienes opiniones sobre los asuntos que afectan a los jóvenes hoy en día?

De momento estamos trabajando juntos para representar las opiniones de la juventud sobre los siguientes temas importantes:

- el terrorismo
- los malos tratos
- las oportunidades para jóvenes
- el medio ambiente
- la inmigración
- la seguridad ciudadana
- el sexo sin riesgos
- la delincuencia
- las drogas
- el tabaco y el alcohol

¿Quieres mejorar tu mundo y ayudar a los demás? Si la respuesta es 'Sí', únete al Foro Juventud y ¡juntos haremos una diferencia!

Busca más información en nuestra página Web **www.osce.org**

CULTURA

El Foro Juventud is the Spanish branch of the European Youth Forum, which works to empower young people to actively participate in the shaping of Europe and the society in which they live.

a 📖 🗻 Estudia esta lista de temas y empareja la palabra o frase española con el inglés adecuado. Usa un diccionario para ayudarte.

el terrorismo	smoking and alcohol
los malos tratos	the environment
oportunidades para jóvenes	immigration
el medio ambiente	terrorism
la inmigración	bullying/abuse
la seguridad ciudadana	safety in the streets
el sexo sin riesgos	opportunities for young people
la delincuencia	drugs
las drogas	safe sex
el tabaco y el alcohol	crime and delinquency

b 📖 Lee lo que dicen estos jóvenes europeos y decide qué tema de la lista del texto les interesa.

Ejemplo: **1** *Marlene — el terrorismo*

Tengo miedo de un ataque terrorista.
Marlene (Alemania)

Me interesa proteger el planeta.
François (Francia)

En mi ciudad hay muchos problemas de delincuencia.
Callum (Reino Unido)

Muchos de mis amigos fuman.
Sven (Suecia)

Hay que ser responsable con las relaciones sexuales.
Marta (España)

Creo que es cada vez más fácil comprar sustancias ilegales.
Giovanni (Italia)

En mi pueblo hay demasiada gente de otros países.
Linda (Holanda)

Tengo problemas en el colegio con los alumnos mayores.
Alex (Polonia)

No sé qué podría hacer en el futuro.
Pietre (Austria)

Quiero salir sin tener miedo de que me pase algo.
Isolde (Dinamarca)

c 💬 Practica este diálogo para saber lo que piensan tus amigos. Pregúntales qué temas de la lista son los más preocupantes.

¿Cuál crees que es más preocupante — el terrorismo o la delincuencia?

Creo que el terrorismo es más preocupante que la delincuencia, pero menos que el problema de abuso del alcohol entre los jóvenes.

2 🎧 Listen to these teenagers telling stories about things that have happened to them. Write notes in English for points 1 to 9 about what happened, and decide which category applies to each of the stories.

What happened: Maria went to her tutor because some children in her class started to pick on her. She says the teacher is going to speak to them, but she doubts if it will do any good.

Category: Bullying (los malos tratos — bullying and abuse)

GRAMÁTICA

Giving opinions

If you want to say 'I don't think…', expressing an opinion that something will not happen, for example 'I don't think it will rain' or 'I doubt if there's a solution', you have to use the subjunctive. The subjunctive is not a tense but a 'mood' of the verb. It can be used in several tenses. The present tense of the subjunctive is formed as follows:

-ar verbs	-er verbs	-ir verbs
comprar	*vender*	*vivir*
compre	*venda*	*viva*
compres	*vendas*	*vivas*
compre	*venda*	*viva*
compremos	*vendamos*	*vivamos*
compréis	*vendáis*	*viváis*
compren	*vendan*	*vivan*

For example:
No creo que compre esa camisa. — I don't think he will buy that shirt.

Es improbable que vendamos nuestra casa. — It is unlikely we will sell our house.

Dudo que viva mucho mi hámster.
I doubt if my hamster will live very long.

There are a number of verbs that are irregular in the subjunctive form. These include *ser* and *estar*:

ser	estar
sea	*esté*
seas	*estés*
sea	*esté*
seamos	*estemos*
seáis	*estéis*
sean	*estén*

For example:
No creo que esté muy contento de momento. — I don't think he/she is very happy at the moment.

Dudo que sean ricos. — I doubt if they are rich.

No quiero que hagas eso. — I don't want you to do that.

Hay (there is/there are), from the verb *haber*, also has a subjunctive form, *haya*. For example:

No creo que haya suficiente comida para todos. — I don't think there will be enough food for everyone.

Es posible que haya nubes. — It's possible that it will be cloudy.

Read these grammar notes carefully, then work out how to say the following phrases and write them down:

Example: I don't think there is a drugs problem in my school.
*No creo que **haya** problema de drogas en mi colegio.*

1 I don't think the environment is very important.
2 I don't think youth crime is a problem.
3 I doubt if we do enough to help the environment.
4 It's not likely there will be a lot of opportunities for young people.
5 I don't believe we buy enough recyclable things.
6 It's unlikely that we'll be living in the same kind of houses in the future.
7 In the Third World I doubt if there is adequate education about safe sex.
8 I don't think my new boyfriend smokes.
9 I doubt if it will rain.
10 Most young people don't believe drugs are good for your health.

3a 📖 Lee estos pósteres y empareja las frases abajo con el póster adecuado (A o B).

Ejemplo: *Trata del medio ambiente. — A*

1 Explica cómo proteger el mundo.
2 Da consejos sobre cómo evitar ataques personales.
3 Dice que debes mantener el contacto.
4 Dice que siempre tienes que tener compañía por las calles.
5 Quiere que ahorres energía.
6 Dice que tienes que dar buen ejemplo.
7 Tienes que presionar a la gente.
8 Dice que no te fíes de los desconocidos.
9 Aconseja que no vayas a sitios donde sería fácil cometer un crimen.
10 Te anima a promocionar la causa.

a

Ayúdenos a mejorar nuestro entorno

- Sea firme con la gente.
- Anímeles a respetar el mundo que es de todos.
- No deje que tiren basura.
- Haga que apaguen los aparatos electrónicos mientras no se usan.
- Sea ejemplar — una persona que evita usar el coche lo máximo posible.

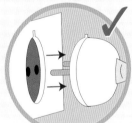

b

¿Sabes cuidarte en las calles?

Sigue estas reglas básicas y podrás salir sin miedo.

¡Que te lo pases muy bien!

- Cuéntales siempre a tus padres donde estás, con quién, cómo vas a volver y a qué hora.
- No salgas solo por la noche — vete por lo menos con otro amigo.
- No vayas a sitios aislados — quédate donde haya luz y gente.
- Si vas a beber hazlo con amigos que te cuiden.
- Nunca pierdas de vista tu bebida y no te vayas nunca solo con alguien desconocido.
- Lleva tu teléfono móvil siempre y ten un plan previsto por si lo pierdes o te quedas sin crédito.

*No te olvides de las reglas
*Que todos lo pasemos bien
*¡Ten cuidado!

b Elige otro de los temas identificados por el Foro Juventud (ver ejercicio 1a) y prepara tu propio póster sobre él. Intenta usar el subjuntivo.

GRAMÁTICA

The imperative and present subjunctive forms

The imperative and the present subjunctive between them supply the Spanish commands (Do this!) and exhortative forms (Let's go! Let him try! May you be sorry!).

Informal (*tú/vosotros*) commands: the imperative form is used only in affirmative *tú/vosotros* commands.

Compra estos vaqueros.	Buy these jeans.
Aprended esta gramática.	Learn this grammar.

All negative commands use the subjunctive form.

No esperes más.	Don't wait any longer.
No desesperes.	Don't despair.

Formal (*usted*) commands: the subjunctive form is always used for formal commands, affirmative and negative.

Siga las instrucciones.	Follow the instructions.
No tire basura.	Don't throw rubbish.

The conjunction *que* generally introduces the exhortative forms in the third person (utterances with an implied 'Let them…')

Que venga ella si quiere.	Let her come if she wants to.
Que compren DVDs.	Let them buy DVDs.

Study the verb forms of the imperative in the singular then do the two tasks that follow it. If you are unsure of the imperative form of a verb, consult the verb tables at the back of the book.

Verb	Imperative (*tú*)	Negative Imperative (*tú*)	Imperative (*usted*), affirmative and negative
mirar (to look at)	*mira*	*no mires*	*mire/no mire*
ser (to be)	*sé*	*no seas*	*sea/no sea*
decidir (to decide)	*decide*	*no decidas*	*decida/no decida*
salir (to go out)	*sal*	*no salgas*	*salga/no salga*

Exercise A: choose the correct form of the singular imperative of the verbs in brackets, using the *tú* form.

Ejemplo: Por favor, _____ (hablar) más despacio.
    Por favor, habla más despacio.

1 _____ (mirar) a aquella chica. Se parece a tu hermana.
2 Javier, ¡_____ (comer) más rápido!
3 _____ (salir) a las ocho si no te llamo antes.
4 Marga, ¡_____ (darme) el boli enseguida!
5 No me _____ (esperar) después de medianoche.
6 ¡_____ (hacer) tus deberes!
7 ¡No _____ (ser) tonta, María!
8 Por favor, _____ (venir) a las ocho en punto.

Exercise B: translate the sentences, using the appropriate form of the singular imperative.

Ejemplo: Look at the picture.   *Mira la imagen.*
    Don't look at the sun.   *No mires el sol.*
    Let him look behind him.   *Que mire hacia atrás.*

1 Don't be stupid.
2 Let her decide what she wants to do.
3 Get out of the room!
4 Look at the film.
5 Let it be a girl!
6 Decide quickly, please.
7 Don't go out alone.
8 Be responsible with your litter.
9 Don't decide the environment isn't important.
10 Let her look where she is going.

4 🎧 📖 Escucha el problema que menciona cada persona. Entonces lee las posibles soluciones. Empareja el problema (1–10) con la imagen (a–j) y con una solución escogida de la lista (i–x). Rellena la tabla.

Problema (1–10)	Imagen (a–j)	Solución (i–xi)
Ejemplo:	*g*	*i*
2		

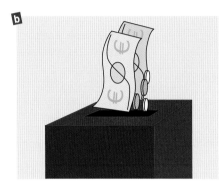

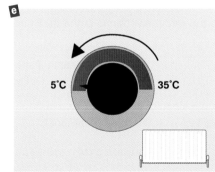

Por un Futuro más limpio, Recicla

Todo Tipo de Vidrio

Soluciones

i Lo que deberíamos hacer es pensar bien en cuanto gastamos. Podríamos ducharnos en vez de bañarnos y poner algo en la cisterna del wáter para reducir el volumen de agua.

ii Debería haber más policías en la calle para evitar problemas, y mejor educación sobre cómo respetar a otras personas — cómo cuidarlas y tratarlas bien. Podríamos apreciar mucho más a los viejos y aprender de ellos. Son muy interesantes.

iii ¡La gente debería ser menos perezosa! Podríamos contaminar menos reduciendo el uso de vehículos que consumen gasolina o gasóleo. En cambio deberíamos andar más, usar el transporte público y sacar la bicicleta. ¡Sería mucho más sano también!

iv El gobierno debería dar más dinero a los científicos que investigan otros combustibles para proporcionar nuestra energía. Sin nuevas tecnologías no vamos a encontrar ninguna solución. Ahora se puede aprovechar el viento y el agua. ¡Hay que espabilarse!

v Podríamos reciclar mucho más. De compras, por ejemplo, podrías devolver tus bolsas de plástico al supermercado para que se reciclen. ¡Todo ayuda!

vi Hay que ocupar a los jóvenes. Las autoridades podrían hacer más para animarles a estudiar o a ayudar a los demás. Muchos dicen que deberíamos empezar de nuevo el servicio militar.

vii Deberíamos seguir el ejemplo de varias religiones del mundo que toman como una obligación moral dar un porcentaje de nuestros bienes a los pobres. Podríamos fácilmente dar un poco cada mes a una institución de caridad, por ejemplo.

viii Podríamos malgastar menos y apreciar más lo que tenemos antes de tirar tanto. Sería muy fácil también comprar cosas de Comercio Justo para ayudar a los pobres. Me gustaría que nadie en este mundo tuviese hambre. ¡Ojalá que no fuera un sueño!

ix Deberíamos prohibir fumar en todos los lugares — dentro y fuera — y deberían poner más difícil el comprar alcohol, sobre todo para los jóvenes.

x Debería ser muy fácil apagar los aparatos cuando no están en uso. Se puede poner aislamiento en las paredes y los techos. ¿Y por qué no regulamos un poquito las temperaturas de la calefacción o el aire acondicionado?

¡ojo!

To give suggestions of possible action rather than orders (using imperative forms), the conditional tense of verbs needs to be used. Before you start the writing activity, check the formation of the conditional tense and note especially the verb endings.

Examples:
Vendería la casa. He/She would sell the house.
Debería ahorrar energía. He/She should save energy.
Viviría en Gran Canaria. I would live in Gran Canaria.

Note down the conditional verbs used in the list of solutions above and write what they mean in English. Use a dictionary to help you.

5a Escribe al Foro Juventud sobre los problemas que existen donde vives y si puedes, ofrece soluciones. Usa los problemas y soluciones de arriba para ayudarte. Empieza tu carta así.

Málaga 6 de enero
Hola chicos del foro,
Les estoy escribiendo para contarles lo que me preocupa de mi pueblo.
En primer lugar ____
____ Yo creo que deberíamos ____ etc.

b Ahora prepara una pequeña presentación de 2 a 3 minutos sobre uno de los temas identificados por el foro. Explica tus opiniones y cómo solucionarías el problema.

Ejemplo: ¡Hola! Me llamo Francisco y tengo dieciséis años.
Me interesa proteger el planeta.
Soy ecólogo.
En mi opinión el medio ambiente es muy, muy importante.
El mundo está en peligro.
En un mundo ideal la gente no consumiría tanta energía…

Paper 1: listening

Hints to answer the question

- Special skills are needed to tackle this type of question:
  - Listen for the speakers' tone of voice as they enthuse about positive points and the reverse for negative points.
  - Positive and negative points may be found at any point of the dialogue.
  - There is frequently more than one way of expressing a correct answer.
- Read the instructions and listen to the extract before you look at the answers. Jot down the positive and negative points and see how many you get right.

Cenar fuera

¿Qué dicen estos chicos?
What do these young people say?

Escribe **en español** en la tabla 3 aspectos positivos y 3 aspectos negativos, según lo que dicen.
Write **in Spanish** in the grid 3 positive aspects and 3 negative aspects, according to what they say.

Aspectos positivos
Ejemplo: La carne es buena.
(i)
(ii)
(iii)
Aspectos negativos
(i)
(ii)
(iii)

(Total for Question = 6 marks)

Sample student answer

Aspectos positivos
Ejemplo: La carne es buena.
(i) El menú es variado
(ii) (Hay) buena relación calidad-precio
(iii) (Usan) productos frescos
Aspectos negativos
(i) (Algunos) camareros (son) antipáticos
(ii) (Hay) demasiada gente
(iii) Hay que esperar mucho

Los precios son razonables or *La calidad es buena* would have been acceptable here too.

Note how in some answers not all the words are obligatory — those in brackets are not.

Paper 2: reading

Here is a multiple-choice reading question relevant to this module, about how to improve our world. For each speaker, one of the three possible answers given is correct.

Jóvenes idealistas

Lee estas opiniones. Read these opinions.

> Es importante el desarme de los países. Deben terminar con los conflictos y promover la paz.

Juan

> Necesitamos una reunión de las grandes naciones en la que trabajen juntas de forma positiva para el bien de todos.

Jorge

> Sólo las personas felices pueden crear un mundo feliz. Esas personas son fuertes y positivas e influyen en los demás.

Cristina

> Lo imprescindible es proteger el medio ambiente y reducir el impacto del cambio climático.

Santi

> Es hora de dar, en vez de pedir tanto, y de pensar en los demás.

Luz

> Para mí, la clave es escuchar a los demás para llegar a entenderse mejor.

Penélope

Escoge la frase que más conviene con el texto.
Choose the sentence which best matches the text.

Ejemplo: Juan

☒	**A** Habla de buscar la paz.
☐	**B** Le gustan los conflictos.
☐	**C** El mundo puede ser feliz sin desarmarse.

(i) Jorge

☐	**A** El bien de todos es un objetivo imposible.
☐	**B** No conseguiremos la paz, aun si todos los ciudadanos del mundo se reúnen.
☐	**C** Es necesaria la cooperación internacional.

(ii) Cristina

☐	**A** Sólo las personas fuertes pueden conseguir la felicidad.
☐	**B** Es necesario influir en la gente feliz para crear un mundo mejor.
☐	**C** La felicidad puede ser contagiosa.

(iii) Santi

☐	**A** La ecología no importa nada.
☐	**B** Hay que cuidar el planeta.
☐	**C** Debemos luchar contra el cambio.

(iv) Luz

☐	**A** Hay que dejar de ser egoísta.
☐	**B** Si no pensamos en nosotros mismos, no conseguiremos nada.
☐	**C** Cambiaremos el mundo si pedimos más.

(v) Penélope

☐	**A** Es imprescindible que los demás escuchen nuestra voz.
☐	**B** El que sabe escuchar bien entiende a los demás.
☐	**C** Hacerse el sordo es una buena manera de salirse con la suya.

(Total for Question = 5 marks)

Hints to answer the question

- The correct answers rephrase ideas that are expressed in the statements.
- Look out for synonyms or phrases that relate to a key idea (e.g. in (iii) *cuidar el planeta* echoes Santi's statement *proteger el medio ambiente*).

Paper 2: writing

Sample student answer

Opinions are important – the candidate goes on to explain at length why he/she has that opinion. Be careful though, *opinión* requires an accent on the 'o'.

Effective use of connective.

Remember that *gente* is always followed by the verb in the singular, unlike 'people' in English.

The student rightly introduces a fresh idea with a new paragraph.

A good phrase, but be careful with the spelling of *posible*. Cognates are not all spelled exactly the same as in English.

Good use of a link phrase for expressing an opinion.

Good use of *gustar* construction.

Wrong gender: many nouns ending in -ma are masculine.

En mi opinion, los gobiernos no hacen lo suficiente por mejorar nuestro mundo. En primer lugar, podrían hacer a los ricos dar dinero a las personas que mueren de hambre. Si los ricos no ayudan, la gente pobre puede sublevarse. Luego, los gobiernos tienen que remediar los conflictos sociales.

Un otro problema es el medio ambiente. Todavía no hacemos todo lo possible para reciclar y deberíamos explorar más las energías alternativas, como la electricidad solar y la energía del viento y del mar. Sé que todos somos responsibles y hay poco tiempo. Si no hacemos nada, el planeta va a calentarse demasiado y entonces el problema será más grave. Desde mi punto de vista, los gobiernos deben hacer más. A muchos políticos del Tercer Mundo les gusta el poder y son corruptos; han utilizado su dinero para construir grandes casas y para comprar propiedades en los países más desarrollados. La sistema en los países subdesarrollados no es siempre democrática; hay que dar más poder a los ciudadanos.

Por is incorrect here and should be *para*. It is wise to revise these prepositions thoroughly so that you don't confuse them.

Good use of the conditional.

Effective use of connective.

A future tense (*tendrán*) or conditional (*tendrían*) could have been used here.

Be careful with *otro*: it is not preceded by an indefinite article. This should be *Otro problema*.

Good, relevant vocabulary.

Be careful with cognates; this should be *responsables*.

This new idea warrants a new paragraph.

Unnecessary, repeated idea; shows a lack of planning.

Consequential error of agreement.

Hints to answer the question

- To achieve the best marks, be sure to cover each of the four points more or less equally.
- Any extensive piece of writing requires *planning*, i.e. putting your ideas in order:
    - Use a new paragraph to introduce a fresh idea.
    - Avoid repeating your ideas.
- Ensure that you express your opinions clearly.

Paper 3: speaking (section B)

Topic area D: The modern world and the environment

Straightforward questions:
- *¿Qué haces en casa para ayudar a cuidar el medio ambiente?*
- *¿Qué haces para ayudar a proteger el medio ambiente en tu instituto?*
- *¿Te parece importante el medio ambiente?*

Extension questions:
- *En tu opinión, ¿cuál es el problema más grave relacionado con el medio ambiente?*
- *¿Crees que los jóvenes pasan demasiado tiempo viendo la televisión?*
- *¿Cuáles son los principales problemas sociales en tu país?*
- *¿Por qué los jóvenes (no) están interesados en las noticias?*
- *En el mundo actual, ¿cuáles son los temas que más interesan a los jóvenes?*

Topic area E: Social activities, fitness and health

Straightforward questions:
- *¿Vas de compras con frecuencia? ¿Adónde? ¿Qué compras?*
- *¿Qué haces para mantenerte en forma?*

Extension questions:
- *¿Qué importancia tienen para ti el deporte y la música?*
- *¿Por qué es importante tener tiempo libre?*
- *¿Cómo se podría mejorar la vida de los jóvenes en tu ciudad/región?*
- *¿Llevas una vida sana?*
- *¿Qué piensas de fumar/del alcohol/de las drogas?*
- *¿Por qué algunas personas son vegetarianas?*

Look through this module. What other questions can you find?

🎧 Listen to the following sample answer for one of the extension questions above. When you have studied it, try preparing a selection of your own responses. Practise them with a classmate.

Sample student answer

¿Cómo se podría mejorar la vida de los jóvenes en tu ciudad?

Good use of conditional.

Variation of tenses – imperfect here.

Acceptable use of colloquialism.

Good use of conditional.

Para mí, sería sencillo mejorar la vida de los jóvenes en mi barrio. Solo tienen que volver a abrir el club que cerraron el año pasado. Lo pasábamos bien allí y había muchas actividades guays. Era un sitio a donde ir en invierno, cuando hacía frío o llovía. Otra cosa que podrían hacer es dar más descuentos a los jóvenes en el transporte público – así podrían hacer más cosas, buscar trabajo o simplemente explorar su ciudad.

Complex structure.

Another example of the imperfect.

Vocabulario

Parts of the body

la **boca** mouth
el **brazo** arm
la **cabeza** head
el **codo** elbow
el **corazón** heart
el **cuello** neck
el **dedo** finger, toe
el **diente**/la **muela** tooth
la **espalda** back
el **estómago** stomach
la **garganta** throat
el **hombro** shoulder
la **lengua** tongue
la **mano** hand
el **músculo** muscle
la **nariz** nose
el **oído**/la **oreja** ear
el **ojo** eye
el **pecho** chest
el **pie** foot
la **piel** skin
la **pierna** leg
la **rodilla** knee

Problems and solutions

Estoy mareado/a. I feel sick.
Me he cortado la mano. I have cut my hand.
Me he cortado. I have cut myself.
Me duele(n)… …hurts.
No me siento bien. I don't feel well.
Tengo el brazo roto/la pierna rota. I have a broken arm/leg.
Tengo dolor de… I have a/an…ache.
Tengo el tobillo torcido/la muñeca torcida. I have a twisted ankle/wrist.
Tengo fiebre. I have a temperature.
Tengo tos. I have a cough.
Tengo un resfriado. I have a cold.
Tengo una insolación. I have sunstroke.
Tengo una picadura. I have a bite.
Tengo una quemadura. I have a burn.
el **comprimido** pill, tablet
la **crema** cream
el **jarabe** syrup
la **pastilla** tablet, pastille, pill
tomar to take

Healthy lifestyles

beber mucha agua to drink a lot of water
comer una dieta variada to eat a varied diet
dormir bien to sleep well
evitar el estrés to avoid stress
hacer ejercicio to do exercise
intentar to try
mantener una vida sana to maintain a healthy lifestyle
no beber alcohol not to drink alcohol

no fumar not to smoke
no tomar drogas not to take drugs

Shops

el **almacén** shop, store
la **carnicería** butcher's
el **centro comercial** shopping centre
el **estanco** tobacconist's
la **farmacia** chemist's
la **frutería** greengrocer's
la **joyería** jeweller's
la **juguetería** toy shop
la **librería** bookshop
el **mercado** market
la **panadería** baker's
la **perfumería** perfumery
la **pescadería** fishmonger's
el **supermercado** supermarket
la **tienda de música** record/music shop
la **tienda de ropa** clothes shop
la **tienda de ultramarinos** grocer's
la **zapatería** shoe shop

Food and drink

el **aceite** oil
la **aceituna** olive
el **agua** (*f*) water
el **ajo** garlic
el **arroz** rice
el **atún** tuna
el **azúcar** sugar
el **bacalao** cod
el **café** coffee
la **carne** meat
la **cebolla** onion
el **cerdo** pork
los **cereales** cereals
la **comida basura** junk food
la **comida rápida** fast food
el **cordero** lamb
la **chuleta** chop
el **champiñón** mushroom
el **dulce** sweet
la **ensalada** salad
los **espaguetis** spaghetti
los **fideos** noodles
el **filete** steak
el **flan** crème caramel
la **fresa** strawberry
la **fruta** fruit
la **galleta** biscuit
las **gambas** prawns
la **gaseosa** fizzy drink
el **gazpacho** chilled tomato soup
los **guisantes** peas
la **hamburguesa** hamburger
el **helado** ice cream
las **hortalizas** vegetables
el **huevo** egg

el **jamón** ham
las **judías verdes** green beans
la **leche** milk
la **lechuga** lettuce
el **limón** lemon
la **limonada** lemonade
el **maíz** corn
la **mantequilla** butter
la **manzana** apple
el **mejillón** mussel
el **melocotón** peach
la **merluza** hake
la **naranja** orange
la **nata** cream
el **pan** bread
el **pan tostado** toasted bread
el **pastel** cake
la **patata** potato
las **patatas fritas** chips, crisps
el **pavo** turkey
el **pepino** cucumber
la **pera** pear
el **perrito caliente** hot dog
el **pescado** fish
el **pimiento** pepper
la **piña** pineapple
el **plátano** banana
el **pollo** chicken
el **pomelo** grapefruit
el **queso** cheese
la **sal** salt
la **sardina** sardine
la **sopa** soup
las **tapas** snacks
el **té** tea
la **ternera** veal
el **tomate** tomato
la **tortilla de patatas** Spanish omelette
la **tostada** toast, piece of toast
las **verduras** green vegetables
el **vino** wine
el **yogur** yoghurt
la **zanahoria** carrot
el **zumo** juice

Quantities

una **barra de** a loaf of
una **botella de** a bottle of
una **caja de** a box of
un **cartón de** a carton of
cien gramos de 100 grams of
una **docena de** a dozen
un **kilo de** a kilo of
una **lata de** a tin of
medio kilo de half a kilo of
un **paquete de** a packet of
un **trozo de** a slice of
un **tubo de** a tube of
un **vaso de** a glass of

Meals and meal times

al mediodía   at midday
beber   to drink
la **cena**   dinner/supper
cenar   to have dinner
comer   to eat
la **comida**   lunch; meal
desayunar   to have breakfast
el **desayuno**   breakfast
la **merienda**   snack, afternoon tea, picnic
por la mañana   in the morning
por la noche   at night
por la tarde   in the afternoon/evening
tomar   to have, take

Eating out

¡Que aproveche!   Enjoy your meal!
¡Salud!   Cheers!
la **cuchara**   spoon
el **cuchillo**   knife
El servicio está incluido.   Service is
   included.
en el rincón   in the corner
en la terraza   on the terrace
entonces   next, then
el **mantel**   tablecloth
Me falta(n)...   I need...
para empezar   to start...
el **plato**   plate
el **postre**   pudding, dessert
el **primer plato**   starter, first course
el **sacacorchos**   corkscrew
salir a cenar   to go out to eat
el **segundo plato**   main course, second
   course
la **servilleta**   napkin
el **tenedor**   knife
tener hambre   to be hungry
tener sed   to be thirsty

Traígame el menú, por favor.   Bring me
   the menu, please.
una mesa para dos   a table for two

The environment

ahorrar   to save
apagar   to switch/turn off
bañarse   to have a bath
la **basura**   rubbish
la **bolsa de plástico**   plastic bag
el **calentamiento global**   global warming
la **capa de ozono**   ozone layer
cerrar   to close
los **combustibles fósiles**   fossil fuels
consumir más/menos   to consume more/
   less
la **contaminación**   pollution
contaminar   to contaminate, pollute
el **contenedor de abono**   compost bin
los **desechos domésticos**   household
   waste
desenchufar   to unplug, turn off
devolver   to return
ducharse   to take a shower
encender   to switch/turn on
la **energía**   energy
estar en peligro   to be in danger
la **gasolina**   petrol
el **humo**   smoke
la **luz**   light
luchar contra/por   to fight against/for
malgastar   to waste
el **medio ambiente**   environment
el **papel**   paper
producir   to produce
prohibir   to forbid
proteger el planeta/el mundo   to protect
   the planet/world
reciclar   to recycle

el **reciclaje**   recycling
reducir   to reduce
respetar   to respect
reutilizar   to reuse
salvar   to save
la **selva**   forest
separar   to separate
ser ecológico/a   to be ecological
utilizar   to use
el **vidrio**   glass

Teenage concerns

abusar   to bully; to abuse
el **acoso escolar**   school bullying
el **alcohol**   alcohol
los **ancianos**   old people
el **botellón**   binge-drinking
debemos   we should/must
la **delincuencia juvenil**   youth crime
el **desempleo**   unemployment
el **dinero**   money
las **drogas**   drugs
el **estrés**   stress
emborracharse   to get drunk
Es necesario...   It is necessary to...
la **guerra**   war
los **inmigrantes**   immigrants
podemos   we can
recaudar dinero   to collect money
la **salud**   health
la **seguridad**   safety
los **sin techo**   homeless people
el **tabaco**   tobacco
el **Tercer Mundo**   Third World
el **terrorismo**   terrorism
tratar mejor   to treat better
la **violencia**   violence

Gramática

Nouns

Gender of nouns

As a general rule, nouns ending in -o are masculine and nouns ending in -a are feminine. However, there are some important exceptions:

el día	day
la mano	hand
el mapa	map
la moto	motorbike
el problema	problem
la radio	radio
el programa	programme
la modelo	(fashion) model
el tema	topic

The following groups of nouns are usually masculine:

- nouns ending in -aje or -or

el garaje	garage
el color	colour

- rivers, seas, mountains, fruit trees, colours, cars, days of the week and points of the compass

el Manzanares	the (river) Manzanares
el Mediterráneo	the Mediterranean
los Alpes	the Alps
el manzano	apple tree
el verde	green
el BMW	BMW
el domingo	Sunday
el norte	north

The following groups of nouns are usually feminine:
- nouns endings in: ión, -dad, -tad, -triz, -tud, -umbre, -anza, -ie

la región	region
la ciudad	town
la dificultad	difficulty
la actriz	actress
la inquietud	concern
la muchedumbre	crowd
la esperanza	hope
la serie	series

- letters of the alphabet

la eñe	the letter ñ

- islands and roads

las (islas) Canarias	the Canary Islands
la M50	the M50

Nouns ending in -ista have no separate masculine or feminine form:

el/la artista	artist
el/la periodista	journalist

Plurals

Spanish nouns form their plurals in various different ways:

- by adding -s, if the noun ends in a vowel, whether stressed or unstressed

el piso — los pisos	flat/s
la mano — las manos	hand/s
el café — los cafés	coffee/s

- by adding -es, if the noun ends in a consonant

el color — los colores	colour/s
el país — los países	country/-ies

- nouns ending in -z change the ending to -ces

la voz — las voces	voice/s

- nouns that have an accent on the last syllable lose the accent in the plural

la región — las regiones	region/s
el inglés — los ingleses	the English

- days of the week, except sábado and domingo, have the same form for singular and plural

el lunes — los lunes	Monday(s)
el sábado — los sábados	Saturday(s)

Articles

Definite article

The definite articles are el/los for the masculine and la/las for the feminine:

	Singular	Plural
Masculine	el día	los días
Feminine	la chica	las chicas

When the masculine singular definite article is preceded by a or de, the preposition combines with it to make one word:

Vamos **al** parque.
Let's go to the park. (a + el = al)

Salieron **del** cine.
They came out of the cinema. (de + el = del)

The other forms of the definite article, *la*, *los* and *las*, are unchanged after *a* and *de*.

The definite article is used in Spanish, but not in English, for:

- nouns used in a general sense

  No me gusta el chocolate.
  I don't like chocolate.

- languages, colours, days of the week (preceded by 'on' in English), the time, percentages, sports teams:

  El español es una lengua muy hermosa.
  Spanish is a beautiful language.

  Me gusta más el rojo que el amarillo.
  I like red better than yellow.

  El miércoles vamos a la piscina.
  On Wednesday we are going to the swimming pool.

  a las dos
  at 2 o'clock

  El 50% de los chicos tiene el pelo rubio.
  50% of the children have blond hair.

  el Real Madrid
  Real Madrid

- abstract nouns

  Todos buscamos la felicidad.
  We are all looking for happiness.

The definite article is omitted in Spanish, but used in English, for:

- the names of monarchs and popes with Roman numerals (when speaking):

  Alfonso XIII (Alfonso trece)
  Alfonso XIII (Alfonso the thirteenth)

- nouns that are in apposition

  José María Aznar, antiguo presidente de España
  José María Aznar, the former prime minister of Spain

The indefinite articles are *un/unos* for the masculine and *una/unas* for the feminine:

	Singular (a/an)	Plural (some)
Masculine	*un piso*	*unos pisos*
Feminine	*una chica*	*unas chicas*

The indefinite article is omitted in Spanish where it is used in English:

- with occupations after *ser*

  Mi padre es enfermero.
  My father is a nurse.

- when the noun is in apposition

  Llegó Juan, amigo de mi padre.
  Juan, a friend of my father, arrived.

- with a number of common words, especially: *otro*, *qué* and *mil*

  El gamberrismo es otro problema.
  Hooliganism is another problem.

  ¡Qué milagro!
  What a miracle!

  Te he dicho mil veces.
  I've told you a thousand times.

The masculine definite and indefinite articles *el* and *un* replace the feminine forms *la* and *una* before feminine nouns in the singular that begin with stressed *a* or *ha*. These nouns remain feminine in gender:

Singular	Plural
el/un agua *el/un hambre*	*las/unas aguas* *las/unas hambres*

Lo + adjective

Lo is used as a neuter article and can act as a noun when followed by an adjective, e.g. *bueno*, *importante*:

  Los exámenes han terminado y eso es lo bueno.
  The exams are over and that's the good thing.

  Lo importante es no perder el tren.
  The important thing is not to miss the train.

Adjectives

Forms

Adjectives that end in *-o* (masculine) or *-a* (feminine) add *-s* for the plural:

	Singular	Plural
Masculine	*limpio*	*limpios*
Feminine	*limpia*	*limpias*

Most adjectives that end in a vowel other than *-o/-a* or a consonant have the same form for masculine and feminine in the singular and plural. In the plural, *-s* is added to those ending in a vowel and *-es* to those ending in a consonant.

	Singular	Plural
Masculine	*triste*	*tristes*
Feminine	*triste*	*tristes*

	Singular	Plural
Masculine	*azul*	*azules*
Feminine	*azul*	*azules*

Adjectives ending in *-z* change the *z* to *c* in the plural:

	Singular	Plural
Masculine	*feliz*	*felices*
Feminine	*feliz*	*felices*

Adjectives denoting region or country that finish in a consonant normally have a feminine form ending in *-a*:

	Singular	Plural
Masculine	*inglés*	*ingleses*
Feminine	*inglesa*	*inglesas*

Adjectives ending in *–or* add *–a* for the feminine singular, *-es* for the masculine plural and *–as* for the feminine plural:

	Singular	Plural
Masculine	*encantador*	*encantadores*
Feminine	*encantadora*	*encantadoras*

Note: comparative adjectives ending in *-or* do not have a separate feminine form:

	Singular	Plural
Masculine	*mejor*	*mejores*
Feminine	*mejor*	*mejores*

When two nouns of different gender stand together, the adjective that qualifies them is masculine plural:

Eva y Jorge están contentos.
Eva and George are happy.

Position

Adjectives are normally placed after nouns:

una lengua difícil
a difficult language

Some common adjectives are often placed before the noun:

bueno
malo
pequeño
gran(de)

Cardinal and ordinal numbers and *último* are placed before the noun:

cien pasajeros
a hundred passengers

el quinto piso
the fifth floor

su última novela
his/her/your (formal) last/latest novel

Shortening (apocopation) of adjectives

Several common adjectives lose the final *-o* when they come before a masculine singular noun. This is called 'apocopation':

alguno — algún	any
primero — primer	first
bueno — buen	good
tercero — tercer	third
malo — mal	bad
uno — un	one, a
ninguno — ningún	no

Volveré algún día. I'll come back some day.
Hace mal tiempo hoy. The weather is bad today.

Grande shortens to *gran* before masculine and feminine singular nouns:

mi gran amiga, Paula my great friend, Paula

Comparison

Types of comparison

There are three basic types of comparison:
- of superiority (more...than) — *más...que*
- of inferiority (less...than) — *menos...que*
- of equality (as...as) — *tan(to)...como*

*Hace **más** frío en Escocia **que** en España.*
It's colder in Scotland than in Spain.

*Hace **menos** frío en España **que** en Escocia.*
It's less cold in Spain than in Scotland.

*Hace **tanto** calor en Madrid **como** en Caracas.*
It's as hot in Madrid as in Caracas.

Comparatives can be adjectives or adverbs.

Irregular adjectives of comparison

Certain common adjectives have special comparative forms:

Adjective	Comparative
bueno (good)	mejor (better)
malo (bad)	peor (worse)
mucho (much)	más (more)
poco (few)	menos (fewer, less)
grande (big, great)	mayor (bigger, greater)
pequeño (little)	menor (less)

Pedro tiene mejor apetito que Enrique.
Pedro has a better appetite than Enrique.

Irregular adverbs of comparison

Certain common adverbs have special comparative forms, which are invariable.

Adverb	Comparative
bien (well)	mejor (better)
mal (bad)	peor (worse)
más (more)	más (more)
poco (not much)	menos (less)

Mi hermano cocina mejor que mi hermana.
My brother cooks better than my sister.

Note: when a number comes after *más* it must be followed by *de* and not *que*:

Hay más de treinta alumnos en la clase.
There are more than 30 pupils in the class.

Superlatives

The way to express the idea of 'most' in Spanish is by placing the definite article before the noun being described and the comparative adjective after the noun:

La montaña más alta de España está en Canarias.
The highest mountain in Spain is in the Canaries.

Chile es el país más largo de América Latina.
Chile is the longest country in Latin America.

To express the idea of a quality possessed to an extreme degree, you can add *-ísimo* to the adjective:

Salamanca es una ciudad hermosísima.
Salamanca is a very beautiful city.

Chile es un país larguísimo.
Chile is an extremely long country.

Note that some *-ísimo* endings, as with the adjective *largo* in the example, require a spelling change to the last consonant of the adjective:

largo — larguísimo
rico — riquísimo
feliz — felicísimo

Demonstrative adjectives

There are three forms of demonstrative adjective in Spanish:
- *este, esta, estos, estas,* meaning 'this'
- *ese, esa, esos, esas,* meaning 'that' (near the listener)
- *aquel, aquella, aquellos, aquellas,* meaning 'that' (distant from both the speaker and the listener)

Masculine singular	Feminine singular	Masculine plural	Feminine plural
este chico (this boy)	esta chica (this girl)	estos chicos (these boys)	estas chicas (these girls)
ese chico (that boy)	esa chica (that girl)	esos chicos (those boys)	esas chicas (those girls)
aquel chico (that boy over there)	aquella chica (that girl over there)	aquellos chicos (those boys over there)	aquellas chicas (those girls over there)

Demonstrative pronouns

The demonstrative pronoun is distinguished from the demonstrative adjective by a written accent, e.g. *ése* ('that one'), *ese* ('that'). The accent is not now necessary, but it is still widely used.

Masculine singular	Feminine singular	Masculine plural	Feminine plural
éste (this (one))	ésta (this (one))	éstos (these (ones))	éstas (these (ones))
ése (that (one))	ésa (that (one))	ésos (those (ones))	ésas (those (ones))
aquél (that (one))	aquélla (that (one))	aquéllos (those (ones))	aquéllas (those (ones))

The neuter forms of the demonstrative pronouns are:

esto	this
eso	that
aquello	that

The neuter form refers to an indeterminate idea and not necessarily to a specific object:

¿Por qué no te gusta eso?
Why don't you like that?

Indefinites

Indefinites are words that refer to persons or things that are not specific. The following words are indefinites:

alguno/a/os/as	some, any
alguien	someone, anyone
algo	something, anything
cada	each, every
otro/a/os/as	(an)other
todo/a/os/as	all, any, every

Algún día visitaré Argentina.
Some day I'll visit Argentina.

Me llamaba cada 2 horas.
He used to ring me every 2 hours.

Alguien llamó a la puerta.
Somebody knocked at the door.

¿Has perdido algo?
Have you lost something?

No hay otra posibilidad.
There isn't another possibility.

Lo sabes todo.
You know it all.

Possessive adjectives

Singular	Plural
mi (my)	*mis* (my)
tu (your)	*tus* (your)
su (his, her, its, your (formal))	*sus* (his, her, its, your (formal))
vuestro/a (your)	*vuestros/as* (your)
su (their, your (formal))	*sus* (their, your (formal))

The possessive adjective agrees in number and gender with the noun that follows it:

Raúl nunca va al colegio con su hermana.
Raúl never goes to school with his sister.

Has dejado tus zapatillas en mi casa.
You've left your trainers at my house.

The possessive adjective *su(s)* can mean his/her/its/their or your (formal):

Deme su pasaporte, señor.
Give me your passport, sir. (formal 'your')

Sabe que su pasaporte está caducado.
He/She knows that his/her passport is out of date.

Tu(s), *vuestro/a/os/as* or *su(s)* can all mean 'your', depending on whether the relationship with the person(s) addressed is familiar or formal:

Tus amigos han llegado, papá.
Your friends have arrived, dad.

Vuestro desayuno está listo, hijos.
Your breakfast is ready, children.

Por favor, abra su maleta, señora.
Open your suitcase, please, madam.

Possessive pronouns

Singular	Plural
mío/a (mine)	*míos/as* (mine)
tuyo/a (yours)	*tuyos/as* (yours)
suyo/a (his, hers, yours (formal))	*suyos/as* (his, hers, yours (formal))
nuestro/a (our)	*nuestros/as* (ours)
vuestro/a (yours)	*vuestros/as* (yours)
suyo/a (theirs, yours (formal))	*suyos/as* (theirs, yours (formal))

Possessive pronouns are used to replace nouns in order to avoid repetition. They agree in number and gender with the object possessed:

Ese boli, ¿es tuyo o mío?
Is that biro yours or mine?

Su coche nuevo no va tan rápido como el nuestro.
Their/your new car doesn't go as fast as ours.

Interrogative adjectives

The interrogative adjectives are:

- *¿qué?* what?

  ¿De qué parte de España eres?
  What part of Spain are you from?

- *¿cuánto/a/os/as?* how much/many?

  ¿Cuántos kilos de patatas deseas?
  How many kilos of potatoes do you want?

Interrogative pronouns

The interrogative pronouns are:

- *¿qué?* what?

  ¿Qué te gustaría hacer esta noche?
  What would you like to do tonight?

- *¿cuál? ¿cuáles?*   which? what?
  (often for choosing between alternatives)

  ¿Cuál de los vestidos prefieres, el azul o el rojo?
  Which dress do you prefer, the blue one or the red one?

- *¿(de) quién/quiénes?*   who, (whose)?

  ¿De quién es esta bici?
  Whose bike is this?

- *¿cómo?*   how? what? why?

  ¿Cómo estás?
  How are you?

- *¿(a)dónde?*   where?

  ¿Adónde vamos este fin de semana?
  Where shall we go this weekend?

- *¿por qué?*   why?

  ¿Por qué no quieres salir con nosotros?
  Why don't you want to come out with us?

- *¿cuándo?*   when?

  ¿Cuándo nació tu hermano?
  When was your brother born?

- *¿cuánto?*   how much?

  ¿Cuánto vale?
  How much is it/How much does it cost?

Notes:
- Interrogative adjectives and pronouns always have a written accent.
- Direct questions in Spanish are preceded by an inverted question mark.

Exclamations

Some of the pronouns and adjctives used for questions are also used for exclamations:

- *¡cuánto(a/os/as)!*   how (much, many)!

  ¡Cuánto calor hace!
  How hot it is!

- *¡qué!*   what a...! how...!

  ¡Qué lástima!
  What a shame!

- *¡cómo!*   how! what!

  ¡Cómo me duele la cabeza!
  How my head aches!

Notes:
- Exclamation words always have a written accent.
- Exclamations are preceded by an inverted exclamation mark.

Relatives

Relatives are words like *que* and *cuyo*, which link two parts, or 'clauses', of a sentence:

- *que* (who, which, that) can be used as subject or object pronoun.

  El chico que está hablando con tu amigo es mi hermano.
  The boy who is speaking to your friend is my brother.

  La chica que ves en la plaza es mi hermana.
  The girl (that) you can see in the square is my sister.

- *el/la/los/las que* (who, which, that) is used mostly after prepositions.

  La casa en la que vivíamos está en las afueras de la ciudad.
  The house that we used to live in is on the outskirts of the town.

- *lo que* (what) refers to an idea rather than a specific noun.

  Haz lo que quieras.
  Do what you like.

- *quien(es)* (who, whom) is used only for people.

  La chica con quien trabajo se marchó ayer.
  The girl (that) I work with left yesterday.

- *cuyo/a/os/as* (whose) is an adjective that agrees in number and gender with the noun it qualifies.

  La chica cuya madre está en el hospital...
  The girl whose mother is in hospital...

Adverbs

Adverbs tell you *when* something is done (time), *how* it is done (manner) and *where* it is done (place).

Many adverbs are formed from the feminine of an adjective, by adding the suffix *-mente*:

Masculine adjective	Feminine adjective	Adverb
claro	clara	claramente
fácil	fácil	fácilmente
feliz	feliz	felizmente

Other common adverbs and adverbial phrases are:

- time

ahora	now
a menudo	frequently
antes	before
a veces	sometimes
después	later, afterwards
en seguida	at once, immediately
entonces	then, at that time
luego	then, later, soon
pronto	soon
siempre	always
tarde	late
temprano	early
todavía	still
ya	already, now

- manner

así	like this, thus
bien	well
de la misma manera	in the same way
de repente	suddenly
despacio, lentamente	slowly
mal	badly

- place

abajo	down, below
adelante	forward(s)
allí, allá	there
aquí, acá	here
arriba	above
atrás	back(wards)
cerca	near(by)
debajo	underneath
delante	in front
(a)dentro	inside
detrás	behind
encima	above, on top
en todas partes	everywhere
(a)fuera	outside
lejos	far

Note: when two *-mente* adverbs come together and are joined by *y*, the first one loses the *-mente* ending:

> *Trabajamos rápida y eficazmente.*
> We worked quickly and effectively.

Quantifiers

A number of adverbs, known as quantifiers, refer to the degree or amount to which something is (done). The most common quantifiers are:

- *bastante*   enough; quite

  > *La película fue bastante buena.*
  > The film was quite good.

- *demasiado*   too

  > *¡Eres demasiado bueno!*
  > You are too good!

- *mucho*   (very) much

  > *Va a hacer mucho más calor.*
  > It's going to get much hotter.

- *muy*   very

  > *El partido fue muy emocionante.*
  > The match was very exciting.

- *(un) poco*   (a) little

  > *Ese político es poco conocido.*
  > That politician is little known.

Personal pronouns

Subject pronouns

The subject pronouns are:

Singular	Plural
yo (I)	*nosotros/as* (we)
tú (you)	*vosotros/as* (you)
él (he, it)	*ellos* (they)
ella (she, it)	*ellas* (they)
usted (you (formal))	*ustedes* (you (formal))

Subject pronouns are used far less than in English. Usually the verb on its own is sufficient to express the meaning: *Habla español* means 'He/She speaks Spanish', without needing a subject pronoun to express 'he/she'.

You might include the subject pronoun, however, if you want to emphasise for some reason who it is who speaks Spanish:

> *Ella habla español, pero él no.*
> **She** speaks Spanish, but **he** doesn't.

Subject pronouns are also used standing on their own:

> *¿Hablas español?*
> Do you speak Spanish?
>
> *Yo no. Y tú?*
> No, I don't. Do you?

There are two forms of the subject pronoun for 'you':
- *tú* and *vosotros* for the familiar mode of address
- *usted* and *ustedes* for the formal mode of address

Note: *usted* and *ustedes* are always used with the third person form of the verb.

> *¿Conoce usted a mi profesor de español?*
> Do you know my Spanish teacher?

In the *tú* form this question would be:

> *¿Conoces a mi profesor de español?*

Direct object pronouns

The direct object pronouns are:

Singular	Plural
me (me)	*nos* (us)
te (you)	*os* (you)
lo/le (him, it, you (formal masc.))	*los/les* (them (masc.), you (formal masc.))
la (her, it, you (formal fem.)	*las* (them (fem.), you (formal fem.))

Note that the third-person direct object pronouns *lo/le*, *la* ('him', 'her') and *los/les/las* ('them') are also used for 'you' (formal).

Lo/los and *le/les* are interchangeable:

> *Lo/le conozco bien.*
> I know him/it/you well.
>
> *La vi en Madrid.*
> I saw her/it/you in Madrid.
>
> *Los/les/las vi en Londres.*
> I saw them/you in London.

Direct object pronouns are usually placed before the verb:

> *Me vio ayer en la calle.*
> He saw me yesterday in the street.

They are always added to the end of the affirmative imperative:

> *¡Míralo!*
> Look at it!

They can be added to the end of an infinitive:

> *Quiero verlos en seguida.*
> I want to see them at once.

However, it is also possible to say:

> *Los quiero ver en seguida.*

They are normally added to the end of a gerund:

> *Está escribiéndola.*
> He's writing it (e.g. a letter).

(Note that *escribiendo* has to have an accent to preserve the stress.)

However, it is also possible to say:

> *La está escribiendo.*

Indirect object pronouns

Singular	Plural
me (to me)	*nos* (to us)
te (to you)	*os* (to you)
le (to him, her, it, you (formal))	*les* (to them, you (formal))

The direct object pronouns receive the action of the verb *directly*, whereas the indirect object pronouns receive it *indirectly*. In the sentence, 'We gave the ball to him', 'the ball' is the direct object and 'to him' is the indirect object: ***Le dimos el balón.***

> *Me vas a decir la verdad.*
> You are going to tell (to) me the truth.
>
> *No te puedo recomendar aquel hotel.*
> I can't recommend that hotel to you.

Like direct object pronouns, indirect object pronouns are always added to the end of the affirmative imperative:

> *Tráigame la cuenta.*
> Bring (to) me the bill.

They can be added to the end of an infinitive:

> *Voy a decirle lo que pienso.*
> I'm going to tell (to) him what I think.

However, it is also possible to say:

> *Le voy a decir lo que pienso.*

They are normally added to the end of a gerund:

> *Está escribiéndoles.*
> He's writing to them. (Note that escribiendo has to have an accent to preserve the stress.)

However, it is also possible to say:

Les está escribiendo.

Order of object pronouns

In sentences that contain both a direct and an indirect object pronoun, the indirect one is always placed first:

Te lo daré mañana.
I'll give it to you tomorrow.

In the above sentence, *te* is the indirect object and *lo* the direct object pronoun.

The indirect object pronoun *le/les* changes to *se* before a third person direct object pronoun:

Se lo di.
I gave it to him/her/you/them.

A él, a ella, a usted, a ellos, a ellas, a ustedes may be added for clarity:

Se lo di a ella.
I gave it to her.

Disjunctive pronouns

Disjunctive pronouns are pronouns that are used after prepositions:

Singular	Plural
mí (me)	*nosotros/as* (us)
ti (you)	*vosotros/as* (you)
él (him, it)	*ellos* (them)
ella (her, it)	*ellas* (them)
usted (you (formal))	*ustedes* (you (formal))

Vamos a visitar el Prado con ellas.
We are going to visit the Prado with them.

Mí, ti and *sí* combine with the preposition *con* to make *conmigo* (with me), *contigo* (with you) and *consigo* (with him/her(self) etc.):

¿Por qué no le deja ir conmigo?
Why don't you let him go with me?

Reflexive pronouns

Reflexive pronouns refer back to the subject of the sentence.

Singular	Plural
me (myself)	*nos* (ourselves)
te (yourself)	*os* (yourselves)
se (himself, herself, yourself (formal))	*se* (themselves, yourselves (formal))

The reflexive pronoun normally precedes the verb but, like the object pronouns, it is added to the end of imperatives, gerunds and infinitives:

Se fue a Venezuela ayer.
He went to Venezuela yesterday.

¡Levántate!
Get up!

Está divirtiéndose.
She's enjoying herself.

Fueron a Las Vegas para casarse.
They went to Las Vegas to get married.

Verbs

Present tense

The present tense is formed by adding the highlighted endings to the stem of the infinitive:
- -*ar* verbs: *hablo, hablas, habla, hablamos, habláis, hablan*
- -*er* verbs: *como, comes, come, comemos, coméis, comen*
- -*ir* verbs: *escribo, escribes, escribe, escribimos, escribís, escriben*

The present tense is used for:

- something that exists at the time of speaking

  Hace frío en Soria.
  It's cold in Soria.

- describing a habit

  Nos reunimos en la discoteca todos los viernes.
  We meet at the disco every Friday.

- general statements

  Los Pirineos están en el norte de España.
  The Pyrenees are in the north of Spain.

- future intention

  ¿Vas a ver el partido?
  Are you going to see the match?

Note: some irregular verbs have a special form in the first person singular:

conocer	to know	*conozco, conoces, conoce...*
construir	to build	*construyo, construyes, construye...*
dar	to give	*doy, das, da...*
decir	to say	*digo, dices, dice...*
estar	to be	*estoy, estás, está...*
hacer	to do/make	*hago, haces, hace...*

ir	to go	*voy, vas, va…*
oír	to hear	*oigo, oyes, oye…*
poner	to put	*pongo, pones, pone…*
salir	to leave	*salgo, sales, sale…*
ser	to be	*soy, eres, es…*
tener	to have	*tengo, tienes, tiene…*
traer	to bring	*traigo, traes, trae…*
venir	to come	*vengo, vienes, viene…*

Note: some of these verbs have other irregularities.

Some verbs change the vowel of the stem in the first three persons of the singular and the third person plural (see also radical-changing verbs, pp. 165–67):

pensar	to think	*pienso, piensas, piensa, pensamos, pensáis, piensan*
encontrar	to find	*encuentro, encuentras, encuentra, encontramos, encontráis, encuentran*
pedir	to ask for	*pido, pides, pide, pedimos, pedís, piden*

Present continuous tense

The present continuous tense is formed by the present tense of verb *estar* plus the gerund. The gerund is the form of the verb that ends in *-ando* (*-ar* verbs) or *-iendo* (*-er* and *-ir* verbs):

This form of the present tense describes actions that are happening *now*:

> *Está hablando con Alex en su móvil.*
> She's talking to Alex on her mobile.

> *Estamos comiendo nuestro desayuno.*
> We're eating our breakfast.

Preterite tense

The preterite tense is formed by adding the highlighted endings to the stem of the infinitive:
- *-ar* verbs: *hablé, hablaste, habló, hablamos, hablasteis, hablaron*
- *-er* verbs: *comí, comiste, comió, comimos, comisteis, comieron*
- *-ir* verbs: *escribí, escribiste, escribió, escribimos, escribisteis, escribieron*

There are many irregular preterites, the most common being:

> *andar — anduve, anduviste, anduvo, anduvimos, anduvisteis, anduvieron*
> *conducir — conduje, condujiste, condujo, condujimos, condujisteis, condujeron*

> *dar — di, diste, dio, dimos, disteis, dieron*
> *decir — dije, dijiste, dijo, dijimos, dijisteis, dijeron*
> *estar — estuve, estuviste, estuvo, estuvimos, estuvisteis, estuvieron*
> *hacer — hice, hiciste, hizo, hicimos, hicisteis, hicieron*
> *ir — fui, fuiste, fue, fuimos, fuisteis, fueron*
> *poder — pude, pudiste, pudo, pudimos, pudisteis, pudieron*
> *poner — puse, pusiste, puso, pusimos, pusisteis, pusieron*
> *querer — quise, quisiste, quiso, quisimos, quisisteis, quisieron*
> *saber — supe, supiste, supo, supimos, supisteis, supieron*
> *ser — fui, fuiste, fue, fuimos, fuisteis, fueron*
> *tener — tuve, tuviste, tuvo, tuvimos, tuvisteis, tuvieron*
> *traer — traje, trajiste, trajo, trajimos, trajisteis, trajeron*
> *venir — vine, viniste, vino, vinimos, vinisteis, vinieron*
> *ver — vi, viste, vio, vimos, visteis, vieron*

Notes on the form of the preterite

- In *-ar* regular verbs, the first person plural has the same form in the preterite as in the present tense.
- The verbs *ir* and *ser* have exactly the same form in the preterite for all persons: *fui, fuiste, fue, fuimos, fuisteis, fueron*.
- The irregular preterite forms should be learned (see also the verb tables on pp. 171–79).

The preterite tense is used to express a *completed* action in the past that happened at a specific time:

> *El Rey de España fue a Argentina en mayo.*
> The King of Spain went to Argentina in May.

These actions are often a series of events within a specific period of time.

> *Ayer* **fui** *con Rosa al bar Manolo. Ella* **tomó** *una coca-cola y yo una cerveza.* **Hablamos** *de las vacaciones. Ella* **dijo** *que odiaba Benidorm y no quería ir allí otra vez. ¡No nos* **pusimos** *de acuerdo! Luego* **llegó** *Roberto. Le* **pregunté** *qué pensaba. Él* **respondió** *que no sabía. ¡Qué lata!*

Yesterday I went to Manolo's bar with Rosa. She had a coke and I had a beer. We spoke about the holidays. She said she hated Benidorm and didn't want to go there again. We didn't agree! Then Roberto arrived. I asked him what he thought. He said he didn't know. What a pain!

Note: students of Spanish who are also studying French often use the Spanish perfect tense (*he hablado*) when they should use the preterite (*hablé*). This is because they don't realise that the French perfect tense (*j'ai parlé* etc.) is similar in its use to the Spanish preterite tense (*hablé* etc.). Thus, 'I spoke to her' in Spanish would normally be '*Hablé con ella*', and not '*He hablado con ella*'.

Gramática

Imperfect tense

The imperfect tense is formed by adding the highlighted endings to the stem of the infinitive:

- -ar verbs: *hablaba, hablabas, hablaba, hablábamos, hablabais, hablaban*
- -er verbs: *comía, comías, comía, comíamos, comíais, comían*
- -ir verbs: *escribía, escribías, escribía, escribíamos, escribíais, escribían*

Three verbs are irregular in the imperfect tense:

  ir — iba, ibas, iba, íbamos, ibais, iban
  ser — era, eras, era, éramos, erais, eran
  ver — veía, veías, veía, veíamos, veíais, veían

The imperfect tense is used for:

- actions that happened regularly in the past, i.e. what we **used to** do

  Mi abuela siempre estaba sentada al lado del fuego.
  My grandma always sat by the fire.

  Íbamos a la playa todos los días.
  We went/used to go to the beach every day.

- descriptions in the past

  José Carlos era un hombre alto.
  José Carlos was a tall man.

Imperfect continuous tense

The imperfect continuous tense is formed by the imperfect tense of the verb *estar* plus the gerund. The gerund is the form of the verb that ends in -*ando* (-*ar* verbs) or -*iendo* (-*er* and -*ir* verbs).

This form of the imperfect tense describes actions that were happening at that time, as in the English sentence:

  Estaba hablando con Alex en su móvil.
  He was talking to Alex on his mobile.

  Estábamos andando en la playa.
  We were walking on the beach.

Future tense

The future tense is formed by adding the highlighted endings to the infinitive of the verb:

- -ar verbs: *hablaré, hablarás, hablará, hablaremos, hablaréis, hablarán*
- -er verbs: *comeré, comerás, comerá, comeremos, comeréis, comerán*
- -ir verbs: *escribiré, escribirás, escribirá, escribiremos, escribiréis, escribirán*

A number of common verbs have an irregular future stem. The most important of these are:

  decir — **dir**é etc
  hacer — **har**é etc.
  poder — **podr**é etc
  poner — **pondr**é etc.
  querer — **querr**é etc.
  saber — **sabr**é etc.
  salir — **saldr**é etc.
  tener — **tendr**é etc.
  venir — **vendr**é etc.

The future tense expresses what *will* happen:

  Volverán de Segovia a las dos.
  They'll return from Segovia at 2 o'clock.

  Hablaré con ella mañana.
  I'll speak to her tomorrow.

Immediate future

The immediate future is formed using *ir a* and the infinitive of the verb. It is often used to express future intention, especially in colloquial Spanish. This form is often interchangeable with the future (see the section above).

  ¿Vas a verle?
  Are you going to see her?

  Voy a buscar pan.
  I'm going to get some bread.

Conditional tense

The conditional tense is formed by adding the highlighted endings to the infinitive of the verb:

- -ar verbs: *hablaría, hablarías, hablaría, hablaríamos, hablaríais, hablarían*
- -er verbs: *comería, comerías, comería, comeríamos, comeríais, comerían*
- -ir verbs: *escribiría, escribirías, escribiría, escribiríamos, escribiríais, escribirían*

A number of common verbs have an irregular form in the conditional. These are the same verbs as those that have an irregular future, i.e. *decir* (*diría* etc.), *hacer* (*haría* etc.), *poder* (*podría*) etc. (See the section above on the future tense.)

The conditional tense expresses what **would** happen:

  ¿Te gustaría pasar el día en el campo?
  Would you like to spend the day in the country?

  ¿Qué preferirías hacer, ir al cine o a la discoteca?
  What would you prefer to do, go to the cinema or the disco?

The conditional is also used to make polite requests:

> *Por favor, ¿podría darme un folleto?*
> Could you please give me a leaflet?

Perfect tense

The perfect tense is a compound tense, formed from the auxiliary verb *haber* plus the past participle of the verb (*hablado, comido, escrito* etc.).

> **he** *hablado/comido/escrito*
> **has** *hablado/comido/escrito*
> **ha** *hablado/comido/escrito,*
> **hemos** *hablado/comido/escrito*
> **habéis** *hablado/comido/escrito*
> **han** *hablado/comido/escrito*

The perfect tense is used to connect past time with present time. It describes actions that have begun in the past and are continuing and/or have an effect now:

> *He empezado a estudiar italiano.*
> I've started to study Italian (and I am continuing to study Italian now).

The perfect tense is also used to express the very recent past, especially events that happened today:

> *Esta mañana me he levantado a las 7.30.*
> I got up this morning at 7.30.

Note: there are a number of irregular past participles of common verbs, which should be learned. These are the most common:

abrir	to open	*abierto*	opened
decir	to say	*dicho*	said
escribir	to write	*escrito*	written
hacer	to do/make	*hecho*	done/made
morir	to die	*muerto*	died
poner	to put	*puesto*	put
romper	to break	*roto*	broken
ver	to see	*visto*	seen
volver	to return	*vuelto*	returned

When used as part of the perfect tense, the past participle never agrees in number or gender with the subject of the sentence:

> *Hemos tenido buena suerte.*
> We've been lucky (i.e. We've had good luck).

> *Tu hermana ha ganado el concurso, ¿no?*
> Your sister has won the competition, hasn't she?

Pluperfect tense

The pluperfect tense is formed from the imperfect tense of *haber* and the past participle of the verb (*hablado, comido, escrito*).

> **había** *hablado/comido/escrito*
> **habías** *hablado/comido/escrito*
> **había** *hablado/comido/escrito,*
> **habíamos** *hablado/comido/escrito*
> **habíais** *hablado/comido/escrito*
> **habían** *hablado/comido/escrito*

This tense expresses what had happened before another action in the past:

> *La fiesta ya había comenzado cuando llegó Jaime.*
> The party had already started when Jaime arrived.

Subjunctive

The subjunctive is one of three moods of the verb (the others are the indicative and the imperative). The subjunctive is used in four tenses: the present, the imperfect, the perfect and the pluperfect. All four tenses of the subjunctive are widely used.

It is important to be able to use the present subjunctive and to be able to recognise the imperfect subjunctive.

Present subjunctive

The present subjunctive is formed by adding the highlighted endings to the stem of the infinitive:

- *-ar* verbs: *habl**e**, habl**es**, habl**e**, habl**emos**, habl**éis**, habl**en***
- *-er* verbs: *com**a**, com**as**, com**a**, com**amos**, com**áis**, com**an***
- *-ir* verbs: *escrib**a**, escrib**as**, escrib**a**, escrib**amos**, escrib**áis**, escrib**an***

The endings of *-ar* verbs are the same as the present indicative endings of *-er* verbs, and those of *-er* and *-ir* verbs are the same as the present indicative endings of *-ar* verbs, with the exception of the first person singular.

The present subjunctive of most irregular verbs is formed by removing the final *-o* from the end of the first person singular of the present indicative and adding the endings listed above. Most irregular verbs keep the final consonant of the first person singular for all persons. For example:

> *hacer — haga, hagas, haga, hagamos, hagáis, hagan.*

See verb tables on pp. 171–79 for more irregular subjunctives.

Gramática

Imperfect subjunctive

The imperfect subjunctive is formed by removing the ending of the third person plural of the preterite tense and adding the highlighted endings:

- -ar verbs: either *hablara, hablaras, hablara, habláramos, hablarais, hablaran*

  or *hablase, hablases, hablase, hablásemos, hablaseis, hablasen*

- -er verbs: either *comiera, comieras, comiera, comiéramos, comierais, comieran*

  or *comiese, comieses, comiese, comiésemos, comieseis, comiesen*

- -ir verbs: either *escribiera, escribieras, escribiera, escribiéramos, escribierais, escribieran*

  or *escribiese, escribieses, escribiese, escribiésemos, escribieseis, escribiesen*

The *-ara/ase* and *-iera/iese* endings are interchangeable.

Perfect subjunctive

The perfect subjunctive is formed from the present subjunctive of *haber* plus the past participle, e.g. *haya hablado, hayas hablado, haya hablado* etc.

Pluperfect subjunctive

The pluperfect subjunctive is formed from the imperfect subjunctive of *haber* plus the past participle, e.g. *hubiera/iese hablado, hubieras/ieses hablado, hubiera/iese hablado* etc.

Uses of the subjunctive

The subjunctive is used in three main areas: subordinate clauses, main clauses and conditional sentences.

Important uses of the subjunctive are:

- after conjunctions of time, such as *cuando* and *mientras*, when expressing the future

  Cuando tenga yo 18 años voy a dar una fiesta enorme.
  When I'm 18 I'm going to have a huge party.

  Hugo tendrá que buscar trabajo temporal mientras viaje por Latinoamérica.
  Hugo will have to look for temporary work while he travels round Latin America

- after verbs of wishing, command, request and emotion

  Laura quiere que le acompañes al cine.
  Laura wants you to go with her to the cinema.

Espero que me escribas pronto.
I hope you will write to me soon.

Te digo que no salgas esta noche.
I'm telling you not to go out tonight.

Pídele que me compre las entradas.
Ask him to buy me the tickets.

- to express purpose, after *para que*

  Te daré la llave para que puedas entrar en el piso.
  I'll give you the key so that you can get into the flat.

- to express possibility, probability and necessity

  Es posible que la selección española gane la copa.
  It's possible that the Spanish team will win the cup.

  No es necesario que ellos vayan a la estación con nosotros.
  It's not necessary for them to go to the station with us.

- to express permission and prohibition

  ¡Déjale que venga!
  Let him come!

- after verbs of saying and thinking used in the negative

  No creo que los estudiantes encuentren fácil el trabajo.
  I don't think the students will find the work easy.

- to express the formal imperative and the negative form of the familiar imperative (for the imperative see the next section)

Imperatives

The imperative mood is for instructions and commands.

Affirmative commands

For regular verbs, the **informal** *tú* imperative is formed by removing the last letter, *s*, from the second person singular of the present indicative:

hablas — habla
comes — come
escribes — escribe

There are nine irregular forms, which have to be learned:

Verb	Tú imperative
decir (to say)	*di*
hacer (to do)	*haz*
ir (to go)	*ve*
oír (to hear)	*oye*
poner (to put)	*pon*
salir (to go out)	*sal*
ser (to be)	*sé*
tener (to have)	*ten*
venir (to come)	*ven*

Escríbeme pronto.
Write to me soon.

Pon el libro en la mesa.
Put the book on the table.

The *vosotros* imperative is formed by replacing the final *-r* of the infinitive with *-d*. Note that the final *-d* is omitted from reflexive forms:

Volved conmigo, amigos.
Come back with me, friends.

¡Levantaos!
Get up!

In the **formal** *usted/ustedes* form, both the singular and the plural are the same as the third person (*usted/ustedes*) of the present subjunctive.

Por favor, firme aquí.
Sign here please.

Dígame lo que ocurre.
Tell me what is happening.

Perdonen, señoras.
Excuse me, ladies.

Negative commands
Negative familiar commands use the second person (*tú/vosotros*) of the present subjunctive:

¡No hables así!
Don't speak like that!

¡No salgas!
Don't go out!

No me lo digáis.
Don't tell me.

Negative *usted/ustedes* commands, like the affirmative ones, use the third person of the present subjunctive:

¡No me diga!
You don't say!

No se molesten.
Don't get upset.

Note: *que* + the subjunctive may be used for wishes and commands. *Que* is sometimes omitted:

(Que) vayan todos.
Let them all go.

¡(Que) viva el Rey!
Long live the King!

Passive

A passive sentence has the same meaning as an active one, but the parts of the sentence are in a different order. For example, 'My handbag was stolen by a thief' is a passive sentence, which can also be expressed actively as 'A thief stole my handbag'.

In a passive sentence, there is normally an agent, usually preceded by the preposition *por*. However, the agent may be omitted from the sentence, as in:

La carta fue escrita ayer.
The letter was written yesterday.

The passive is formed from *ser* plus the past participle, which agrees in number and gender with the subject of the sentence:

El acuerdo fue firmado por el presidente.
The agreement was signed by the president.

La novela será publicada mañana.
The novel will be published tomorrow.

Gerund
The gerund expresses the idea of the *duration* of the action of the verb.

To form the gerund, add *-ando* to the stem of *-ar* verbs and *-iendo* to the stem of *-er* and *-ir* verbs. The gerund is invariable in form.

hablar — hablando
comer — comiendo
escribir — ecribiendo

The gerund is used for actions that take place at the same time as the main verb:

Van corriendo por la calle.
They go running along the street.

It is used for the continuous form of the verb:

Estaban mirando el cielo para ver si iba a llover.
They were looking at the sky to see if it was going to rain.

Continuar, seguir and *llevar* are followed by the gerund to emphasise the duration of the verb:

Por favor, sigue hablando.
Carry on talking, please.

Llevamos 3 años viviendo en Barcelona.
We've been living in Barcelona for 3 years.

Note: don't confuse the English present participle ending in –*ing* (e.g. 'eating') with the Spanish gerund. The English -*ing* form after a preposition is translated by an infinitive:

> *Después de terminar mis deberes, me acosté.*
> After finishing my homework, I went to bed.

Ser and estar

These two verbs both mean 'to be', but they are used in different circumstances.

Ser refers to characteristics that are 'inherent' to a person, thing or idea, such as identity, permanent features, occupation, time:

> *Soy gallego.*
> I'm Galician.
>
> *Madrid es la capital de España.*
> Madrid is the capital of Spain.
>
> *Es policía.*
> He's a policeman.
>
> *Son las nueve y media.*
> It's half past nine.

Estar refers to a temporary state or to where a person or thing is, whether temporarily or permanently:

> *Estamos contentos.*
> We're happy (but this is a momentary feeling).
>
> *Málaga está en el sur de España.*
> Malaga is in the south of Spain.

Ser and estar with adjectives

Some adjectives are always used with *ser*, others always with *estar*:

Ser		Estar	
(in)justo/a	(un)fair	*bien/mal/fatal*	good/bad/terrible
(in)necesario/a	(un)necessary	*de buen/mal humor*	in a good/mad mood
(in)conveniente	(in)appropriate	*enfadado/a*	angry
importante	important	*enfermo/a*	ill
inteligente	intelligent	*ocupado/a*	busy

Some adjectives can be used with either *ser* or *estar*, but their meaning is different. *Ser* meanings always reflect permanent characteristics; *estar* meanings refer to temporary states. The most common of these adjectives are:

Adjective	Used with *ser*	Used with *estar*
aburrido	boring	bored
listo	clever	ready
malo	bad, evil	ill
nervioso	nervous (disposition)	nervous (temporarily)
triste	sad (disposition)	sad (temporarily)

Impersonal verbs

Verbs such as *gustar, encantar, costar, doler, faltar, hacer falta, interesar* and *molestar* are used with a special construction that is the reverse of the English one. The sentence:

> *Me gusta la dieta mediterránea.*
> I like the Mediterranean diet.

can be broken down literally in English as follows:

Indirect object	Third person verb	Subject
Me	*gusta*	*la dieta mediterránea*
To me	is pleasing	the Mediterranean diet

If the subject is plural, the verb must also be plural, as in:

> *Le gustan los tomates.*
> He likes tomatoes. (Literally 'To him are pleasing the tomatoes.')

Frequently, the person concerned is emphasised by adding *a* plus a personal pronoun:

> *A mí me gustan los tomates.*
> I like tomatoes.

The same construction can be seen in the following examples:

> *¿Te duele la cabeza?*
> Have you got a headache?
>
> *Les encanta la playa.*
> They love the beach.
>
> *Me costó un dineral.*
> It cost me a bomb.
>
> *¿A ti te molesta que venga Julio?*
> Are you bothered that Julio's coming?

Reflexive verbs

In Spanish, reflexive verbs are always accompanied by a reflexive pronoun, which changes according to the subject of the verb. For example:

levantarse	to get up
me levanto	I get up
te levantas	you get up
se levanta	he/she/it/you (formal) gets up
nos levantamos	we get up
os levantáis	you get up
se levantan	they/you (formal) get up

Reflexive verbs often do not have a reflexive pronoun when translated into English, for example: *acostarse* to go to bed; *afeitarse* to shave; *casarse* to marry.

Infinitives

Many common verbs are followed by a preposition, usually either *a*, *de*, *en*, *con*, *para* or *por*, before an infinitive. Some of the most common of these verbs are given below.

Verb + *a* + infinitive

acercarse a	to get near to
aprender a	to learn to
ayudar a	to help to
comenzar a	to begin to
decidirse a	to decide to
empezar a	to begin to
enseñar a	to teach to
invitar a	to invite to
ir a	to go to
volver a	to (do) again

Por favor, ayúdame a preparar la cena.
Help me to prepare dinner, please.

Comenzaron a entrar a las 9.00.
They started to go in at 9.00.

Verb + *de* + infinitive

acabar de	to finish (doing); to have just
acordarse de	to remember
alegrarse de	to be pleased about
olvidarse de	to forget to
terminar de	to stop (doing)
tratar de	to try to

Me alegro de saber eso.
I'm pleased to know that.

¡Trata de hacerlo!
Try to do it!

Verb + *en* + infinitive

dudar en	to hesitate to
insistir en	to insist on (doing)
interesarse en	to be interested in (doing)
tardar en	to take time in (doing)

El tren tardaba mucho en salir.
The train was very late departing.

Verb + *con* + infinitive

amenazar con	to threaten to
contentarse con	to be happy to
soñar con	to dream of (doing)

Sueña con ser piloto.   He dreams about being a pilot.

Verb + *para* + infinitive

prepararse para	to prepare oneself to
faltar para	to have time/distance to go

Se está preparando para hacer el examen.
He's preparing to take the exam.

Falta poco para llegar a Zaragoza.
It's not far to Zaragoza.

Verb + *por* + infinitive

comenzar por	to begin by (doing)
empezar por	to begin by (doing)
luchar por	to fight/struggle to

Comenzamos la tarde por comer tapas.
We started the evening by eating tapas.

Three special constructions with the infinitive

- *Al* + the infinitive is used with the meaning 'when…', referring to an action that happens at the same time as that of the main verb:

  Al llegar a la estación vio que el tren había salido.
  When he got to the station he saw that the train had left.

- *Volver* followed by *a* + the infinitive means 'to do something again':

  No he vuelto a verle.
  I haven't seen him again.

- *Acabar* followed by *de* + the infinitive means 'to have just (done something)':

  Acaban de volver.
  They have just come back.

Radical-changing verbs

Radical-changing verbs are so called because they make changes to the 'root' or stem of the verb. Many Spanish verbs are of this type.

For example, in the verb *pensar* (to think) the stem is *pens-* (the infinitive without the *-ar* ending). In this verb, the *-e* of the stem changes to *–ie*; 'I think' is *pienso*.

Radical changes affect *-ar*, *-er* and *-ir* verbs. It is not easy to predict whether a given verb will have a stem change or not, so the radical-changing verbs have to be learned.

Conjugation of radical-changing verbs

In the present indicative tense of *-ar* and *-er* verbs, the main vowel of the stem splits into two when it is stressed. The vowel changes from *e* to *ie* and *o* to *ue* in the first, second and third persons singular and the third person plural:

cerrar (to close)	encontrar (to find)	perder (to lose)	volver (to return)
cierro	encuentro	pierdo	vuelvo
cierras	encuentras	pierdes	vuelves
cierra	encuentra	pierde	vuelve
cerramos	encontramos	perdemos	volvemos
cerráis	encontráis	perdéis	volvéis
cierran	encuentran	pierden	vuelven

The stem also changes in the *tú* (familiar) form of the imperative:

cierra

encuentra

pierde

vuelve

Other common -*ar* and -*er* verbs that follow the same pattern are:

e > ie:

-ar verbs	-er verbs
calentar (to heat)	defender (to defend)
comenzar (to begin)	encender (to switch on, to light)
despertar (to wake)	entender (to understand)
empezar (to begin)	querer (to wish, to want)
*nevar (to snow)	
pensar (to think)	
recomendar (to recommend)	
sentarse (to sit down)	

*nevar is used only in the third person singular

o > ue

-ar verbs	-er verbs
acordarse de (to remember)	doler (to hurt)
acostarse (to go to bed)	*llover (to rain)
contar (to count, to tell)	mover (to move)
costar (to cost)	poder (to be able)
probar (to prove, taste, try (on))	soler (to do habitually)
recordar (to remember)	torcer (to turn, twist)
soñar (to dream)	
volar (to fly)	

*llover is used only in the third person singular

Note: *jugar* (to play), with stem vowel *u*, follows the same pattern as verbs with stem vowel *o*: *juego, juegas, juega, jugamos, jugáis, juegan.*

-ir verbs

There are three types of radical-changing -*ir* verbs:

- those that change the stem vowel in the present tense from *e* to *i*, such as *pedir* (to ask for)
- those that change the stem vowel in the present tense from *e* to *ie*, such as *sentir* (to feel, be sorry)
- those that change the stem vowel in the present tense from *o* to *ue*, such as *dormir* (to sleep)

In the present indicative, the changes take place in the first, second and third persons singular and the third person plural, when the stress falls on the stem:

e > i	e > ie	o > ue
pedir	sentir	dormir
pido	siento	duermo
pides	sientes	duermes
pide	siente	duerme
pedimos	sentimos	dormimos
pedís	sentís	dormís
piden	sienten	duermen

In the stem of the preterite, in the third persons singular and plural, *e* changes to *i* and *o* changes to *u*:

pedí	sentí	dormí
pediste	sentiste	dormiste
pidió	sintió	durmió
pedimos	sentimos	dormimos
pedisteis	sentisteis	dormisteis
pidieron	sintieron	durmieron

The stem also changes in the *tú* (familiar) form of the imperative, following the pattern of the present indicative:

pide

siente

duerme

In the gerund, the stem changes from *e > i* or *o > u*:

pidiendo

sintiendo

durmiendo

Other common verbs which follow the *e > i* pattern are:

conseguir	to succeed
corregir	to correct
despedir	to dismiss, say goodbye to
elegir	to choose
impedir	to prevent
medir	to measure
reír	to laugh (*río, ríes, ríe...*)
reñir	to quarrel
repetir	to repeat
seguir	to follow
sonreír	to smile (*sonrío, sonríes, sonríe...*)
vestir	to dress

Other common verbs that follow the *e > ie* pattern are:

convertir	to convert
divertir	to entertain
herir	to wound
mentir	to lie
preferir	to prefer
referir	to refer

The only verbs to follow the *o > ue* pattern are:

dormir	to sleep
morir	to die

Spelling changes in verbs

Some Spanish verbs make spelling changes in order to comply with the rules of Spanish pronunciation. These changes are of two types and affect:

- the consonant immediately before the verb ending, which changes in order to keep the correct sound
- the use of the accent, which is needed in order to keep the required stress on a vowel

Changes to the spelling of the final consonant:

For *-ar* verbs, these changes occur before the vowel *-e*:

- *c > qu*   *buscar*   to look for

  present subjunctive: *busque, busques, busque* etc.
  preterite: *busqué, buscaste* etc.

- *g > gu*   *llegar*   to arrive

  present subjunctive: *llegue, llegues, llegue* etc.
  preterite: *llegué, llegaste* etc.

- *z > c*   *empezar*   to begin

  present subjunctive: *empiece, empieces, empiece* etc.
  preterite: *empecé, empezaste* etc.

For *-er* and *-ir* verbs, these changes occur before the vowel *-o* in the first person singular of the present indicative and before *-a* in the present subjunctive:

- *c > z*   *vencer*   to conquer

  present indicative: *venzo, vences* etc.
  present subjunctive: *venza, venzas, venza* etc.

- *g > j*   *coger*   to take, catch

  present indicative: *cojo, coges* etc.
  present subjunctive: *coja, cojas* etc.

- *gu > g*   *seguir*   to follow

  present indicative: *sigo, sigues* etc.
  present subjunctive: *siga, sigas, siga* etc.

Addition of an accent in order to keep the correct stress

Verbs ending in *-uar* and *-iar* do not have an accent in their infinitive form but they add an accent in the first, second and third persons singular and in the third person plural of the present indicative, the present subjunctive and in the *tú* form of the imperative:

continuar (to continue)		
Present indicative	**Present subjunctive**	**Imperative**
continúo	*continúe*	
continúas	*continúes*	*continúa*
continúa	*continúe*	
continuamos	*continuemos*	
continuáis	*continuéis*	
continúan	*continúen*	

enviar (to send)		
Present indicative	**Present subjunctive**	**Imperative**
envío	*envíe*	
envías	*envíes*	*envía*
envía	*envíe*	
enviamos	*enviemos*	
enviáis	*enviéis*	
envían	*envíen*	

Negatives

It is usual in Spanish for the negative to be expressed by two words (with the exception of *no* meaning 'not'). All the negatives below can, however, be expressed either:

- as two words, with *no* before the verb and the negative word after it, or
- as one word placed before the verb, eliminating the need for *no*

For example, 'They say that it never snows in Malaga' can be translated as:

*Dicen que **no** nieva **nunca** en Málaga.*

or

*Dicen que **nunca** nieva en Málaga.*

Negative	Example
no	*No viene.* (He isn't coming.)
nunca	*No llueve nunca.* (It never rains.)
jamás	*No voy a volver jamás.* (I'm never going to come back.)
tampoco	*Tampoco lo sabían ellos.* (They didn't know either.)
ni...ni...	*Ayer no vinieron ni Carlos ni Pepe.* (Neither Carlos nor Pepe came yesterday.)
nada	*No sabe nada.* (He doesn't know anything.)
nadie	*No hay nadie aquí.* (There is nobody here.)
ninguno	*No hay ninguna persona en la calle.* (There is no one in the street.)

Prepositions

a

a translates the English word 'at' when it refers to time or rate:

> *a la una*
> at one o'clock

> *Están viajando a solo 20 kilómetros por hora.*
> They are only travelling at 20 kph.

de

de means 'of', indicating possession, and 'from', indicating origin. It can also mean 'by', 'about' and 'in':

> *Están hablando de ti.*
> They are talking about you.

> *Vienen de Almagro.*
> They are coming from Almagro.

en

en means 'in' and 'at' of location:

> *en casa*
> at home

> *Estaba esperando en la estación.*
> He was waiting at the station.

enfrente de and frente a

These two prepositional phrases mean 'opposite':

> *La oficina de turismo está enfrente de/frente a la catedral.*
> The tourist office is opposite the cathedral.

para

para means 'for' and '(in order) to' in the sense of destination or purpose:

> *Tomamos una botella de agua fría para el viaje.*
> We're taking a bottle of cold water for the journey.

> *Voy a utilizar mi tarjeta de crédito para pagar el hotel.*
> I'm going to use my credit card to pay for the hotel.

por

por is used for cause and origin. The English equivalents of *por* are 'by', 'through', 'on behalf of' and 'because of':

> *Lo compré por Internet.*
> I bought it through the internet.

> *Hablaremos por teléfono.*
> We'll speak on the phone.

> *Salió por la puerta principal.*
> He went out by the main door.

> *Contesté por él.*
> I answered on his behalf.

por is also used to introduce the agent in passive sentences (see p. 163):

> *Aquel poema fue escrito por García Lorca.*
> That poem was written by García Lorca.

sobre

sobre means 'on (top of)', 'above' or 'over':

> *El avión voló sobre mi casa.*
> The plane flew over my house

> *Tus postales están sobre la mesa.*
> Your postcards are on the table.

sobre is also used to indicate an approximate time or number:

> *Llegarán sobre las nueve.*
> They'll arrive around 9 o'clock.

Conjunctions

Conjunctions are words that link phrases and sentences. Examples of conjunctions are:

y	and
o	or
pero	but
porque	because
cuando	when

> *Quiero ir al cine pero mi madre no me deja salir.*
> I want to go to the cinema but my mother won't let me go out.

> *Ha venido porque quiere hablar con el profesor.*
> He's come because he wants to speak to the teacher.

Note: *y* becomes *e* before 'i' and 'hi':

> *Pedro es serio e inteligente.*
> Pedro is serious and intelligent.

o becomes *u* before 'o' and 'ho':

> *siete u ocho*
> seven or eight

Numbers

Cardinal numbers

The numbers that are used for counting are called cardinal numbers:

1	*uno/una*
2	*dos*
3	*tres*
4	*cuatro*
5	*cinco*
6	*seis*
7	*siete*
8	*ocho*
9	*nueve*
10	*diez*
11	*once*
12	*doce*
13	*trece*
14	*catorce*
15	*quince*
16	*dieciséis*
17	*diecisiete*
18	*dieciocho*
19	*diecinueve*
20	*veinte*
21	*veintiuno/una*
22	*veintidós*
23	*veintitrés*
24	*veinticuatro*
25	*veinticinco*
26	*veintiséis*
27	*veintisiete*
28	*veintiocho*
29	*veintinueve*
30	*treinta*
31	*treinta y uno*
32	*treinta y dos*
40	*cuarenta*
50	*cincuenta*
60	*sesenta*
70	*setenta*
80	*ochenta*
90	*noventa*
100	*cien(to)*
101	*ciento uno/una*
102	*ciento dos*
153	*ciento cincuenta y dos*
200	*doscientos/as*
300	*trescientos/as*
400	*cuatrocientos/as*
500	*quinientos/as*
600	*seiscientos/as*
700	*setecientos/as*
800	*ochocientos/as*
900	*novecientos/as*
1000	*mil*
1001	*mil uno/una*
4.005	*cuatro mil cinco*
7.238	*siete mil doscientos treinta y ocho*
1.000.000	*un millón*
9.000.000	*nueve millones*

Notes:

- Numbers up to 30 are written as one word.
- *uno* becomes *un* before a masculine singular noun:

  un billete
  one ticket

  cuarenta y un años
  forty-one years

- Cardinal numbers containing *un(o)* and multiples of *ciento* have a masculine and a feminine form; other numbers do not:

  trescientas libras
   three hundred pounds

- *Ciento* is shortened to *cien* before a noun or an adjective but not before another number, except *mil*:

  cien kilómetros
  a hundred kilometres

  ciento veinte litros
  a hundred and twenty litres

- There is no indefinite article before *cien* and *mil*, unlike the English 'a hundred' and 'a thousand':

  mil euros
  a thousand euros

- *Un millón* (a million) is preceded by the indefinite article, as in English, and is followed by *de*:

  un millón de habitantes
  a million inhabitants

- Numbers over a thousand are frequently written with a dot after the figure for a thousand. This sometimes happens with dates:

20.301	20,301
2.009	2009

Gramática

Ordinal numbers

Ordinal numbers indicate the order or sequence of things (1st, 2nd, 3rd, 4th, etc.):

1st	$1°/1^a$	*primero/a*
2nd	$2°/2^a$	*segundo/a*
3rd	$3°/3^a$	*tercero/a*
4th	$4°/4^a$	*cuarto/a*
5th	$5°/5^a$	*quinto/a*
6th	$6°/6^a$	*sexto/a*
7th	$7°/7^a$	*séptimo/a*
8th	$8°/8^a$	*octavo/a*
9th	$9°/9^a$	*noveno/a*
10th	$10°/10^a$	*décimo/a*

Ordinal numbers agree with the noun in number and gender:

las primeras horas de la mañana
the first hours of the morning

Primero and *tercero* drop the final *-o* before a masculine singular noun:

el primer día de la primavera
the first day of spring

el tercer piso
the third floor

Ordinal numbers are normally used up to 10, after which cardinal numbers are used:

Carlos V (read '*quinto*')
Charles V (the fifth)

but

el siglo XXI (read '*veintiuno*')
the twenty-first century

Time, dates and years

Clock time

Cardinal numbers are used to tell the time. With *la una*, the singular of *ser* is used; the plural is used with all other times:

¿Qué hora es?
What time is it?

Es la una y media.
It's half past one.

Son las ocho y media.
It's half-past eight.

Note that the 24-hour clock is used for timetables:

El tren salió a las 20.45.
The train left at 8.45 p.m.

The phrases '*de la mañana*' (a.m.) and '*de la tarde/ noche*' (p.m.) are often placed after the number:

las seis de la mañana
6 a.m.

las diez y cuarto de la noche
10.15 p.m.

Dates

For dates, cardinal numbers are used except for the first of the month, where the ordinal number is used:

el 4 de julio
4th July

el primero de enero
1st January

Note that when writing the date it is usual to insert *de* before the month and year:

el 3 de marzo de 1995
3rd March 1995

Years

In Spanish, years are expressed by listing thousands, hundreds, tens and units.

mil novecientos cincuenta y nueve
nineteen hundred and fifty nine

dos mil diez
two thousand and ten

Time expressions

The idea of 'for' with a period of time can be expressed by using *desde hace* plus the time expression:

Vivimos en Méjico desde hace 3 años.
We've lived in Mexico for 3 years.

or *llevar* followed by the gerund:

Llevamos 3 años viviendo en Méjico.

Note that this construction involves a change of tense from the English perfect to the Spanish present. Similarly, the pluperfect tense in English is translated by the imperfect tense in Spanish:

Vivíamos en Méjico desde hacía 3 años
or
Llevábamos 3 años viviendo en Méjico.
We had lived in Mexico for 3 years.

Verb tables

Regular verbs

hablar

		Gerund: *hablando*	Past principle: *hablado*
Imperative familiar	**Present indicative**	**Imperfect indicative**	**Preterite**
habla	hablo	hablaba	hablé
hablad	hablas	hablabas	hablaste
	habla	hablaba	habló
	hablamos	hablábamos	hablamos
	habláis	hablabais	hablasteis
	hablan	hablaban	hablaron
Future	**Conditional**	**Present subjunctive**	**Imperfect subjunctive**
hablaré	hablaría	hable	hablara/ase
hablarás	hablarías	hables	hablaras/ases
hablará	hablaría	hable	hablara/ase
hablaremos	hablaríamos	hablemos	habláramos/ásemos
hablaréis	hablaríais	habléis	hablarais/aseis
hablarán	hablarían	hablen	hablaran/asen

comer

		Gerund: *comiendo*	Past principle: *comido*
Imperative familiar	**Present indicative**	**Imperfect indicative**	**Preterite**
come	como	comía	comí
comed	comes	comías	comiste
	come	comía	comió
	comemos	comíamos	comimos
	coméis	comíais	comisteis
	comen	comían	comieron
Future	**Conditional**	**Present subjunctive**	**Imperfect subjunctive**
comeré	comería	coma	comiera/ese
comerás	comerías	comas	comieras/eses
comerá	comería	coma	comiera/ese
comeremos	comeríamos	comamos	comiéramos/ésemos
comeréis	comeríais	comáis	comierais/eseis
comerán	comerían	coman	comieran/esen

escribir

		Gerund: *escribiendo*	Past principle: *escrito*
Imperative familiar	**Present indicative**	**Imperfect indicative**	**Preterite**
escribe	escribo	escribía	escribí
escribid	escribes	escribías	escribiste
	escribe	escribía	escribió
	escribimos	escribíamos	escribimos
	escribís	escribíais	escribisteis
	escriben	escribían	escribieron
Future	**Conditional**	**Present subjunctive**	**Imperfect subjunctive**
escribiré	escribiría	escriba	escribiera/ese
escribirás	escribirías	escribas	escribieras/eses
escribirá	escribiría	escriba	escribiera/ese
escribiremos	escribiríamos	escribamos	escribiéramos/ésemos
escribiréis	escribiríais	escribáis	escribierais/eseis
escribirán	escribirían	escriban	escribieran/esen

Common irregular verbs

conocer		Gerund: *conociendo*	Past principle: *conocido*
Imperative familiar	**Present indicative**	**Imperfect indicative**	**Preterite**
conoce	conozco	conocía	conocí
conoced	conoces	conocías	conociste
	conoce	conocía	conoció
	conocemos	conocíamos	conocimos
	conocéis	conociáis	conocisteis
	conocen	conocían	conocieron

Future	**Conditional**	**Present subjunctive**	**Imperfect subjunctive**
conoceré	conocería	conozca	conociera/ese
conocerás	conocerías	conozcas	conocieras/eses
conocerá	conocería	conozca	conociera/ese
conoceremos	conoceríamos	conozcamos	conociéramos/ésemos
conoceréis	conoceríais	conozcáis	conocierais/eseis
conocerán	conocerían	conozcan	conocieran/esen

dar		Gerund: *dando*	Past principle: *dado*
Imperative familiar	**Present indicative**	**Imperfect indicative**	**Preterite**
da	doy	daba	di
dad	das	dabas	diste
	da	daba	dio
	damos	dábamos	dimos
	dais	dabais	disteis
	dan	daban	dieron

Future	**Conditional**	**Present subjunctive**	**Imperfect subjunctive**
daré	daría	dé	diera/ese
darás	darías	des	dieras/eses
dará	daría	dé	diera/ese
daremos	daríamos	demos	diéramos/ésemos
daréis	daríais	deis	dierais/eseis
darán	darían	den	dieran/esen

decir		Gerund: *diciendo*	Past principle: *dicho*
Imperative familiar	**Present indicative**	**Imperfect indicative**	**Preterite**
di	digo	decía	dije
decid	dices	decías	dijiste
	dice	decía	dijo
	decimos	decíamos	dijimos
	decís	decíais	dijisteis
	dicen	decían	dijeron

Future	**Conditional**	**Present subjunctive**	**Imperfect subjunctive**
diré	diría	diga	dijera/ese
dirás	dirías	digas	dijeras/eses
dirá	diría	diga	dijera/ese
diremos	diríamos	digamos	dijéramos/ésemos
diréis	diríais	digáis	dijerais/eseis
dirán	dirían	digan	dijeran/esen

estar

		Gerund: estando	Past principle: estado
Imperative familiar	**Present indicative**	**Imperfect indicative**	**Preterite**
está	estoy	estaba	estuve
estad	estás	estabas	estuviste
	está	estaba	estuvo
	estamos	estábamos	estuvimos
	estáis	estabais	estuvisteis
	están	estaban	estuvieron

Future	**Conditional**	**Present subjunctive**	**Imperfect subjunctive**
estaré	estaría	esté	estuviera/ese
estarás	estarías	estés	estuvieras/eses
estará	estaría	esté	estuviera/ese
estaremos	estaríamos	estemos	estuviéramos/ésemos
estaréis	estaríais	estéis	estuvierais/eseis
estarán	estarían	estén	estuvieran/esen

haber (auxilary verb)

		Gerund: habiendo	Past principle: habido
Imperative familiar	**Present indicative**	**Imperfect indicative**	**Preterite**
Imperative not used	he	había	hube
	has	habías	hubiste
	ha	había	hubo
	hemos	habíamos	hubimos
	habéis	habíais	hubisteis
	han	habían	hubieron

Future	**Conditional**	**Present subjunctive**	**Imperfect subjunctive**
habré	habría	haya	hubiera/ese
habrás	habrías	hayas	hubieras/eses
habrá	habría	haya	hubiera/ese
habremos	habríamos	hayamos	hubiéramos/ésemos
habréis	habríais	hayáis	hubierais/eseis
habrán	habrían	hayan	hubieran/esen

hacer

		Gerund: haciendo	Past principle: hecho
Imperative familiar	**Present indicative**	**Imperfect indicative**	**Preterite**
haz	hago	hacía	hice
haced	haces	hacías	hiciste
	hace	hacía	hizo
	hacemos	hacíamos	hicimos
	hacéis	hacíais	hicisteis
	hacen	hacían	hicieron

Future	**Conditional**	**Present subjunctive**	**Imperfect subjunctive**
haré	haría	haga	hiciera/ese
harás	harías	hagas	hicieras/eses
hará	haría	haga	hiciera/ese
haremos	haríamos	hagamos	hiciéramos/ésemos
haréis	haríais	hagáis	hicierais/eseis
harán	harían	hagan	hicieran/esen

ir — Gerund: *yendo* — Past principle: *ido*

Imperative familiar	Present indicative	Imperfect indicative	Preterite
ve	voy	iba	fui
id	vas	ibas	fuiste
	va	iba	fue
	vamos	íbamos	fuimos
	vais	ibais	fuisteis
	van	iban	fueron

Future	Conditional	Present subjunctive	Imperfect subjunctive
iré	iría	vaya	fuera/se
irás	irías	vayas	fueras/eses
irá	iría	vaya	fuera/ese
iremos	iríamos	vayamos	fuéramos/ésemos
iréis	iríais	vayáis	fuerais/eseis
irán	irían	vayan	fueran/esen

leer — Gerund: *leyendo* — Past principle: *leído*

Imperative familiar	Present indicative	Imperfect indicative	Preterite
lee	leo	leía	leí
leed	lees	leías	leíste
	lee	leía	leyó
	leemos	leíamos	leímos
	leéis	leíais	leísteis
	leen	leían	leyeron

Future	Conditional	Present subjunctive	Imperfect subjunctive
leeré	leería	lea	leyera/ese
leerás	leerías	leas	leyeras/eses
leerá	leería	lea	leyera/ese
leeremos	leeríamos	leamos	leyéramos/ésemos
leeréis	leeríais	leáis	leyerais/eseis
leerán	leerían	lean	leyeran/esen

oír — Gerund: *oyendo* — Past principle: *oído*

Imperative familiar	Present indicative	Imperfect indicative	Preterite
oye	oigo	oía	oí
oíd	oyes	oías	oíste
	oye	oía	oyó
	oímos	oíamos	oímos
	oís	oíais	oísteis
	oyen	oían	oyeron

Future	Conditional	Present subjunctive	Imperfect subjunctive
oiré	oiría	oiga	oyera/ese
oirás	oirías	oigas	oyeras/eses
oirá	oiría	oiga	oyera/ese
oiremos	oiríamos	oigamos	oyéramos/ésemos
oiréis	oiríais	oigáis	oyerais/eseis
oirán	oirían	oigan	oyeran/esen

pedir

		Gerund: *pidiendo*	Past principle: *pedido*

Imperative familiar	Present indicative	Imperfect indicative	Preterite
pide	pido	pedía	pedí
pedid	pides	pedías	pediste
	pide	pedía	pidió
	pedimos	pedíamos	pedimos
	pedís	pedíais	pedisteis
	piden	pedían	pidieron

Future	Conditional	Present subjunctive	Imperfect subjunctive
pediré	pediría	pida	pidiera/ese
pedirás	pedirías	pidas	pidieras/eses
pedirá	pediría	pida	pidiera/ese
pediremos	pediríamos	pidamos	pidiéramos/ésemos
pediréis	pediríais	pidáis	pidierais/eseis
pedirán	pedirían	pidan	pidieran/esen

poder

		Gerund: *pudiendo*	Past principle: *podido*

Imperative familiar	Present indicative	Imperfect indicative	Preterite
Imperative not used	puedo	podía	pude
	puedes	podías	pudiste
	puede	podía	pudo
	podemos	podíamos	pudimos
	podéis	podíais	pudisteis
	pueden	podían	pudieron

Future	Conditional	Present subjunctive	Imperfect subjunctive
podré	podría	pueda	pudiera/ese
podrás	podrías	puedas	pudieras/eses
podrá	podría	pueda	pudiera/ese
podremos	podríamos	podamos	pudiéramos/ésemos
podréis	podríais	podáis	pudierais/eseis
podrán	podrían	puedan	pudieran/esen

poner

		Gerund: *poniendo*	Past principle: *puesto*

Imperative familiar	Present indicative	Imperfect indicative	Preterite
pon	pongo	ponía	puse
poned	pones	ponías	pusiste
	pone	ponía	puso
	ponemos	poníamos	pusimos
	ponéis	poníais	pusisteis
	ponen	ponían	pusieron

Future	Conditional	Present subjunctive	Imperfect subjunctive
pondré	pondría	ponga	pusiera/ese
pondrás	pondrías	pongas	pusieras/eses
pondrá	pondría	ponga	pusiera/ese
pondremos	pondríamos	pongamos	pusiéramos/ésemos
pondréis	pondríais	pongáis	pusierais/eseis
pondrán	pondrían	pongan	pusieran/esen

querer — Gerund: *queriendo* — Past principle: *querido*

Imperative familiar	Present indicative	Imperfect indicative	Preterite
quiere	quiero	quería	quise
quered	quieres	querías	quisiste
	quiere	quería	quiso
	queremos	queríamos	quisimos
	queréis	queríais	quisisteis
	quieren	querían	quisieron

Future	Conditional	Present subjunctive	Imperfect subjunctive
querré	querría	quiera	quisiera/ese
querrás	querrías	quieras	quisieras/eses
querrá	querría	quiera	quisiera/ese
querremos	querríamos	queramos	quisiéramos/ésemos
querréis	querríais	queráis	quisierais/eseis
querrán	querrían	quieran	quisieran/esen

saber — Gerund: *sabiendo* — Past principle: *sabido*

Imperative familiar	Present indicative	Imperfect indicative	Preterite
sabe	sé	sabía	supe
sabed	sabes	sabías	supiste
	sabe	sabía	supo
	sabemos	sabíamos	supimos
	sabéis	sabíais	supisteis
	saben	sabían	supieron

Future	Conditional	Present subjunctive	Imperfect subjunctive
sabré	sabría	sepa	supiera/ese
sabrás	sabrías	sepas	supieras/eses
sabrá	sabría	sepa	supiera/ese
sabremos	sabríamos	sepamos	supiéramos/ésemos
sabréis	sabríais	sepáis	supierais/eseis
sabrán	sabrían	sepan	supieran/esen

salir — Gerund: *saliendo* — Past principle: *salido*

Imperative familiar	Present indicative	Imperfect indicative	Preterite
sal	salgo	salía	salí
salid	sales	salías	saliste
	sale	salía	salió
	salimos	salíamos	salimos
	salís	salíais	salisteis
	salen	salían	salieron

Future	Conditional	Present subjunctive	Imperfect subjunctive
saldré	saldría	salga	saliera/ese
saldrás	saldrías	salgas	salieras/eses
saldrá	saldría	salga	saliera/ese
saldremos	saldríamos	salgamos	saliéramos/ésemos
saldréis	saldríais	salgáis	salierais/eseis
saldrán	saldrían	salgan	salieran/esen

seguir
Gerund: *siguiendo* **Past principle:** *seguido*

Imperative familiar	Present indicative	Imperfect indicative	Preterite
sigue	sigo	seguía	seguí
seguid	sigues	seguías	seguiste
	sigue	seguía	siguió
	seguimos	seguíamos	seguimos
	seguís	seguíais	seguisteis
	siguen	seguían	siguieron

Future	Conditional	Present subjunctive	Imperfect subjunctive
seguiré	seguiría	siga	siguiera/ese
seguirás	seguirías	sigas	siguieras/eses
seguirá	seguiría	siga	siguiera/ese
seguiremos	seguiríamos	sigamos	siguiéramos/ésemos
seguiréis	seguiríais	sigáis	siguierais/eseis
seguirán	seguirían	sigan	siguieran/esen

sentir
Gerund: *sintiendo* **Past principle:** *sentido*

Imperative familiar	Present indicative	Imperfect indicative	Preterite
siente	siento	sentía	sentí
sentid	sientes	sentías	sentiste
	siente	sentía	sintió
	sentimos	sentíamos	sentimos
	sentís	sentíais	sentisteis
	sienten	sentían	sintieron

Future	Conditional	Present subjunctive	Imperfect subjunctive
sentiré	sentiría	sienta	sintiera/ese
sentirás	sentirías	sientas	sintieras/eses
sentirá	sentiría	sienta	sintiera/ese
sentiremos	sentiríamos	sintamos	sintiéramos/ésemos
sentiréis	sentiríais	sintáis	sintierais/eseis
sentirán	sentirían	sientan	sintieran/esen

ser
Gerund: *siendo* **Past principle:** *sido*

Imperative familiar	Present indicative	Imperfect indicative	Preterite
sé	soy	era	fui
sed	eres	eras	fuiste
	es	era	fue
	somos	éramos	fuimos
	sois	erais	fuisteis
	son	eran	fueron

Future	Conditional	Present subjunctive	Imperfect subjunctive
seré	sería	sea	fuera/ese
serás	serías	seas	fueras/eses
será	sería	sea	fuera/ese
seremos	seríamos	seamos	fuéramos/ésemos
seréis	seríais	seáis	fuerais/eseis
serán	serían	sean	fueran/esen

Verb tables

tener		Gerund: *teniendo*		Past principle: *tenido*

Imperative familiar	Present indicative	Imperfect indicative	Preterite
ten	tengo	tenía	tuve
tened	tienes	tenías	tuviste
	tiene	tenía	tuvo
	tenemos	teníamos	tuvimos
	tenéis	teníais	tuvisteis
	tienen	tenían	tuvieron

Future	Conditional	Present subjunctive	Imperfect subjunctive
tendré	tendría	tenga	tuviera/ese
tendrás	tendrías	tengas	tuvieras/eses
tendrá	tendría	tenga	tuviera/ese
tendremos	tendríamos	tengamos	tuviéramos/ésemos
tendréis	tendríais	tengáis	tuvierais/eseis
tendrán	tendrían	tengan	tuvieran/esen

traer		Gerund: *trayendo*		Past principle: *traído*

Imperative familiar	Present indicative	Imperfect indicative	Preterite
trae	traigo	traía	traje
traed	traes	traías	trajiste
	trae	traía	trajo
	traemos	traíamos	trajimos
	traéis	traíais	trajisteis
	traen	traían	trajeron

Future	Conditional	Present subjunctive	Imperfect subjunctive
traeré	traería	traiga	trajera/ese
traerás	traerías	traigas	trajeras/eses
traerá	traería	traiga	trajera/ese
traeremos	traeríamos	traigamos	trajéramos/ésemos
traeréis	traeríais	traigáis	trajerais/eseis
traerán	traerían	traigan	trajeran/esen

venir		Gerund: *viniendo*		Past principle: *venido*

Imperative familiar	Present indicative	Imperfect indicative	Preterite
ven	vengo	venía	vine
venid	vienes	venías	viniste
	viene	venía	vino
	venimos	veníamos	vinimos
	venís	veníais	vinisteis
	vienen	venían	vinieron

Future	Conditional	Present subjunctive	Imperfect subjunctive
vendré	vendría	venga	viniera/ese
vendrás	vendrías	vengas	vinieras/eses
vendrá	vendría	venga	viniera/ese
vendremos	vendríamos	vengamos	viniéramos/ésemos
vendréis	vendríais	vengáis	vinierais/eseis
vendrán	vendrían	vengan	vinieran/esen

ver

Gerund: *viendo*   **Past principle:** *visto*

Imperative familiar	Present indicative	Imperfect indicative	Preterite
ve	veo	veía	vi
ved	ves	veías	viste
	ve	veía	vio
	vemos	veíamos	vimos
	veis	veíais	visteis
	ven	veían	vieron

Future	Conditional	Present subjunctive	Imperfect subjunctive
veré	vería	vea	viera/ese
verás	verías	veas	vieras/eses
verá	vería	vea	viera/ese
veremos	veríamos	veamos	viéramos/ésemos
veréis	veríais	veáis	vierais/eseis
verán	verían	vean	vieran/esen

volver

Gerund: *volviendo*   **Past principle:** *vuelto*

Imperative familiar	Present indicative	Imperfect indicative	Preterite
vuelve	vuelvo	volvía	volví
volved	vuelves	volvías	volviste
	vuelve	volvía	volvió
	volvemos	volvíamos	volvimos
	volvéis	volvíais	volvisteis
	vuelven	volvían	volvieron

Future	Conditional	Present subjunctive	Imperfect subjunctive
volveré	volvería	vuelva	volviera/ese
volverás	volverías	vuelvas	volvieras/eses
volverá	volvería	vuelva	volviera/ese
volveremos	volveríamos	volvamos	volviéramos/ésemos
volveréis	volveríais	volváis	volvierais/eseis
volverán	volverían	vuelvan	volvieran/esen

Vocabulario

The following abbreviations are used in this section:

(*coll.*)   colloquial
(*f*)   feminine
(*LA*)   Latin America
(*Sp*)   Spain

A

a (su) alcance   within (their) reach
a causa de   because of
a comienzos de   at the beginning of
a diario   daily
a eso de   around
a finales de   at the end of
a la derecha   to the right
a la izquierda   to the left
a la semana   per week, weekly
al aire libre   in the open air
al contrario   on the contrary
al día siguiente   the next day
al final de   at the end of
al lado de   next to
al lado del mar   by the seaside
al mismo tiempo   at the same time
a lo alto de   at the top of
a lo largo de   along, throughout
a lo mejor   maybe
a menudo   often
a partir de   from, starting on
a pesar de   in spite of
¿a qué hora?   at what time?
a toda hora   at all times
a través de   across
a veces   sometimes
abajo   below, down(stairs)
el **abanico**   fan
abierto/a   open
el/la **abogado/a**   lawyer
el **abrazo**   hug
el **abrigo**   coat
abril   April
abrir   to open

el/la **abuelo/a**   granddad/ grandma
aburrido/a   boring, bored
aburrirse   to get bored
abusar   to bully; to abuse
acá   here
acabar   to finish
acabar de   to have just
el **acantilado**   cliff
el **accidente**   accident
la **acción**   action
el **aceite de oliva**   olive oil
el **aceite**   oil
la **aceituna**   olive
aceptar   to accept
acerca de   about
acercarse a   to near, to approach
acompañar   to go with, to accompany
aconsejar   to advise
el **acontecimiento**   event
acordarse de   to remember
el **acoso escolar**   school bullying
acostarse   to go to bed
la **actitud**   attitude
la **actividad**   activity
las **actividades deportivas**   sporting activities
las **actividades extraescolares**   extra-curricular activities
activo/a   active
el **actor**   actor
el **actor secundario**   supporting actor
la **actriz**   actress
actuar   to act
adecuado/a   suitable, appropriate

además   moreover
además de   as well as
adentro   inside, within
admitir   to admit
el/la **adolescente**   teenager
¿adónde?   where to?
adoptar   to adopt
el **adulto**   adult
aeróbico/a   aerobic
el **aeropuerto**   airport
afeitarse   to shave
afortunado/a   fortunate
afuera   outside
la **agencia de viajes**   travel agency
agosto   August
agradable   pleasant
agradecer   to thank
agresivo/a   aggressive
el/la **agricultor/a**   farmer
el **agua** (*f*) **bendita**   holy water
el **agua** (*f*) **con gas**   fizzy/ sparkling water
el **agua** (*f*) **esterili- zada**   sterilised water
el **agua** (*f*) **mineral**   mineral water
el **aguacate**   avocado
aguantar   to put up with, to bear
ahí   there
ahora   now
ahorrar   to save
el **aire**   air
el **aire acondicionado**   air conditioning
aislado/a   isolated
aislante   insulating
el **ajedrez**   chess
el **ajo**   garlic
alargado/a   extended, long
el **albañil**   builder

el **albergue juvenil**   youth hostel
alcanzar   to reach
la **aldea**   village
alegre   happy, cheerful
la **alegría**   happiness, merriment
Alemania   Germany
el **alemán**   German (language/subject)
alemán/alemana   German
la **alergia**   allergy
alérgico/a   allergic
algo   something, anything
algo así   something like this/that
¿algo más?   anything else?
el **algodón**   cotton
alguien   someone
algún, alguno/a   some, any
algunas veces   sometimes
alimentar   to feed
el **alimento**   food
allí   there
el **almacén**   shop, store
la **almendra**   almond
el **alojamiento**   accommodation, lodging
el **alpinismo**   mountain/rock climbing
alojarse   to lodge, to stay
alquilar   to hire, to rent
alrededor de   around
los **alrededores**   outskirts
alterar   to alter
alto/a   tall
la **altura**   height
alucinante   fantastic, amazing
el/la **alumno/a**   pupil
el **ama** (*f*) **de casa**   housewife
amable   kind, friendly
amar   to love
amarillo/a   yellow
la **ambición**   ambition
ambicioso/a   ambitious
el **ambiente**   atmosphere, environment
ambos/as   both
la **amenaza**   threat
amenazar   to threaten

América Latina   Latin America
el/la **amigo/a**   friend
la **amistad**   friendship
el/la **amo/a de casa**   housewife/husband
amplio/a   roomy, spacious
ancho/a   wide
anciano/a   old
los **ancianos**   old people
andando   on foot, walking
andar   to walk
el **andén**   platform
el/la **anfitrión/anfitriona**   host(ess)
el **anillo**   ring
animado/a   lively
el **animal salvaje**   wild animal
animar   to encourage
anoche   last night
anteayer   the day before yesterday
la **antena**   aerial
antes (de)   before
anticuado/a   old-fashioned
las **antigüedades**   antiques
antiguo/a   former; ancient
antipático/a   unpleasant; unkind
el **anuncio**   advertisement
añadir   to add
el **año**   year
apagar   to switch/turn off
el **aparador**   sideboard
el **aparato**   machine
el **aparcamiento**   parking
aparcar   to park
aparecer   to appear
la **apariencia**   appearance
el **apartamento**   flat, apartment
aparte de   apart from
el **apellido**   surname
apenas   scarcely
apetecer   to appeal, to fancy
aprender (a)   to learn (to)
el **aprendizaje**   apprenticeship
aprobar   to pass (examinations)

apropiado/a   appropriate
aprovechar   to use, to make use of
aproximadamente   about, approximately
apuntar   to note
el **apunte**   note
aquí   here
árabe   Arabic
la **araña**   spider
el **árbol**   tree
archivar   to file
archivo   file
el **área** (*f*)   area
la **arena**   sand
Argentina   Argentina
el **argumento**   argument
el **armario**   wardrobe; cupboard
el **arpa** (*f*)   harp
el/la **arqueólogo/a**   archaeologist
el/la **arquitecto/a**   architect
arquitectónico/a   architectural
arreglar   to arrange, to put right, to tidy
arriba   above, up(stairs)
la **arroba**   @
el **arroz**   rice
el **arte dramático**   drama
las **artes marciales**   martial arts
la **artesanía**   crafts
el **artículo**   article
el/la **artista**   artist
la **asamblea**   assembly
asar   to roast
el **ascensor**   lift
asegurar   to assure
el **aseo**   toilet
asequible   achievable
así   thus
así que   and so
el **asiento**   seat
el/la **asesor/a**   consultant
la **asignatura**   (school) subject
asistir a   to attend
la **aspiradora**   vacuum cleaner
el **asunto**   topic
asustar   to frighten

el **ataque** attack
atar to tie
aterrizar to land
el **ático** attic
el **atletismo** athletics
atracar to mug
la **atracción** attraction
el **atraco** mugging
atrevido/a daring
atropellar to knock down
el **atún** tuna
el **aula** (*f*) classroom
aumentar to increase
el **aumento** increase
aun even
aún still, yet
aunque although
Austria Austria
el **autobús** bus
el **autocar** coach
la **autopista** motorway
las **autoridades** authorities
el/la **auxiliar de vuelo** flight
attendant
el **avance** advance
el **ave** (*f*) bird
la **aventura** adventure
la **avería** breakdown
averiguar to find out
el **avión** plane
el **aviso** warning
la **avispa** wasp
ayer yesterday
la **ayuda** help
ayudar to help
el **ayuntamiento** town hall
el/la **azafato/a** flight attendant
el **azafrán** saffron
el **azúcar** sugar
azul blue

B

el **bacalao** cod
bailar to dance
el **baile** dance
bajar to go down

bajo beneath, under
bajo/a low, short
el **bádminton** badminton
el **baile** dance
el **balcón** balcony
el **baloncesto** basketball
el **balonmano** handball
el **banco** bank
la **banda sonora** soundtrack
la **bandera** flag
bañarse to have a bath; to
bathe
bañarse en el mar to swim
in the sea
la **bañera** bath
el **baño** bath(room)
barato/a cheap
la **barba** beard
la **barbacoa** barbecue
el **barco** boat
la **barra** loaf
barrer el suelo to sweep the
floor
el **barrio** neighbourhood, area
¡basta! (that's) enough!
bastante quite, enough, a little
bit
bastar to be enough
la **basura** rubbish
el **basurero** bin
la **batalla** battle
la **batería** drumkit
el/la **bebé** baby
beber to drink
la **bebida** drink
el **béisbol** baseball
el **belén** crib
Bélgica Belgium
la **belleza** beauty
bello/a beautiful
el **beneficio** benefit
besar to kiss
el **beso** kiss
la **biblioteca** library
la **bicicleta, bici** (*coll.*) bicycle,
bike
bien educado/a
well-mannered, polite

los **bienes** goods, possessions
el **bienestar** well-being
bienvenido/a welcome
el **bigote** moustache
el **billar** billiards
el **billete** ticket (travel)
el **billete de ida y**
vuelta return ticket
el **billete sencillo** single ticket
la **biología** biology
el/la **bisabuelo/a** great-
granddad/great-grandma
el **bistec** steak
blanco/a white
el **bloc** pad
el **bloque** block
la **blusa** blouse
bobo/a silly
la **boca** mouth
el **bocadillo** sandwich
la **boda** wedding
la **bodega** wine cellar; winery
la **bola de nieve** snowball
la **bolera** bowling alley
el **bolígrafo, boli** (*coll.*) biro
el **bollo** bread roll
la **bolsa** bag
la **bolsa de plástico** plastic
bag
el **bolsillo** pocket
el **bolso** handbag
el/la **bombero/a** firefighter
bonito/a pretty
el **bono de lotería** lottery ticket
borracho/a drunk
borrar to delete
la **borrachera** drunkenness
el **bosque** wood
la **bota** boot
el **bote** can, tin
la **botella** bottle
el **botellón** binge-drinking
el **botiquín** first-aid kit
el **botón** button
el **boxeo** boxing
el **brazo** arm
Brasil Brazil
breve brief, short

brevemente briefly
brindar to drink a toast
el bricolaje DIY
británico/a British
bronceado/a tanned
broncearse to get brown
el buceo (scuba)diving
buenísimo/a very good
bueno/a good
el buen tiempo good weather
¡buen viaje! have a good journey!
la bufanda scarf
buscar to look for
buscar un trabajo to look for a job
la búsqueda search
la butaca seat, armchair
el buzón post-box

C

el caballo horse
la cabeza head
la cabina booth
la cacerola saucepan
cada each
cada día each/every day
cada vez más more and more
la cadena chain, channel
caer to fall
la caída fall
el café coffee
la cafetería café, coffee shop
la caja box; till
el/la cajero/a cashier
el cajero automático cash point
la cala cove
los calamares squid
los calcetines socks
la calculadora calculator
el caldo soup, broth
la calefacción heating
el calentamiento global global warming
la calidad quality

cálido/a hot (climate)
caliente hot
callado/a quiet
callarse to be quiet
la calle street
callejero/a (of the) street
el calor heat
caluroso/a hot, warm
calvo/a bald
la cama bed
la cámara camera
la camaradería camaraderie
el/la camarero/a waiter/waitress
cambiar to change
cambiarse to get changed
el cambio bureau de change
el camino road
el camión lorry
la camisa shirt
la camiseta T-shirt
la campana bell
el/la campeón/ campeona champion
el camping campsite
el campo the country(side)
el campo de deportes sports field
Canadá Canada
el canario canary
la canción song
el/la canguro babysitter
cansado/a tired
cansar to tire
el/la cantante singer
cantar to sing
la cantidad amount, quantity
cantidad de a lot of
la cantina canteen
la capacidad capacity
la capa de ozono ozone layer
la capa polar polar ice-cap
capaz capable
la capital capital (city)
la cara face
el caracol snail
el carácter character
caracterizarse por to be characterised by

el caramelo sweet
la caravana caravan
el carbón carbon; coal
la cárcel prison
la caridad charity
el cariño affection
cariñoso/a affectionate, loving
la carne meat
la carnicería butcher's
caro/a expensive
la carpeta folder
el/la carpintero/a carpenter, joiner
la carrera career; race
la carretera (main) road, highway
la carta letter
el/la cartero/a postman/ postwoman
el cartón carton; cardboard
la casa house
la casa de mis sueños dream house
casado/a married
casarse to get married
el casco helmet
casi almost
el caso case
castaño/a brown, chestnut (colour)
castigar to punish
el castigo detention; punishment
el castillo castle
la catarata waterfall
catastrófico/a catastrophic
el catarro cold
la catedral cathedral
católico/a catholic
la caza hunting
la cebolla onion
la celebración celebration
celebrar to celebrate
los celos jealousy
celoso/a jealous
la cena evening meal, dinner
cenar to have dinner

el **centímetro**   centimetre

céntrico/a   central

el **centro**   centre

el **centro comercial**   shopping centre

cepillarse los dientes   to brush one´s teeth

la **cerámica**   ceramics

cerca de   near (to)

cercano/a   near

el **cerdo**   pig; pork

los **cereales**   cereals

la **cerilla**   match

cerrar   to shut, to close (down)

la **cerveza**   beer

el **chalet**   house, cottage, bungalow

el **champán**   champagne

el **champiñón**   mushroom

el **champú**   shampoo

el **chantaje**   blackmail

la **chaqueta**   jacket

chatear   to chat

el/la **chico/a**   boy/girl

el **chicle**   chewing-gum

Chile   Chile

la **chinchilla**   chinchilla

Chipre   Cyprus

el **chófer**   driver

el **chubasco**   shower (of rain)

la **chuleta**   chop

el **ciclismo**   cycling

ciego/a   blind

el **cielo**   sky, heaven

cien(to)   a hundred

la **ciencia ficción**   science fiction

las **ciencias**   science

el/la **científico/a**   scientist

cierto/a   certain, true

la **cifra**   figure

el **cine**   cinema

el/la **cineasta**   film director

la **cinta**   ribbon, tape

la **cintura**   waist

el **cinturón**   belt

el/la **cirujano/a**   surgeon

la **cita**   date, appointment

la **ciudad**   town; city

la **civilización**   civilisation

claro/a   clear, light

la **clase**   class; lesson

el **clavo**   clove; nail

el/la **cliente**   customer

el **clima**   climate

el **club de jóvenes**   youth club

la **cobaya**   guinea pig

cocer   to cook

el **coche**   car

el **coche de carreras**   racing car

la **cocina**   kitchen; cooking; cooker

cocinar   to cook

el/la **cocinero/a**   cook, chef

el **codo**   elbow

coger   to take; to catch

coger recados   to take messages

cogerse un año sabático   to take a year out

coger un tren   to catch a train

coleccionar   to collect

el/la **colega**   colleague

el **colegio, cole** (*coll.*)   school (often independent)

el **colegio de primaria**   primary school

el **colegio de secundaria**   secondary school

el **collar**   necklace

colocar   to place

Colombia   Colombia

los **combustibles fósiles**   fossil fuels

la **comedia**   comedy

el **comedor**   dining room; canteen

comenzar (a)   to begin (to)

comer   to eat

el **Comercio Justo**   Fair Trade

cometer un crimen   to commit a crime

la **comida**   food; lunch-time meal

la **comida basura**   junk food

la **comida rápida**   fast food

la **comisaría**   police station

como   like, as, since

como es debido   properly, as it should be done

la **cómoda**   chest of drawers

cómodo/a   convenient, comfortable

el/la **compañero/a**   companion

la **compañía**   company

el **compartimiento**   compartment

compartir   to share

el **compás**   compass

los **complementos**   accessories

completar   to complete

el **comportamiento**   behaviour

comportarse   to behave

comprar   to buy

comprensivo/a   understanding

el **comprimido**   pill, tablet

común   common

la **computadora** (*LA*)   computer

las **comunicaciones**   communications

comunicar   to communicate

la **comunidad**   community

con   with

con respecto a   with respect to, concerning

con vistas al mar   with views of the sea

la **concentración**   concentration

concentrarse   to concentrate

el **concierto**   concert

el **concurso**   competition; game show

el **condado**   county

conducir   to drive, to lead

la **conducta**   behaviour

el/la **conductor/a**   driver

el **conejo**   rabbit

la **confianza** confidence, trust
el **conflicto** conflict
el **congelador** freezer
los **congelados** frozen products
conocer to know (a person/
place etc.)
conocido/a (well) known
los **conocimientos** knowledge
conquistar to overcome, to
conquer
la **consecuencia** consequence,
result
conseguir to obtain
el **consejo** (piece of) advice
consistir en to consist of
constipado/a having a cold
construir to build
consumir energía to
consume energy
el/la **contable** accountant
el **contacto** contact
la **contaminación** pollution
contaminado/a polluted
contaminar to contaminate,
pollute
contar to tell; to narrate; to
count
contar con to rely on
contener to contain
el **contenedor de**
abono compost bin
los **contenidos** contents
contento/a happy, content
el **contestador**
automático answer
machine
contestar to answer
(en) **contra (de)** against
la **contraseña** password
el **contrato** contract
contribuir to contribute
convencer to convince
convenir to suit
la **conversación** conversation
convertirse en to turn into
la **copa** glass, drink
la **copia** copy
el **corazón** heart

la **corbata** tie
el **cordero** lamb
la **corneta** cornet
el **coro** choir
la **correa** lead (dog's)
correcto/a correct
el **corrector líquido** correcting
fluid
corregir to correct
el **correo** mail
el **correo electrónico** e-mail
Correos post office
correr to run
la **corrida de toros** bullfight
cortar to cut
cortés courteous, polite
la **cortesía** politeness
corto/a short
el **cortometraje** short film
la **cosa** thing
la **costa** coast
costero/a coastal
la **costumbre** custom
cotidiano/a daily
crear to create
creativo/a creative
crecer to grow
creciente growing
el **crecimiento** growth
los **créditos** credits
la **creencia** belief
crear to create
creer to believe, to think
creído/a conceited
la **crema** cream
la **crema antiséptica** antiseptic
cream
la **crema de sol** sun cream
el **críquet** cricket
el **crimen** crime
el **cristal** glass
cristiano/a Christian
la **crítica de cine** film review
el **cruce** crossroads
cruzar to cross
el **cuaderno** exercise book
cuadrado/a square
¿cuál? which?, what?

la **cualidad** quality
las **cualificaciones** qualifications
cualquiera anyone
el **cuarto** quarter; room
el **cuarto de baño** bathroom
cubierto/a covered
la **cuchara** spoon
el **cuchillo** knife
el **cuello** neck
la **cuenta** bill
la **cuerda** rope, cord
el **cuero** leather
el **cuerpo** the body
cuesta mucho it costs a lot
¡cuidado! careful!
cuidadoso/a careful
cuidar to look after
la **culpa** fault
cultivar to grow
la **cultura** culture
el **cumpleaños** birthday
cumplir to fulfil
el/la **cuñado/a** brother-in-law/
sister-in-law
el **curso** course; school year

D

da vergüenza it's a disgrace
dado que since, given that
dañar to harm, to damage
el **daño** harm, damage
la **danza** dance
dar to give
dar a to overlook
dar de comer to feed
dar la lata to tell (someone)
off
dar las gracias to thank
dar miedo to frighten
dar un paseo to go for a
walk
los **dardos** darts
darse cuenta de to realise
darse prisa to hurry
de acuerdo OK, agreed
de buen/mal humor in a
good/bad mood

Vocabulario

de moda fashionable

de momento at present

de nada don't mention it

de nuevo again

de paso by the way

de pie standing up

de primera/segunda clase first/second class

de prisa quickly, in a hurry

¿de qué color? what/which colour?

¿de quién? whose?

de repente suddenly

de talla media medium size

de todos modos in any case, anyway

de veras really

de vez en cuando from time to time

debajo de below, beneath

deber to have to, to owe

los **deberes** homework

decidir to decide

decir to say

la **decisión** decision

el **dedo** finger; toe

dejar to let, to leave

dejar el colegio to leave school

delante de in front of

delgado/a thin, slim

delicioso/a delicious

la **delincuencia juvenil** youth crime

los **demás** others, other people

demasiado/a too much, too many

demostrar to show, to demonstrate

el/la **dentista** dentist

dentro (de) inside

el **departamento** department

depender de to depend on

el/la **dependiente/a** shop assistant

el **deporte** sport

los **deportes acuáticos** water sports

el/la **deportista** sportsperson

deportivo/a sporty

derecho/a straight, right

derribar to knock down, to demolish

desafortunadamente unfortunately

desagradable unpleasant

desarrollarse to develop

el **desastre** disaster

desayunar to have breakfast

el **desayuno** breakfast

descansar to rest, relax

el **descanso** break

la **descongelación** melting

el/la **desconocido/a** stranger

describir to describe

descubrir to discover, to reveal

descuidarse to neglect, to be careless

desde from

desde...hasta... from...to...

desde luego of course

desear to want, to wish

los **desechos domésticos** household waste

el **desempleo** unemployment

desenchufar to unplug, turn off

el **desorden** disorder

desordenado/a untidy, messy

el **despacho** office, study

despacio slowly

despectivo/a derogatory

despegar to take off (aeroplane)

el **despertador** alarm clock

despertarse to wake up

despistado/a forgetful

después (de) after

el **destino** destination

destruir to destroy

el **detalle** detail

detener to arrest

detenerse to stop

detestar to detest

detrás (de) behind

devolver to give back, return

el **día** day

el **Día de la Madre** Mother's Day

el **día escolar** school day

el **día festivo** holiday

el **diario** newspaper

diario/a daily

dibujar to draw

el **dibujo** art

el **dibujo animado** cartoon

el **diccionario** dictionary

diciembre December

el **diente** tooth

la **dieta equilibrada** balanced diet

la **diferencia** difference

diferente different

difícil difficult

la **dificultad** difficulty

dígame hello (on telephone)

Dinamarca Denmark

el **dinero** money

la **dirección** direction; address

el/la **director/a** headteacher

el/la **director/a de cine** film director

el **disco** CD, disk

el **disco duro** hard disk

la **discoteca** club; disco

la **discriminación** discrimination

discutir to argue

el/la **diseñador/a** designer

el **diseño** design

los **disfraces** dressing-up clothes

el **disfraz** disguise, costume

disfrazar to disguise

disfrutar to enjoy

disminuir to diminish, to lessen

disponible available

dispuesto/a ready

distinto/a different

distraer to distract

distraerse to get distracted

la **diversión** fun, entertainment

divertido/a funny, entertaining

dividir to divide

divorciado/a divorced

doblar to bend, fold

doble double

la **docena** dozen

el **documental** documentary

doler to hurt

el **dolor** pain

el **domicilio** residence, abode

el **domingo** (on) Sunday

donde where

dorarse to turn golden brown

dormir to sleep

dormirse to go to sleep

el **dormitorio** bedroom

el **drama** drama

la **droga** drug

la **ducha** shower

ducharse to have a shower

dudar to doubt

el/la **dueño/a** owner

dulce sweet

los **dulces** sweets

el **dúplex** maisonette

durante during, for

durar to last

duro/a hard

E

e and (before i, hi and y)

echar to put on, to show (programme, film); to throw

echar la siesta to have a siesta

ecológico/a ecological

el/la **ecólogo/a** ecologist

el/la **economista** economist

la **edad** age

el **edificio** building

la **educación** education

la **educación cívica** PHSE

la **educación física** physical education

los **efectos especiales** special effects

eficaz effective

egoísta selfish

el **ejemplar** copy

el **ejemplo** example

el **ejercicio** exercise

la **elección** choice

el/la **electricista** electrician

elegante smart

elegir to choose

elevado/a high

embarazada pregnant

el **embutido** sausage

emborracharse to get drunk

la **emoción** excitement, emotion

emocionante exciting

la **empanada** pasty

emparejar to match, to pair

empezar (a) to begin (to)

el/la **empleado/a** employee

el/la **empleado/a temporal** temporary employee

el **empleo** job

la **empresa** company, business

el/la **empresario/a** employer

en bicicleta by bicycle

en coche by car

en el centro de in the centre of

en el extranjero abroad

en el fondo at the bottom, deep down

¡enhorabuena! congratulations!

en las afueras in the outskirts

en paro out of work

en realidad in fact

enseguida, en seguida at once

en vivo live (e.g. music)

enamorarse de to fall in love with

encantado/a pleased to meet you, enchanted

el **encanto** charm

encender to light, to turn/switch on

enchufado/a connected

el **encierro** running of the bulls festival

encima de on (top of)

encontrar to find

encontrarse to be found/situated

la **encuesta** survey

el/la **enemigo/a** enemy

la **energía** energy

enero January

enfadarse to get angry

la **enfermedad** illness

el/la **enfermero/a** nurse

el/la **enfermo/a** sick person

enfrente (de) opposite

el **enlace** link

enorme enormous

la **ensalada** salad

ensayar to rehearse

la **enseñanza** teaching

enseñar (a) to teach (to); to show

ensimismado/a engrossed, absorbed

entender to understand

enterarse de to find out

entero/a entire, whole

enterrar to bury

entonces then

el **entorno** environment

la **entrada** entrance; ticket (film etc.)

entrar to go in, to enter

entre between

el **entrenador** trainer

el **entrenamiento** training, exercise

entrenarse to train

entretenido/a entertaining, enjoyable

la **entrevista** interview

el/la **entusiasta** enthusiast

enviar to send

el **equipaje** luggage

el **equipo** team

equivocado/a wrong

la **equitación** horse riding

la **escalera** staircase, stairs

escapar to escape

el **escaparate** shop window

escaso/a scarce

la **escena** scene

escoger to choose

esconder to hide

escribir to write

el/la **escritor/a** writer

escuchar to listen (to)

la **escuela** school

la **escultura** sculpture

es decir that is

la **esgrima** fencing

el **espacio** space

los **espaguetis** spaghetti

la **espalda** back

España Spain

el **español** Spanish (language/ subject)

español/española Spanish

especializado/a specialised

especialmente especially

el/la **espectador/a** spectator

el **espejo** mirror

esperar to hope; to expect; to wait for

las **espinacas** spinach

el/la **esposo/a** husband; wife

el **esquí** skiing

el **esquí acuático** water-skiing

esquiar to ski

la **esquina** corner

esta mañana this morning

esta tarde this afternoon

estable stable

la **estación** season; station

la **estación de trenes** railway station

la **estación de autobuses** bus station

el **estadio** stadium

los **Estados Unidos** USA

la **estancia** stay

el **estanco** tobacconist's

la **estantería** bookcase

estar to be

estar a favor de to be in favour of

estar al teléfono to be on the phone/taking a call

estar contento/a to be happy/contented

estar de acuerdo to agree

estar de broma to be joking

estar de moda to be fashionable

estar de pie to be standing up

estar de prisa to be in a hurry

estar en contra de to be against

estar en forma to keep fit

estar harto/a to be fed up

estar mareado/a to feel sick

el **este** east

el **estilo** style

Estimado señor Dear Sir

estirar to stretch

el **estómago** stomach

estrecho/a narrow

la **estrella** star

la **estrella de cine** film star

el **estrés** stress

estresante stressful

estricto/a strict

estropear to break, to damage

el **estuche** pencil case

el/la **estudiante** student

estudiar to study

el **estudio** study

estudioso/a studious

¡estupendo! great!

estúpido/a stupid

la **evaluación** assessment

evitar to avoid

exacto/a exact, accurate

exagerado/a excessive, extravagant

el **examen,** *pl.* **exámenes** examination

excepto except

la **excusa** excuse

el **éxito** success

exitoso/a successful

la **experiencia** experience

explicar to explain

la **exposición** exhibition

extenderse to extend

extranjero/a foreign

extraño/a strange

extraordinario/a extraordinary

los **extras** extras

extrovertido/a extrovert

F

la **fábrica** factory

la **fábrica de galletas** biscuit factory

fácil easy

la **facultad** faculty

la **falda** skirt

las **Fallas** Fallas (fiesta in Valencia)

el **fallo** defect, fault

falso/a false

la **falta** fault, error

faltar to be lacking/missing

la **fama** fame

la **familia** family

el/la **familiar** family member

famoso/a famous

el/la **farmacéutico/a** chemist, pharmacist

la **farmacia** chemist's

fatal terrible, badly

favorito/a favourite

febrero February

la **fecha de nacimiento** date of birth

la **felicidad** happiness

feliz happy

¡feliz cumpleaños! happy birthday!

¡fenomenal! fantastic!

feo/a ugly

la **feria** festival, fair

la **Feria de Abril** Feria (fiesta in Seville)

el **ferrocarril** railway

fiarse de to trust

la **fibra** fibre

los **fideos** noodles

la **fiesta** party; festival; holiday

el **filete** steak

el **fin** end

el **fin de semana** weekend

finalmente finally

las **finanzas** finance

la **física** physics

físicamente physically

físico/a physical

el **flan** crème caramel

la **flauta** flute

el **flamenco** type of dance

la **flor** flower

la **florería** florist

la **floristería** florist

el **folleto** brochure

el/la **fontanero/a** plumber

el **footing** jogging

la **formación** training

el **formulario** from

la **foto** photo

el **francés** French (language/subject)

francés/francesa French

Francia France

la **frase** sentence

frecuente frequent

el **fregadero** kitchen sink

fregar to wash, to scrub, to mop

fregar los platos to wash the dishes

freír to fry

la **fresa** strawberry

fresco/a fresh

frío/a cold

frito/a fried

la **frontera** border, frontier

la **fruta** fruit

la **frutería** fruit shop

el **fuego** fire

los **fuegos artificiales** fireworks

la **fuente** fountain

fuera (de) outside

fuera de (su) alcance out of (one's) reach

fuerte strong

la **fuerza** strength

fumar to smoke

fundado/a funded

furioso/a furious, violent

el **fútbol** football

el **futbolín** table football

el/la **futbolista** footballer

el **futuro** future

G

las **gafas** glasses

las **gafas de sol** sun glasses

Gales Wales

la **galleta** biscuit

la **gama** range

las **gambas** prawns

ganar to win, to earn

ganar dinero to earn money

la **ganga** bargain

el **garaje** garage

la **garganta** throat

la **gasolina** petrol

la **gaseosa** fizzy drink

gastar to spend

gastar dinero to spend money

el **gato** cat

el **gazpacho** chilled tomato soup

el/la **gemelo/a** twin

generoso/a generous

¡genial! great!

la **gente** people

la **geografía** geography

el **gerbo** gerbil

la **gimnasia** gymnastics

el **gimnasio** gymnasium

el **golf** golf

la **goma** rubber

gordo/a fat

la **gorra** cap

gracias a thanks to

graciosamente funnily

gracioso/a funny

el **grado** degree

el **gramo** gramme

grande big

los **grandes almacenes** department store

la **granja** farm

el **granjero** farmer

la **grapadora** stapler

la **grasa** fat

gratis free

grave serious

Grecia Greece

gris grey

gritar to shout

grosero/a rude

grueso/a thick

el **grupo** group

el **guante** glove

guapo/a good-looking

guardar to keep, to save (document)

el **guardarropa** cloakroom

guay (coll.) cool

la **guerra** war

la **guía** guidebook

el/la **guía** guide

el/la **guionista** scriptwriter

el **guisante** pea

el **guiso** stew

la **guitarra** guitar

gustar to like

el **gusto** taste

H

haber to have (auxiliary verb)

hábil skilful

la **habilidad** skill

la **habitación** room

el/la **habitante** inhabitant

hablador/a talkative
hablar to speak, to talk
hace (una semana) (a week) ago
hace buen tiempo the weather is good
hace frío it's cold
hace sol it's sunny
hace viento it's windy
hacer to do, to make
hacer bricolaje to do DIY
hacer caso a to take notice of
hacer de canguro to babysit
hacer deporte to play sports
hacer el café to make the coffee
hacer falta to need
hacer la cama to make the bed
hacer la compra to go shopping
hacer las prácticas de trabajo to do work experience
hacer los deberes to do homework
hacer surf to go surfing
hacer transbordo (en) to change (e.g. trains)
hacer un aprendizaje to do an apprenticeship
hacer vela to go sailing
hacerse to become
hacia towards
hacia atrás back(wards)
hacia delante forwards
la **halterofilia** weightlifting
el **hambre** (f) hunger
la **hamburguesa** hamburger
el **hámster** hamster
hasta until; up to; even
hasta luego bye
hay there is, there are
el **helado** ice cream
el **hemisferio** hemisphere
la **herencia** heritage

el/la **hermanastro/a** stepbrother/ stepsister
el/la **hermano/a mayor** older brother/sister
el/la **hermano/a menor** younger brother/sister
los **hermanos** brothers and sisters
hermoso/a beautiful
la **hermosura** beauty
el **héroe** hero
la **heroína** heroine; heroin
hervir to boil
el **hielo** ice
el **higo** fig
el/la **hijastro/a** stepson/ stepdaughter
el **hijo único/la hija única** only child
el **hipermercado** hypermarket
hispanohablante Spanish-speaking
la **historia** story, history
histórico/a historic(al)
el **hockey** hockey
el **hogar** home
la **hoguera** bonfire
el **hojaldre** puff pastry
el **hombre** man
el **hombre de negocios** businessman
el **hombro** shoulder
hondo/a deep
honesto/a honest
honrado/a honest
la **hora** time, hour
la **hora de comer** lunch time
la **hora de llegar** time of arrival
la **hora de salir** time of departure
el **horario** timetable
el **horno** oven
horroroso/a dreadful
las **hortalizas/ verduras** vegetables
el **hospital** hospital

la **hostelería** hotel business
hoy today
hoy en día nowadays
el **huevo** egg
húmedo/a wet
el **humo** smoke
Hungría Hungary

la **idea** idea
el **idioma** language
la **iglesia** church
igual equal
la **igualdad** equality
ilegal illegal
la **imagen,** pl. **imágenes** image, picture, photo
la **imaginación** imagination
imaginar to imagine
impaciente impatient
el **imperdible** safety pin
importante important
imposible impossible
imprescindible essential, indispensable
impresionante impressive
improbable unlikely
incendio fire
incluido/a included
incluir to include
incluso even
incómodo/a uncomfortable, inconvenient
increíble incredible
indicar to indicate
la **industria** industry
industrial industrial
inequívoco/a unequivocal
la **infancia** childhood
la **información** information
la **informática** ICT
la **información** information
el **informativo** news programme

el/la **ingeniero/a** engineer
Inglaterra England
el **inglés** English (language/ subject)
inglés/inglesa English
injusto/a unjust, unfair
inmediatamente immediately
la **inmigración** immigration
el/la **inmigrante** immigrant
insistir to insist
la **insolación** sunstroke
insoportable unbearable
inspirar to inspire
las **instalaciones** facilities
el **instituto** high school
inteligente intelligent
intentar to try
el **interés** interest
interesante interesting
interesarse en/por to be interested in
interior interior, internal
(el/la) **Internet** internet
interrumpir to interrupt
la **inundación** flood
inútil useless
el **invierno** winter
invitar to invite
ir to go
ir a la universidad to go to university
ir al extranjero to go abroad
ir a reuniones to go to meetings
ir de compras to go shopping
ir de excursion to go hiking; to go on a trip
ir de viaje to go travelling
ir en monopatín to go skateboarding
ir de paseo to go for a walk
Irlanda Ireland
irse to go away
irse de juerga to live it up
isla island
Islandia Iceland

J

Italia Italy
el **italiano** Italian (language/ subject)

el **jabón** soap
jamás never, ever
el **jamón** ham
el **jarabe** syrup
el **jardín** garden
la **jardinería** gardening
el **jefe/**la **jefa** boss
el **jerbo** gerbil
la **jornada** working day
el/la **joven** young (person)
los **jóvenes** young people
la **joyería** jeweller's
jubilado/a retired
la **judía** bean
las **judías verdes** green beans
el **juego** game
los **juegos de azar** games of chance
el **jueves** (on) Thursday
el/la **jugador/a** player
jugar to play
el **juguete** toy
la **juguetería** toy shop
julio July
junio June
juntarse to gather, to come together
junto con together with
justo/a fair, right
la **juventud** youth
juzgar to judge

K

el **kárate** karate
el **kilo** kilo
el **kilómetro** kilometre

L

el **laboratorio** laboratory
los **lácteos** dairy products
el **lago** lake
la **lagartija** small lizard
el **lagarto** lizard
la **lágrima** tear
la **lámpara** lamp
la **lana** wool
el **lapicero** pencil
el **lápiz** pencil
el **lápiz de color** coloured pencil
largo/a long
la **lata** tin
el **latín** Latin (language/ subject)
latinoamericano/a Latin American
los **lavabos** toilets
la **lavadora** washing machine
el **lavaplatos** dishwasher
lavar el pelo to wash hair
lavar el coche to wash the car
lavar(se) to wash, to clean
leal loyal, faithful
la **leche** milk
la **lechuga** lettuce
el/la **lector/a** reader
la **lectura** reading
leer to read
las **legumbres** pulse
lejos far
la **lengua** language; tongue
lento/a slow
la **letra** letter
levantarse to get up
la **libertad** freedom
libre free
la **librería** bookshop
el **libro** book
el **libro de texto** textbook
la **licenciatura** degree
ligeramente lightly
ligero/a light

el **límite**   limit

el **limón**   lemon

la **limonada**   lemonade

limpiar   to clean

limpiar los cristales   to clean the windows

limpiar el polvo   to do the dusting

la **limpieza**   cleaning

limpio/a   clean

la **limusina**   limousine

la **linterna**   torch

liso/a   smooth, straight (hair)

listo/a   ready, clever

la **literatura**   literature

el **litro**   litre

la **llamada**   telephone call

llamarse   to be called

la **llave**   key

llegar   to get (to a place), to arrive

llenar   to fill

lleno/a de   full of

llevar   to wear; to take (e.g. by car)

llevar una vida dura   to lead a hard life

llevar uniforme   to wear a uniform

llorar   to cry

llover   to rain

la **lluvia**   rain

lo bueno de   the good thing about

lo malo de   the bad thing about

lo mejor   the best thing

lo peor   the worst thing

lo siento   I'm sorry

lo único   the only thing

el **local**   premises

loco/a   mad

la **locura**   madness

lograr   to gain, to succeed (in)

el **logro**   success, achievement

la **loncha**   slice

el **loro**   parrot

la **lucha**   struggle; wrestling

luchar (contra)   to struggle (against)

luego   then, next

el **lugar**   place

los **lugares de interés**   places of interest

la **luna**   moon

el **lunes**   (on) Monday

Luxemburgo   Luxembourg

la **luz**   light

M

la **madera**   wood

la **madrastra**   stepmother

la **madre**   mother

el/la **madrileño/a**   citizen of Madrid

la **madrugada**   the early hours of the morning

mágico/a   magic

el **maíz**   corn, maize

majo/a   good-looking, nice, lovely

mal   badly

el **mal tiempo**   bad weather

maleducado/a   badly behaved

la **maleta**   suitcase

el **maletín** (*Sp*)   briefcase

malgastar   to waste

el **malgasto**   waste

malo/a   bad

los **malos tratos**   physical abuse

el **maltrato**   abuse

mañana   morning; tomorrow

mandar   to send

mandar un fax   to send a fax

la **manera**   way, manner

la **mano**   hand

el **mantel**   tablecloth

mantener   to maintain, to keep

mantenerse en forma   to keep fit

mantenerse sano   to keep healthy

la **mantequilla**   butter

la **manzana**   apple; block (of houses)

el **mapa**   map

el **maquillaje**   make-up

maquillarse   to put on one's make-up

la **máquina**   machine

el **mar**   sea

la **maravilla**   wonder

maravilloso/a   marvellous

marcar un gol   to score a goal

mareado/a   sick, dizzy

el **marido**   husband

el/la **marinero/a**   sailor

el **marisco**   shellfish

marrón   brown

marrón claro/a   light brown

marrón oscuro/a   dark brown

Marruecos   Morocco

el **martes**   (on) Tuesday

marzo   March

más   more

más adelante   further on

más de   more than (followed by a number)

más...que   more...than

la **masa**   dough

la **mascota**   pet

masticar   to chew

matar   to kill

las **matemáticas**   maths

el **matrimonio**   marriage

mayo   May

mayor   larger; older

la **mayoría**   majority

la **mayoría de la gente**   most people

la **mayoría del tiempo**   most of the time

el/la **mecánico/a**   mechanic

el **mechero**   cigarette lighter

la **media**   stocking

la **media naranja**   ideal partner

la **medianoche**   midnight

(la) **media pensión**   half board

el/la **médico/a** doctor
medio half, mid
el **medio ambiente** environment
el **mediodía** midday
los **medios (de comunicación)** media
medir to measure
Méjico Mexico
el **mejillón** mussel
mejor better
mejorar to improve
el **melocotón** peach
mencionar to mention
menor smaller; younger
menos less, except
menos...que less...than
el **mensaje** message
el **mensaje de texto** sms, text message
la **mente** mind
mentir to lie
la **mentira** lie
mentiroso/a lying, false
el **mercadillo** street market
el **mercado** market
la **merienda** snack, afternoon tea, picnic
el **mérito** merit
la **merluza** hake
el **mes** month
la **mesa** table
mestizo/a mixed race
meter goles to score goals
meter to put
el **método** method
el **metro** metre; underground
la **mezcla** mixture
mezclar to mix
el **microondas** microwave
el **miedo** fear
mientras (que) while
el **miércoles** (on) Wednesday
mil a thousand
el **minuto** minute
la **misa** mass
mismo/a same; (one)self
la **mitad** half

la **mochila** school bag, backpack
la **moda** fashion
el/la **modelo** model
el **modo de transporte** means of transport
el **modo de vivir** way of life
¡mola mazo! fantastic!
molestar to bother, to annoy, to upset
el **momento** moment
la **moneda** coin; currency
el **monedero** purse
la **montaña** mountain
montañoso/a mountainous
montar a caballo to ride a horse
montar en bici to go for a bike ride
moreno/a dark
morir to die
morir de hambre to die of hunger
mostrar to show
la **moto** motorbike
mover to move
el **móvil** mobile phone
el/la **muchacho/a** boy/girl
la **muchedumbre** crowd
mucho/a much, a lot
mucho gusto pleased to meet you
mudarse to move house
mudo/a dumb
los **muebles** furniture
la **muela** tooth
muerto/a de hambre starving
la **mujer** woman; wife
la **mujer de negocios** businesswoman
mundial worldwide
el **mundo** world
la **muñeca** doll
el **músculo** muscle
el **museo** museum
el **museo de arte** art gallery
la **música** music

musulmán/ musulmana Moslem
muy very

N

nacer to be born
el **nacimiento** birth
la **nación** nation
la **nacionalidad** nationality
nada nothing, anything
nadar to swim
nadie no one, anyone
la **naranja** orange
la **nariz** nose
la **nata** fresh cream
la **natación** swimming
naturalmente naturally
navegar to navigate
navegar por/en Internet to surf the internet
Navidad(es) Christmas
navideño/a (of) Christmas
necesario/a necessary
necesitar to need
negro/a black
nervioso/a nervous
nevar to snow
la **nevera** fridge
ni...ni... neither...nor...
ni siquiera not even
la **niebla** fog
el/la **nieto/a** grandson/grand-daughter
la **nieve** snow
ningún, ninguno/a no
el/la **niño/niña** boy/girl
el **nivel** level
no importa it doesn't matter
no obstante nevertheless
la **noche** night
la **Nochebuena** Christmas Eve
el **nombre** name
el **nombre de pila** first name
el **noreste** northeast
la **norma** rule
el **noroeste** northwest

el **norte** north

la **nota** note; mark

las **noticias** news

la **novia** girlfriend; bride

noviembre November

el **novio** boyfriend; bridegroom

nublado/a cloudy

la **nuera** daughter-in-law

Nueva Zelanda New Zealand

la **nuez** nut, walnut

nunca never

O

o or

obediente obedient

objetos perdidos lost property

obligar to oblige

obligatorio/a obligatory, compulsory

la **obra de teatro** play

el/la **obrero/a** labourer

obtener to obtain, to get

obvio/a obvious

el **océano** ocean

ocho días a week

el **ocio** leisure

octubre October

ocupado/a busy, engaged

ocurrir to happen

odiar to hate

el **oeste** west

ofender to offend

la **oficina** office

la **oficina de turismo** tourist office

el/la **oficinista** office worker

ofrecer to offer

el **oído** ear

oír to hear

ojalá if only

el **ojo** eye

oler to smell

el **olor** smell

olvidarse de to forget

ondulado/a wavy

opinar to have an opinion

la **opinión** opinion

la **oportunidad** opportunity

optimista optimistic

el **ordenador** (*Sp*) computer

la **oreja** ear

organizar to organise

orgulloso/a proud

el **origen** origin

originarse to originate

el **oro** gold

la **orquesta** orchestra

oscuro/a dark

el **otoño** autumn

otro/a other

otra vez again

el/la **oyente** listener

P

la **paciencia** patience

paciente patient

padecer to suffer

el **padrastro** step-father

los **padres** parents

el **padrino** godfather

pagar to pay

la **página** page

la **página web** webpage

el **país** country

el **paisaje** countryside

los **Paises Bajos** the Netherlands

el **pájaro** bird

la **palabra** word

el **palacio** palace

pálido/a pale

el **pan** bread

la **panadería** baker's

el **panecillo** roll

los **pantalones** trousers

el **pan toastado** toasted bread

el **pañuelo de papel** paper handkerchief

el **papagayo** parrot

el **papel** paper

el **papel (de cine)** role

el **papel higiénico** toilet paper

la **papelería** stationer's

el **paquete** packet

para for, in order to/that

la **parada de autobús** bus stop

el **parador** (*Sp*) state-run hotel

el **paraguas** umbrella

parar to stop

parece mentira que I can't believe that, it's unbelievable

parecer to appear, to seem

parecido/a similar

la **pared** wall

la **pareja** partner, pair

los **parientes** relatives

el **parque** park

el **parque de atracciones** amusement park

el **parque temático** theme park

la **parte** part

el **partido** match (e.g. football)

el **patrimonio** patrimony

la **pasa** raisin

el **pasado** past

pasado/a de moda outdated, old-fashioned

el/la **pasajero/a** passenger

el **pasaporte** passport

pasar to happen

pasar de largo to go straight past

pasar la aspiradora to hoover

pasarlo bomba to have a great time

el **pasatiempo** hobby, pastime

la **Pascua** Easter

pasear el perro to walk the dog

pasearse to go for a stroll

el **paseo** walk

el **pasillo** corridor

la **pasta de dientes** toothpaste

el **pastel** cake

la **pastelería** cake shop

la **pastilla** tablet, pastille, pill

la **patata**   potato

las **patatas fritas**   chips; crisps

el **patín**   skate

el **patinaje**   skating

patinar   to skate

patinar sobre ruedas   to roller-skate

el **patio**   patio; playground

el **pavo**   turkey

la **paz**   peace

la **peca**   freckle

el **pedazo**   piece

pediatra   pediatric

pedir   to ask for

pegar   to strike, to hit; to stick

el **pegamento**   glue

peinarse   to comb one's hair

pelar   to peel

pelear(se)   to fight

la **película**   film

la **película de acción**   action film

la **película de amor**   romantic film

la **película de aventura**   adventure film

la **película de ciencia ficción**   science-fiction film

la **película de espionaje**   spy film

la **película de fantasía**   fantasy film

la **película de guerra**   war film

la **película del Oeste**   Western

la **película de terror**   horror film

la **película de vaqueros**   western

la **película histórica**   historical film

la **película musical**   musical

la **película policíaca**   detective/ crime film

la **película romántica**   romantic film

el **peligro**   danger

peligroso/a   dangerous

pelirrojo/a   red-haired

el **pelo**   hair

la **peluquería**   hairdresser's

el/la **peluquero/a**   hairdresser

la **pena**   pity, sorrow, shame

el **pendiente**   earring

la **península**   peninsula

la **pensamiento**   thought

pensar   to think, to intend

pensativo/a   thoughtful

la **pensión**   cheap hotel

(la) **pensión completa**   full board

el **pepino**   cucumber

pequeño/a   little, small

los **pequeños**   little children

la **pera**   pear

perder   to miss; to lose

la **pérdida**   loss

la **pérdida de tiempo**   waste of time

perdido/a   lost

perdón   excuse me

perdonar   to forgive

perezoso/a   lazy

perfecto/a   perfect

la **perfumería**   perfumery

el **perico**   parakeet

el **periódico**   newspaper

el/la **periodista**   journalist

el **permiso**   permission

permitir   to allow, to permit

peor   worse

el **perro**   dog

el **perro caliente**   hot dog

perseguir   to pursue

la **persona**   person

la **personalidad**   personality

pertenecer   to belong

Perú   Peru

la **pesadilla**   nightmare

pesado/a   boring, tedious

pesar   to weigh

las **pesas**   weight-training

la **pesca**   fishing

la **pescadería**   fishmonger's

el **pescado**   fish (to eat)

pesimista   pessimistic

el **peso**   weight

el **pez**   fish (in water)

el **pez dorado**   goldfish

el **piano**   piano

picado/a   chopped

la **picadura**   bite

picar   to sting; to prick; to nibble

a **pie**   on foot

el **pie**   foot

la **piel**   skin

la **pierna**   leg

la **pila**   battery

pillar (*coll.*)   to catch

el **piloto**   pilot

el **pimiento**   pepper

la **piña**   pineapple

pintar   to paint

pintoresco/a   picturesque

las **pinzas**   tweezers

el **piragüismo**   canoeing

el **piropo**   compliment

la **piscina**   swimming pool

el **piso**   flat; floor

la **pista**   track; slope

la **pista de hielo/de patinaje**   ice rink

la **pista de tenis**   tennis court

la **pistola**   baguette

planchar la ropa   to iron clothes

planear   to plan

el **planeta**   planet

el **plano**   plan

la **planta**   floor, storey

la **planta baja**   ground floor

el **plástico**   plastic

el **plátano**   banana

los **platillos**   cymbals

el **plato**   plate, dish

la **playa**   beach

la **plaza**   square, place

la **plaza de toros**   bullring

la **plaza mayor**   main square

la **pluma**   fountain pen

pobre   poor

la **pobreza**   poverty

pocas veces   seldom, rarely

poco/a   little, not much

un **poco**   a little

poco a poco   gradually

poco interestante   uninteresting, dull

pocos/as   few

poder to be able

el/la **policía** policeman/woman

el **polideportivo** sports centre

el/la **político/a** politician

el **pollo** chicken

Polonia Poland

el **pomelo** grapefruit

poner to put on, to show (programme, film)

poner la mesa to lay the table

ponerse to put on (clothes)

ponerse de acuerdo to agree

poquito a little bit

por by, because of, along

por cierto certainly

por día each/per day

por eso therefore

por la mañana in the morning

por la noche in the evening/ at night

por la tarde in the afternoon/ evening

por lo menos at least

por medio de by means of

por otra parte on the other hand

por otro lado on the other hand

por parte de (mi madre etc.) on (my mother's etc.) side

por supuesto of course

por todas partes everywhere

por una parte on the one hand

por un lado on the one hand

el **porcentaje** percentage

porque because

el **portafolio** (*LA*) briefcase

el/la **portero/a** caretaker

¿por qué? why?

posible possible

la **posibilidad** possibility

la **posición** position

la **postal** postcard

el **póster** poster

el **postre** pudding, dessert

el **pozo** well

la **práctica de trabajo** work experience

practicar to practise

práctico/a practical

el **precio** price, cost

precioso/a beautiful, lovely

la **precipitación** rainfall

precipitarse to rush

la **preferencia** preference

preferible preferable

preferir to prefer

preguntar to ask (a question)

el **prejuicio** prejudice

premiado/a prize-winning

el **premio** prize

la **prensa** press

la **preocupación** worry

preocupado/a anxious

preocupante worrying

preocuparse por to worry about

prepararse para to prepare for

el/la **presentador/a** presenter

la **primavera** spring

primero/a first

el/la **primo/a** cousin

principal main, principal

principalmente mainly

el **principio** beginning

probar to try, to taste

el **problema** problem

la **procesión** procession

producir to produce

el **producto** product

el **productor** producer

la **profesión** job, profession

el/la **profesor/a, profe** (*coll.*) teacher

profundo/a deep, profound

el **programa** program(me)

la **programación** viewing guide

prohibir to forbid

prometer to promise

el **pronóstico** weather forecast

pronto soon

propio/a own

proporcionar to give, to provide

la **protección** protection

proteger to protect

provocar to cause

próximo/a next

la **prueba** test, proof

la **publicidad** publicity; advertising

público/a public

pueblerino/a rustic

el **pueblo** small town; village

el **puente** bridge

la **puerta** door

la **puerta de embarque** departure gate

el **puerto** port, harbour

pues then, well

el **puesto** stall

la **pulgada** inch

el **pulso** pulse

Q

quedarse to stay, to remain

quedarse en el cole to stay on at school

quedarse en la cama to stay in bed

la **queja** complaint

quejarse to complain

la **quemadura** burn

quemar to burn

querer to wish, to want, to love

querer decir to mean

querido/a dear

el **queso** cheese

¡Que aproveche! Enjoy your meal!, Bon appetit!

¡Qué pena! What a shame!

¿Qué pasa? What's happening?

¿Qué tal? How are you/ things?

quien who, whom

la **química**   chemistry

quince días   a fortnight

las **quinielas**   football pools

el **quiosco**   kiosk

quitar   to take away

quitar la mesa   to clear the
  table

quizás   perhaps

R

la **ración**   portion, helping

la **radio**   radio

la **rana**   frog

rápidamente   quickly

rápido/a   rapid, quick

raro/a   strange

el **rasgo**   trait

el **rato**   time, while

la **rata**   rat

el **ratón**   mouse

la **razón**   reason

razonable   reasonable

recaudar dinero   to collect
  money

la **recepción**   reception

el/la **recepcionista**   receptionist

rechazar   to reject

recibir   to receive

recibir una llamada   to
  receive a call

el **recibo**   receipt

reciclable   recyclable

reciclar   to recycle

recién hecho/a   just made/
  done

reciente   recent

el **recipiente**   container

recomendar   to recommend

reconocer   to recognise

recordar   to remember

el **recreo**   break

el **recuerdo**   souvenir, memory

los **recursos**   resources

la **red**   network, web

redondo/a   round

reducir   to reduce

el **refresco**   soft drink

la **regla**   rule, ruler

el **regalo**   present

regar las plantas   to water
  the plants

el **régimen,** *pl.*
  regímenes   diet; regime

la **región**   region

la **regla**   ruler

regresar   to return

regresar a casa   to go home

el **regreso**   return

la **reina**   queen

el **Reino Unido**   United Kingdom

reír   to laugh

reírse de   to laugh at, to mock

la **relación**   relation, relationship

relajado/a   relaxed

relajarse   to relax

el **relámpago**   lightning

la **religión**   religion

religioso/a   religious

rellenar   to fill

el **reloj**   clock, watch

el **remedio**   cure, remedy

remover   to stir

remunerar   to remunerate

el **rendimiento escolar**   school
  performance

repartir el correo   to deliver
  the post

el **reparto**   cast

repasar   to revise

repentino/a   sudden

repetir   to repeat

repetitivo/a   repetitive

el **reportaje**   report

el/la **reportero/a**   reporter

requerir   to require

la **reserva**   reservation

reservar   to book, to reserve

respetar   to respect

la **respiración**   breathing

respirar   to breathe

resplandeciente   radiant,
  shining

responder   to respond, to
  answer

la **responsabilidad**
  responsibility

responsable   responsible

la **respuesta**   reply, response

el **resultado**   result

el **retraso**   delay

el **retrete**   toilet

la **reunión**   meeting

reunirse   to meet (up)

reutilizar   to reuse

la **revista**   magazine

el **rey**   king

los **Reyes Magos**   Magi,
  Three Kings

rico/a   rich, tasty (of food)

el **riesgo**   risk

el **rincón**   corner

el **río**   river

la **risa**   laughter

rizado/a   curly

robar   to steal

el **robo**   robbery

rodeado/a de   surrounded by

la **rodilla**   knee

el **rollo**   bore

romántico/a   romantic

la **ropa**   clothes

la **ropa de moda**   fashionable
  clothes

rosa   pink

roto/a   broken

el **rotulador**   felt-tip pen;
  marker pen

rubio/a   blond(e)

el **rugby**   rugby

el **ruido**   noise

ruidoso/a   noisy

rural   rural

la **ruta**   route

la **rutina**   routine

S

el **sábado**   (on) Saturday

saber   to know

el **sabor**   taste

sabroso/a   tasty

el **sacapuntas**   pencil sharpener
sacar   to take out
el **sacacorchos**   corkscrew
sacar la basura   to take out the rubbish
sacar fotos   to take photos
el **saco de dormir**   sleeping bag
la **sal**   salt
la **sala**   room
la **sala de espera**   waiting room
la **sala de estar**   living room
la **sala de profesores**   staff room
la **salchicha**   sausage
la **salida**   exit; departure
salir   to go out
salir de casa   to leave the house
el **salón**   lounge, living room
saltar   to jump
el **salto**   jump
la **salud**   health
¡Salud!   Cheers!
saludable   healthy
saludar   to greet
el **saludo**   greeting
salvar   to save
salvo   except
la **sangre**   blood
sano/a   healthy
San Valentín   Valentine's day
la **sardina**   sardine
la **sartén**   frying pan
satisfecho/a   satisfied
el **saxofón**   saxophone
secarse   to get dry
la **sección**   department (in store), section
seco/a   dry
el/la **secretario/a**   secretary
la **seda**   silk
seguir   to continue, to follow
seguir estudiando   to carry on studying
según   according to
segundo/a   second

la **seguridad**   safety, security
seguro/a   sure
el **sello**   stamp
la **selva**   forest
el **semáforo**   traffic light
la **semana**   week
la **semana pasada**   last week
la **semana que viene**   next week
(la) **Semana Santa**   Holy Week
semejante   similar
la **señal**   signal, sign
señalar   to point out
sencillo/a   simple; single (ticket)
sensible   sensitive
sentado/a   seated
sentarse   to sit down
el **sentido común**   common sense
el **sentido del humor**   sense of humour
el **sentimiento**   feeling
sentir   to feel
separar   to separate
separado/a   separated
septiembre   September
la **sequía**   drought
ser   to be
ser aficionado/a a   to be keen on
ser ecológico/a   to be ecological
ser licenciado/a   to have a degree
serio/a   serious
la **serpiente**   snake
el **servicio**   toilet, washroom
la **servilleta**   serviette, napkin
servir   to serve
severo/a   strict
si   if
siempre   always
la **sierra**   mountain range
el **siglo**   century
significar   to mean, to signify
significativo/a   significant
siguiente   following, next

la **silla**   chair
el **sillón**   armchair
el **símbolo**   symbol
simpático/a   nice, kind
sin   without
sincero/a   sincere
sin duda   without doubt
sin embargo   however
sino   but
los **sin techo**   homeless people
el **sistema**   system
el **sitio**   place, site, pitch
la **situación**   situation
situarse   to be situated
sobre   on, about (of time)
sobre todo   especially
sobrevivir   to survive
el/la **sobrino/a**   nephew/niece
el/la **socio/a**   member
el **socorro**   help
el **sofá**   sofa
el **sol**   sun
solamente   only
soler   to do as a habit/usually
solicitar un puesto   to apply for a job
solo/a   alone, on one's own
solo   only
soltero/a   single, unmarried
la **sombra**   shadow
el **sombrero**   hat
el **sonido**   sound
sonriente   smiling
la **sonrisa**   smile
soñar (con)   to dream (about/of)
la **sopa**   soup
sordo/a   deaf
sorprendentemente   surprisingly
la **sorpresa**   surprise
el **sótano**   basement
suave   mild
suavemente   gently, smoothly
la **subida**   rise
subir   to rise, to go up
los **subtítulos**   subtitles
sucio/a   dirty

Sudáfrica South Africa

Suecia Sweden

el/la **suegro/a** father-in-law/
    mother-in-law

el **sueldo** salary

el **suelo** ground

el **sueño** sleep, dream

suficiente enough, suffcient

sufrir to suffer

la **sugerencia** suggestion

sugerir to suggest

Suiza Switzerland

superar to overcome

superguapo/a very
    good-looking

el **supermercado** supermarket

suponer to suppose

el **sur** south

el **sureste** southeast

surfear Internet to surf the
    internet

surgir to arise

el **suroeste** southwest

el **surtido** selection, range

suspender un examen to
    fail an exam

sustituir to substitute

T

el **tabaco** tobacco

la **talla** size

el **taller** workshop

tal vez perhaps

el **tamaño** size

también also

el **tambor** drum

tampoco neither

tan...como as...as

tanto/a...como as/so
    much...as

la **taquilla** box office, ticket
    office

tardar (en) to be late

tarde late

la **tarea** task

la **tarea de casa** household
    task/chore

la **tarjeta** card

la **tarjeta móvil** mobile card

la **tarta** tart, cake

el **taxi** taxi

la **taza** cup(ful)

el **té** tea

el **teatro** theatre; drama

el **tebeo** comic

el **techo** roof

el **teclado** keyboard

el/la **técnico/a** technician

la **tecnología** technology

la **tela** fabric, cloth

el **telediario** news

telefonear to telephone

el **(telefóno) móvil** mobile
    phone

la **telenovela** soap opera

el **televisor** television set

el **tema** topic, theme

temer to fear, to be afraid

el **temor** fear

la **temperatura** temperature

la **temporada** season

temporal temporary

temprano/a early

el **tenedor** fork

tener to have

tener celos to be jealous

tener cuidado to be careful

tener dolor de cabeza to
    have a headache

tener dolor de muelas to
    have toothache

tener éxito to be successful

tener fiebre to have a
    temperature/fever

tener ganas de to want to

tener hambre to be hungry

tener lugar to take place

tener miedo to be afraid

tener que to have to

tener razón to be right

tener sed to be thirsty

tener sueño to be sleepy

tener suerte to be lucky

tener tos to have a cough

tener una insolación to
    have sunstroke

tener una picadura to have
    a bite

tener una quemadura to
    have a burn

tener un resfriado to have a
    cold

el **tenis** tennis

el **tenis de mesa** table tennis,
    ping pong

la **terapia** therapy

el **Tercer Mundo** Third World

tercero/a third

terminar to finish

el **termómetro** thermometer

la **ternera** veal

la **terraza** terrace, balcony

el **terrorismo** terrorism

el **tiempo** weather; time

el **tiempo libre** free time

la **tienda** shop; tent

la **tienda de música** record/
    music shop

la **tienda de ropa** clothes shop

la **tienda de ultramarinos**
    greengrocer's

la **tierra** land

las **tijeras** scissors

tímido/a shy

la **tinta** ink

el/la **tío/a** uncle/aunt

típico/a typical

el **tipo** type, kind

tirar to throw away

la **tirita** plaster

el **tiro con arco** archery

los **titulares** headlines

el **título** title; qualification

la **toalla** towel

el **tobillo** ankle

tocar to play (an instrument);
    to touch

todo/a all

todavía still

todo el mundo everybody

todo el rato all the time

todos los días each/every
    day

tomar to take

tomar el aire fresco to take in the fresh air

tomar el sol to sunbathe

el **tomate** tomato

tonto/a stupid, crazy

torcer to turn, to twist

el/la **torero/a** bullfighter

la **tormenta** storm

la **tortilla** omelette

la **tortilla de patatas** Spanish omelette

la **tortuga** tortoise

la **tos** cough

la **tostada** toast, piece of toast

trabajador/a hardworking

trabajar to work

el **trabajo de mis sueños** my dream job

la **tradición** tradition

tradicional traditional

traer to bring, to get, to fetch

el **tráfico** traffic

tragar to swallow

el **traje** dress, suit

tranquilo/a calm

el **tratamiento** treatment

tratar de to be about

tratar mejor to treat better

travieso/a naughty

la **trayectoria** route

el **tren** train

el **tren de cercanías** suburban/ commuter train

el **trimestre** term

triste sad

el **trombón** trombone

la **trompeta** trumpet

trozear to cut into pieces

el **trozo** slice, piece

el **trueno** thunder

el **tubo** tube

el **túnel** tunnel

el **turismo** tourism

el/la **turista** tourist

turístico/a tourist

el **turrón** (*Sp*) nougat

el/la **tutor/a** tutor

la **tutoría** tutorial

U

u or (before *o* and *ho*)

último/a last

los **ultramarinos** groceries

único/a only

el **uniforme** uniform

unir to join

la **universidad** university

usar to use

útil useful

utilizar to use

la **uva** grape

V

la **vaca** cow

las **vacaciones** holidays

vaciar el lavavajillas to empty the dishwasher

vacío/a empty

vago/a lazy

vale OK

vale la pena it's worth while

valiente brave

valioso/a useful

el **valle** valley

el **valor** value

los **vaqueros** jeans

la **variedad** variety

el **vaso** glass

el/la **vecino/a** neighbour

la **vela** candle; sailing

vencer to beat, conquer

la **venda** bandage

el **vendaval** gale

vender to sell

Venezuela Venezuela

venir to come

la **venta** sale

la **ventaja** advantage

la **ventana** window

ver to see

ver la televisión to watch television

el **verano** summer

la **verbena** open-air celebration, festival

la **verdad** truth

verdaderamente really, truly

verdadero/a true

verde green

las **verduras** green vegetables

verter to pour (out)

el **vestido** dress

vestirse to dress/get dressed

el/la **veterinario/a** vet

la **vez** time

una **vez** once

viajar to travel

el **viaje** journey, trip

el/la **viajero/a** traveller

vibrar to vibrate

la **vida** life

el **videoclub** video-rental shop

los **videojuegos** video games

el **vidrio** glass

viejo/a old

el **viento** wind

el **viernes** (on) Friday

el **villancico** Christmas carol

el **vino** wine

la **violencia** violence

el **violín** violin

visitar to visit

la **víspera** night before

la **vista** view

vistas al mar sea views

viudo/a widowed

la **vivienda** dwelling

vivir to live

vivir a tope to live life to the full

vivo/a bright, vivid

volar to fly

el **volcán** volcano

el **voleibol** volleyball

voltear to turn over

el **volumen** volume

voluntario/a voluntary worker

volver to return

volver a + infinitive   to (do) again

la **voz**   voice

el **vuelo**   flight

la **vuelta**   return

W

el **windsurf**   windsurfing

Y

ya   now, already

ya no   no longer

ya que   since

el **yerno**   son-in-law

el **yogur**   yogurt

Z

la **zanahoria**   carrot

la **zapatería**   shoe shop

la **zapatilla**   slipper

las **zapatillas (de deporte)**   trainers

el **zapato**   shoe

la **zona**   area, region

el **zumo**   juice